Civic Republicanism and Civic Education

Also by Andrew Peterson

THE ROUTLEDGE COMPANION TO EDUCATION (co-edited) (*forthcoming*)

Civic Republicanism and Civic Education

The Education of Citizens

Andrew Peterson
Canterbury Christ Church University, UK

First published 2011 by
PALGRAVE MACMILLAN

Palgrave Macmillan in the UK is an imprint of Macmillan Publishers Limited,
registered in England, company number 785998, of Houndmills, Basingstoke,
Hampshire RG21 6XS.

Palgrave Macmillan in the US is a division of St Martin's Press LLC,
175 Fifth Avenue, New York, NY 10010.

Palgrave Macmillan is the global academic imprint of the above companies
and has companies and representatives throughout the world.

Palgrave® and Macmillan® are registered trademarks in the United States,
the United Kingdom, Europe and other countries.

ISBN 978–0–230–25194–6 hardback

This book is printed on paper suitable for recycling and made from fully
managed and sustained forest sources. Logging, pulping and manufacturing
processes are expected to conform to the environmental regulations of the
country of origin.

A catalogue record for this book is available from the British Library.

Library of Congress Cataloging-in-Publication Data

Peterson, Andrew, 1976–
    Civic republicanism and civic education : the education of citizens /
Andrew Peterson.
        p. cm.
    Includes index.
    ISBN 978–0–230–25194–6 (hardback)
        1. Citizenship – Study and teaching. 2. Civics – Study and teaching.
    3. Democracy – Study and teaching. 4. Democracy and education. I. Title.

LC1091.P48 2011
372.83'2044—dc22   2011004891

10 9 8 7 6 5 4 3 2 1
20 19 18 17 16 15 14 13 12 11

Printed in the United States of America

For Jessica and Oliver

Contents

Acknowledgements

Whilst at times writing a book is a solitary experience, it is an endeavour which cannot be achieved alone. I have a number of people to thank for their advice and support. First, I would like to thank the following colleagues who each offered me thoughts, comments and critical reflections on the ideas found in this book: Professor James Arthur, Professor Ian Davies, Professor John Annette, Dr Lynn Revell and Bob Bowie. Second, I would like to thank colleagues at Palgrave Macmillan for supporting this project and helping me through the stages from proposal to publication. Third, and most importantly, I would like to thank my fiancée Jessica and my son Oliver for their unswerving love, support and understanding. They have helped me more than they can know, and for this I am eternally grateful.

Foreword

Since the 1990s there has been a revival of civic republican political thinking within Western political thought. In his book 'Civic Republicanism and Civic Education' Andrew Peterson offers a sophisticated and remarkably clear analysis of this revival in relation not only to the debate between liberalism and communitarianism but also to the way in which civic republicanism can offer a public philosophy which can address contemporary public policy issues. He also links this revival to the equally recent development of the rethinking of the history of political thought and the reconstruction of the civic humanist or republican 'tradition' of political thinking from Aristotle and Cicero via the 'Machiavellian Moment' to the foundations of the American Republic and beyond that to the elision of liberal and civic republican thinking in the nineteenth century exemplified by J. S. Mill. He provides a nuanced interpretation which allows for the diversity and complexity of civic republican thinking.

This is a remarkable book in terms of its clarity and its ability to address some of the key issues in civic republican political theory. I was greatly impressed by the author's consideration of some of the core themes in civic republican theory: the nature of civic obligation, the awareness of the common good, the role of civic virtue and the commitment to deliberative democratic engagement. The chapter on deliberative engagement and the analysis of the civic republican conception of citizenship as a practice of active and participatory engagement is to be welcomed.

What makes this book particularly original is that it probably is the first in-depth consideration of how the key themes of civic republicanism have influenced and can shape for the future the development of civic education in Western democratic nations. For this alone this book makes an original and substantial contribution to the literature on civic education, while it can also be read as an important contribution to our understanding of contemporary civic republican political theory.

PROFESSOR JOHN ANNETTE,
Birkbeck, University of London

Introduction

Any programme, initiative or curriculum for civic education must be built on a particular model (or models) of citizenship if it is to be meaningful and effective. For this reason civic education in our schools and classrooms should be neither distinct nor independent from philosophical discussions about the nature of citizenship. It is the role of political scientists interested in citizenship to spell out the educational importance of their work, and it is the job of the range of professionals involved in civic education (including teachers, school leadership teams, policy makers and academics) to ensure that what happens in schools and classrooms is not blind to important philosophical debates about what citizenship is and what it means to be a good citizen. The aim of this book is to make such links between political science and civic education in the light of what has become known as the 'civic republican revival' in political theory.

It is both necessary and useful to define from the outset the main terms and scope of this book. The term 'civic education' refers to any formative attempt to teach the knowledge, skills or dispositions required for citizenship. Civic education comes in many guises, ranging from what is often characterized as the passive rote-learning of civics to more active and participatory forms of learning. Moreover, whilst civic education incorporates classroom-based lessons, such learning reaches outside the classroom and incorporates not only the structures and ethos of schools themselves, but activities within the community as well. A theme which runs throughout the analysis of civic republicanism presented in this book is that civic education is a diffuse process which involves not just formal schooling, but the whole system of laws, institutions and, indeed, civic participation within political communities (Barber, 2003: 233).[1] In other words, civic education does not stop

1

when a pupil leaves school; it continues throughout adulthood through a complex system of formative processes. Notwithstanding this, the main focus here is on the formal teaching and learning of civic education in schools (particularly that which relates to pupils between the ages of 11 and 16).

There has been a renewed sense of interest in civic education across a number of nations in the last two decades. A central feature of such developments has been the role of the concept of 'citizenship' as a key organising and framing principle. Usually called 'citizenship education' or 'education for citizenship', the civic education programmes and initiatives that have developed in the last two decades in a number of Western democracies have been notable for the extent to which they have sought to engender not simply knowledge of the respective political systems and an understanding and respect for rights, but a more active and participatory model of citizenship that recognizes the existence of citizen responsibilities. This has involved a bringing together of civics knowledge with service learning (Boyte, 2003: 88). It is not enough to know what it means to be a citizen – one has to put this knowledge into action in a responsible way as a member of a political community. The reasons for this renewed interest in civic education are multiple, complex and inter-related,; they can broadly be understood as being three-fold. First, there is a belief in many Western democracies that the political awareness, understanding and activity of young people is in decline.[2] This has been coupled with the belief that such political apathy is associated with, and is even the cause of, increased social and moral deviancy.[3] The influence of this deficit model has been persuasive in encouraging policy makers to seek, at least in part, to remedy this 'decline' through civic education. The second reason has to do with the increasingly complex and heterogeneous nature of Western societies, and the cultural, ethnic and religious diversity which this brings. The third reason relates to the increasingly complex political and social world in which young people live. Forces such as globalisation, fast-paced technological changes and new forms of media mean that young people are subject to a range of forces (and possibly opportunities) which are inherently different from those of three or more decades ago. The recent resurgence in interest in civic education can, then, be understood as an attempt to engage young people in the lives of their political communities and to support them in handling the challenges raised by the complexities of contemporary life. In other words, it is an attempt to ensure that young people are educated so that they can actively and meaningfully participate in public life. As used in this book, the term 'public life' refers to a sphere of relationships and activities which is much wider than simply the public sector, and which has both a civic and civil element. The British intellectual David Marquand (2004: 27) provides a useful definition of what comprises public life:

> It is best understood as a dimension of social life, with its own norms and decision rules, cutting across sectoral boundaries: as a set of activities, which can be (and historically has been) carried out by private individuals, private charities and even private firms as well as public agencies. It is symbiotically linked to the notion of public interest, in principle distinct from private interests; central to it are the values of citizenship, equity and service. In it goods are distributed on the basis of need and not of personal ties or access to economic resources. It is a space, protected from the adjacent market and private domains, where strangers encounter each other as equal partners in the common life of society – a space for forms of human flourishing which cannot be bought in the market-place or found in the tight-knit community of the clan or family or group of intimates.

Alongside the increasing attention paid to the need for civic education, there has been a great deal of intellectual interest in the political theory of civic republicanism. In common usage the term 'republic' is mainly used to refer to a state which is not led by a monarch. Republicanism as a field of thought is, however, much richer than this. Ancient in origin, republican ideas have witnessed a revival (Sunstein, 1988; Gey, 1993; Dagger, 2004) within political theory since the late 1980s. Whilst some have made reference to and sought to delineate what might be seen as a civic republican 'tradition', others have attested to the amorphous nature of the field. Understood in broad terms, civic republicanism embodies an active conception of what it means to be a citizen, with citizenship defined *as a practice*. To be a citizen is to act in a particular way and within a particular political community. The concept of citizenship acts as the organising principle of contemporary republican ideas. Drawing on historical notions identified as deriving from the civic republican tradition, this active understanding of 'citizenship as practice' advocated by contemporary proponents of the theory incorporates a commitment to four inter-related principles. First, that citizens possess and should recognize certain *civic obligations*; second, that citizens must develop an awareness of *the common good*, which exists over and above their private self-interests; third, that citizens must possess and act in accordance with *civic virtue*; and fourth, that civic engagement in democracy should incorporate a *deliberative* aspect. Whilst these themes are treated separately throughout this book for the purposes of analytical clarity, it should be remembered that '[T]hese principles are related to one another; each republican commitment serves to inform and define the others' (Sunstein, 1988: 1541). In this sense the core republican commitments are interdependent.

Although the broad commitment to civic obligations, the common good, civic virtue and deliberative civic engagement is common to civic republican positions, it does not entail a shared understanding of either the basis or the substantive nature of such principles. As a result, civic republicanism does not denote a single, coherent idea, but permits multiple interpretations. For this reason, it makes sense to refer to 'republicanisms, rather than one unitary theory' (Maynor, 2003: 4; cf. Sunstein, 1988; Dagger, 2004). As one of the leading contemporary civic republican theorists – Michael Sandel (1998: 325) – points out however, '[T]hat republicanism is sufficiently capacious to inform different political and economic outlooks is no argument against it'. Those interested in civic education have much to gain from interrogating civic republicanism, and from seeking to understand the different arguments which republicans put forward. It is with these differences, and the questions and issues to which they give rise, that the analysis of this book concerns itself. What, then, is the link between civic education and civic republicanism? On a rather superficial level, the revival in interest in the latter has coincided with a renewed sense of vigour in the former. More presciently, most, if not all, programmes and initiatives in civic education in Western democratic nations over the last twenty years have either been explicitly premised on what might be termed a 'civic republican' model of citizenship or have at least been strongly sympathetic to such an approach. What is less clear is what such a 'civic republican' model of citizenship involves, particularly when we look more deeply at the broad commitments cited above. When we do so, and as the analysis of this book hopes to demonstrate, we find that there are important and measurable differences within civic republican political thought which raise pertinent issues for those engaged with civic education. This book is premised on my concern that civic republican ideas are being used to frame and inform the aims and purposes of civic education, as well as its curricular content, without always being accompanied by a sound and clear understanding of the true nature and complexities of contemporary civic republican thought, including the historical tradition upon which this is based.[4] It should be noted from the outset that civic republicans do not provide a clear and cohesive strategy for civic education; rather, the education of citizens represents only one aspect of their work amongst many. Whilst analyses of the implications of other political theories (most notably liberal and communitarian thought) for education, and civic education more specifically, are reasonably common, there is currently little detailed exploration of the links between civic republicanism and education and how such links might help to build a better understanding of the purposes and content of civic education. This book aims to, in some way, remedy this lack of attention.

It is necessary to address at the start what is perhaps the most obvious objection to any claim that civic republican models of citizenship may be of use and relevance to contemporary societies. This is the suggestion that, because they seek to excavate ideas from historical contexts and scholars, civic republican writers cannot escape from the vestiges of that past; namely the elements of historical republican thought that tolerated inequality and restricted citizenship to a few wealthy men. Such arguments miss the significant claim of contemporary republicans: that these ancient ideas are re-interpreted so as to discard the inequality of historical ideas and recognize political equality and pluralism. As Sherry (1995: 136) makes clear in her analysis of the civic republican revival, recent representations of the theory have 'lost some of its less savoury historical aspects, especially those associated with elitism and exclusionary limits on citizenship'. This book is not, however, intended as an uncritical manifesto for a civic republican informed approach to civic education. I am sympathetic to civic republican ideas, but do not view the field as being without problems. As I hope to show throughout the arguments expressed here, these problems are mainly due to the definitional and conceptual ambiguity (though this should not be confused with definitional and conceptual complexity) within civic republicanism as a field of political thought. Moreover, the book is premised on my view that whilst civic republican theory has a great deal to offer educational theory, policy and practice, its supporters need to be much clearer about the importance to their endeavour of formal civic education in schools. No form of civic republican political community can be sustained, much less operate effectively, unless young people in schools come to understand the nature of and the basis for active citizenship. Equally, any form of civic education which seeks to impart to young people the knowledge, skills and dispositions necessary for that citizenship stands to gain a great deal from civic republican accounts of citizenship. For this reason, I view the relationship between civic republican theory and civic education in symbiotic terms.

In summary, this book is concerned with civic republicanism and its potential for casting light on the purposes, content and focus of civic education programmes in contemporary Western democracies. Recognising that no curriculum, much less any curriculum for civic education, is neutral, the analysis provided here interrogates the nature of contemporary civic republican thought and explores the implications of this for current and future educational practice in this area. The book is divided into the following seven chapters. In Chapter 1 the context for the revival of civic republican ideas is considered in terms of political theory and public policy. Attention is also given to the links between this revival and recent interest in civic education. Chapter 2 comprises an exploration of ideas which fall within what has been called the civic republican 'tradition' of political ideas. The next three chapters consider the main commitments of contemporary civic republican political and moral thought. In Chapter 3 civic republican commitments to civic obligation and the common good are analysed and reviewed. Chapter 4 considers the basis and nature of republican concerns for civic virtue. Chapter 5 investigates the civic republican commitment to deliberative forms of political participation and civic engagement. Chapter 6 picks up in more detail, and analyses in a critical manner, the issues raised for civic education in Western democratic nations by civic republican commitments. Chapter 7 provides a summary of the main arguments of the book, offers some thoughts about further work required in determining more detailed civic republican models of citizenship for civic education, and finally presents a number of concluding thoughts.

1
The Civic Republican Revival

Beyond the broad republican commitments identified in the Introduction – commitments to civic obligations, the common good, civic virtue and civic deliberation – civic republicanism is a diverse theoretical field and cannot be reduced to a singular or unified set of commitments (from this point on the term 'civic republican' will be used with specific reference to contemporary writers unless otherwise indicated). Instead, civic republicanism is better understood as a broad philosophical and political position which permits a number of interpretations. This chapter is concerned with the reasons for the recent revival of interest in civic republican ideas. Its purpose is to establish the context in which civic republican theories have surfaced through a consideration, first, of civic republicanism's relationship to the liberal-communitarian debate and, second, its relationship to public philosophy. The chapter provides a brief overview of contemporary civic republican thought and locates it in relation to the two standpoints that have dominated political theory over the last forty years – namely liberalism and communitarianism. It goes on to establish links between civic republican ideas and recent developments in civic education, most notably the increase in approaches to civic education framed around the concept of citizenship. The analysis offered in this chapter provides the framework for the deeper exploration of civic republican ideas presented in the remaining chapters of the book.

Why the revival?

The late 1980s and early 1990s witnessed a 'revival' in civic republican thinking within Western political philosophy. If we are to understand contemporary civic republicanism, it is important that some initial attention be paid to the differing (if interrelated) forms which this revival has comprised. These are three-fold. First, since at least the 1960s a number of what might be termed *civic republican historians* have sought to trace key republican ideas through the work of a wide historical corpus of thinkers, texts and ideas (see, for example, Raab, 1965; Pocock, 1975; Skinner, 1990a, 1990b, 1997, 1998, 2002; Bock et al. 1990; Rahe, 1992; Held, 1996, 1997; Honohan, 2002). A central aspect of this work has been the developing sense in which a 'tradition' of civic republican thought has been identified. This is examined further in Chapter 2, but typically the civic republican tradition has been characterized as starting in ancient times in the work of Aristotle and Cicero and then developing through the work of a range of political thinkers including Niccolò Machiavelli, James Harrington, Jean-Jacques Rousseau and James Madison. The second form is the work of *civic republican* theorists who seek to relate historical ideas to tensions which they identify within contemporary Western democratic states in order to put forward normative political theories (cf. Honohan, 2002: 7–8). Initially, appeals to civic republicanism were located within the field of legal theory in the United States. Writers such as Thomas Pangle (1988), Frank Michelman (1986, 1988) and Cass Sunstein (1988) expounded republican ideas in order to restate the importance of civic republicanism as a set of ideas within American legal and constitutional thought. As Sunstein (1988: 1539) has pointed out, for republican theorists, 'the task is not simply one of excavation' but is instead the employment of republican ideas and principles to inform debates within public affairs as well as political philosophy. Since 1990 a number of political and public philosophers have sought to provide more detailed and extensive theories of contemporary civic republicanism. Prominent and important examples of such work include Adrian Oldfield's *Citizenship and Community: Civil Republicanism in the Modern World* (1990), Michael Sandel's *Democracy's Discontent: America in Search of a Public Policy* (1996), Philip Pettit's *Republicanism* (1999) and John Maynor's *Republicanism in the Modern World* (2003). Civic republican ideas and principles also figure in the work of a number of political theorists who draw on republican themes but do not present their ideas as necessarily constituting a republican theory (see, for example, Arendt, 1958; Pitkin, 1981; Barber, 1984, 1998, 2003; Bellah et al., 1985; Marquand, 1994; Macedo et al., 2005). The American political scientist Benjamin Barber's (1998: 38) theory of 'Strong Democracy', which he cites as 'cousin' of civic republicanism, is illustrative of such work. Third, and to some extent less developed, is the increasing reference to civic republican ideas which can be identified within political and public policy debate. This tendency, which is explored in more detail later in the chapter, is most clearly illustrated in the policies and discourse of two national governments. First, the political agenda and reasoning of the Spanish Socialist Workers' Party (*Partido Socialista Obrero Español*) governments led by José Luis Rodrìguez Zapatero in Spain since 2004, and, second, the policies and discourse of the successive New Labour governments in the United Kingdom between 1997 and 2010. The referencing and, to some extent, the application of civic republican ideas within national policy is significant, and attests to the growing role of republican ideas of in public life, as well as in political theory. There is a concern, however, that civic republican ideas are being operationalized in public policy without due attention being paid to their meanings, historical roots and complexities (cf. Maynor, 2003).

That civic republican thought has witnessed a 'revival' in political and public philosophy over the last three decades is difficult to dispute, but why has this been so? The two single most important reasons have been, first, the belief by its proponents that civic republican theory can add to and advance what is widely termed the liberal-communitarian debate within political philosophy and, second, the public policy view that civic republicanism ideas are useful in responding to perceived tensions within contemporary liberal Western democratic societies (cf. Dagger, 2004: 167).

The liberal-communitarian debate

A common starting point for those seeking to define civic republican ideas is to locate them within the context of the liberal-communitarian debate that has shaped Western political philosophy over the last four decades. This debate has been pervasive, and a number of positions have developed within both liberal and communitarian thought which make it unwise to conflate distinct standpoints within each field without some recognition that these terms are, themselves, diverse rather than unitary (Keeney, 2007). Nevertheless, there are certain basic ideas that have fundamentally divided liberals and communitarians and that are important in seeking to understand the development of recent republican thinking.

Since the 1970s two main forms of liberalism have been prominent in Western political philosophy: 'contractual' (Patten, 1996) or 'procedural' liberalism (Taylor, 1995; Sandel, 1996) and 'libertarian' liberalism. Whilst sharing some commonalities, the two forms of liberalism differ in their view of how far the state should provide for the welfare of its citizens. Whilst libertarian liberals trust the free market to secure justice, contractual liberals accept that the state has an important role to play in securing this end (see Kymlicka, 2002 for a detailed and accessible analysis of the differences between these two forms of liberalism). Of these two types of liberalism, it is the contractual form that has been most prominent in shaping political and philosophical debate in Western nations since the appearance of three highly influential texts in the 1970s: John Rawls' *A Theory of Justice* (1971), Robert Nozick's *Anarchy, State and Utopia* (1977), and Ronald Dworkin's *Taking Rights Seriously* (1978a). Collectively, these texts reinvigorated the Kantian transcendental self within the contemporary context and depicted the individual citizen as essentially prior to any social or communal form of organization, and it is Rawls whose ideas most fundamentally accounted for this development. In *A Theory of Justice* (1971: 560), Rawls argued that, in its natural state, the self is 'unencumbered' by any communal ties and obligations, observing that 'we should ... reverse the relation between the right and the good proposed by teleological doctrines and view the right as prior'. On the basis that all societal commitments are secondary to the pre-societal self, contractarian liberals are typically sceptical of any attempt by the state to adopt a formative role regarding a particular view of the best form of living. They argue that individuals should be free to choose and follow their own conception of the good life rather than having a conception of the good imposed upon them. To this extent, the state remains neutral and it does not privilege one conception of the good over another. Furthermore, individuals possess important rights to protect them from interference, whether from the state or from other citizens, in the pursuit of their chosen ends. Rawls (1980: 544; cf. Kymlicka, 2002: 215), for example, argues that:

> As free persons, citizens recognize one another as having the moral power to have a conception of the good. This means that they do not view themselves as inevitably tied to the pursuit of the particular conception of the good and its final ends which they espouse at any given time. Instead, as citizens, they are regarded as, in general, capable of revising and changing this conception on reasonable and rational grounds. Thus it is held to be permissible for citizens to stand apart from conceptions of the good and to survey and assess their various final ends. (Rawls, 1980: 544)

On the basis that the self is conceptualized as being prior to society, contemporary liberals have typically viewed rights as prior to the good.

Dworkin (1978b: 35) illustrates this stance when he contends that 'if someone has a right to do something, then it is wrong for the government to deny it to him even though it would be in the general interest to do so'. For procedural liberals, self-determination in the choice and pursuit of final ends represents the 'only way to respect individuals fully as human beings' (Kymlicka, 2002: 212–3).

Based on the understanding of individuals as able to rationally choose and revise their own ends, liberals have advanced a negative understanding of freedom in terms of non-interference. According to Berlin's (1998: 194) classic conception of negative freedom, an individual is 'said to be free to the degree to which no man or body of men interferes with [his] activity'. This liberal understanding of freedom as non-interference developed from the work of classical liberals such as Hobbes, Paley and Bentham, and is concerned with removing unnecessary constraints on the actions of citizens. The principle of non-interference in turn informs a basic set of civil liberties such as freedom of religion, freedom of speech and freedom of movement. This concept of freedom as non-interference features within contemporary liberal theories. Any attempt by the state to restrict the actions of citizens, including through the law, represents a transgression of individual liberty. However, such interference is legitimized through the principle of a social contract, and to the extent to which it accords with a more general principle of liberal equality. In this sense, for contemporary liberals such as Rawls, the concept of liberty, whilst important, remains secondary to a wider theory of justice. From this liberal perspective, citizenship is necessary in the sense that without a degree of citizen action, liberal institutions would cease to be effective, but it is both voluntary and temporary. As Barber (2003: 8) points out in his characterization of the liberal requirements of the citizen, '[C]itizenship is an artificial role that the natural man prudently adopts in order to safeguard his solitary humanity'. Individuals enter the realm of citizenship for particular purposes and at particular times, and are free to retreat into the realms of private life and the market as they so wish.

In the 1980s a number of 'communitarian theorists' (MacIntyre, 1981, 1988; Walzer, 1983; Sandel, 1984; Bellah et al., 1985; Taylor, 1985) critiqued the main tenets of the liberal position and sought to provide a more robust account of social membership and bonds. In rejecting the concept of the unencumbered self, communitarian theorists contested the liberal principle that communal ties were optional. Instead, they argued that the self was essentially 'situated' or 'embedded' in the social groupings and practices to which it belongs (Sandel, 1982; 1996;

cf. Kymlicka, 2002: 221). In other words, we are constituted by our communities. The influential communitarian moral philosopher Alasdair MacIntyre (1981: 204–205) explains this in the following way:

> we all approach our own circumstances as bearers of a particular social identity. I am someone's son or daughter, someone else's cousin or uncle; I am a citizen of this or that city, a member of this or that guild or profession; I belong to this clan, that tribe, this nation. Hence what is good for me has to be good for one who inhabits these roles. As such, I inherit from the past of my family, my city, my tribe, my nation, a variety of debts, inheritances, rightful expectations and obligations. These constitute the given way of my life, my moral starting point.

Similarly, in *Liberalism and the Limits of Justice* Michael Sandel (1982: 18–19; emphasis in original) argues that in constructing humans as unencumbered, liberals mistakenly deny the possibility of individuals possessing '*constitutive* ends': roles or commitments that 'could define one so completely that I could not understand myself without [them]'. Founded on their questioning that the self was essentially prior to society, communitarian theorists dispute the liberal position regarding rights. In prioritizing individual rights over the common good, liberals such as Rawls argue, firstly, that certain rights were so important that it could never be justifiable to override them in favour of the general welfare of the community and, secondly, that the understanding of justice that underpinned individual rights should not appeal to any specific conception of the good life. It is on this second claim that communitarian scholars largely focus. Therefore, communitarians contend that the notion of the common good is one that has value and merit within contemporary society. The communitarian response to the liberal commitment to freedom as non-interference has been two-fold. First, communitarians have critiqued liberal theories as incorporating an overly individualistic or 'atomistic' understanding of human agency (Taylor, 1995). Second, on the basis of this critique, communitarians suggest that true freedom can only be understood in collective terms, and can only be achieved through engagement in the common enterprise of a community. For communitarians freedom is, as Taylor (1979: 157) puts it, 'situated'.

There has been a great deal of work which has sought to draw out the implications of recent liberal and communitarian political thought in relation to both education and, more specifically, civic education.[5]

Theobald and Snauwaert (1995: 2) encapsulate the educational differences between the two approaches:

> The fundamental purpose of communitarian education is the transmission of cultural heritage, and with it enculturation into an ethic of association wherein there are fundamental obligations to the common good. In contrast, the fundamental purpose of liberal education is preparation for defining and pursuing one's own conception of the good life and with it enculturation into an ethic of tolerance wherein there is respect for the equal rights of others.

The differences highlighted in this passage have clear implications for civic education. A liberal informed civic education concerns itself primarily with an understanding of the rights of a citizen and the development of certain capacities, such as critical thinking, tolerance and respect, required to secure and protect such individual rights. The type of civic education which liberals typically have in mind is 'rather minimal' (Victoria Costa, 2004: 1; for a clear and concise account of liberal political and civic education see Levinson, 1999). In the American context, Harry Boyte (2003: 88) has identified this liberal approach as predominating in civic education. He suggests that 'the focus is on the state, on the one side, describing departments of government, processes of legislation and the like. On the other side, the focus is on the individual, who is conceived as a bearer of rights. The role of the government is to secure such rights and ensure a fair or just distribution of goods and resources, as well as to maintain the rule of law'. According to Boyte, this liberal dominance has been challenged recently by what Arthur (2000) has termed the 'communitarian agenda in education'. Communitarian models of civic education prompt schools to consider the importance of teaching young people about their obligations to the community and to the common good, largely through service to their communities. Also central to communitarian civic education programmes is the development of character traits that can also be formed and expressed by providing pupils with the opportunity to learn in community settings.

Civic republicanism and the liberal-communitarian debate

The growth in interest in civic republicanism can be understood largely as a response to the tensions between liberalism and communitarianism, and as growing out of the debate between the proponents of these two schools of thought (cf. Frazer, 1999; Little, 2002). To identify commonalities and distinctions between contemporary liberals or communitarians and civic republicans is a complex task. First and foremost, the labels themselves can be problematic. Michael Sandel's work in the 1980s, for example, was widely identified as 'communitarian' – an ascription with which he (alongside other notable communitarians such as Michael Walzer and Alasdair MacIntyre) has not always been happy. Since the 1990s, however, Sandel has been very clear regarding the civic republican essence of his thinking. It is also true that many liberal writers, including Will Kymlicka, William Galston, Joseph Raz, John Gray, and, in his later work, John Rawls, reference elements of republican thought to supplement (though, importantly, not to replace) the liberal orientation of their work. This has aimed at providing liberal political theory with a more robust account of community and citizenship so that liberal notions of autonomy, choice and freedom become connected to certain features and benefits of communal forms of living. Furthermore, whilst some commentators have made links between certain forms of republican thinking and communitarianism (Frazer, 1999), others have looked to differentiate the two fields (Honohan, 2002; Kymlicka, 2002; Dagger, 2004). The relationship with liberal thought is even more complex. Whilst some interpret contemporary republicanism as a reaction to liberalism, others see certain forms of republican arguments as essentially liberal in nature. Sunstein (1988: 1541, 1567, 1589), for example, argues that his own republican ideas are 'not antiliberal at all' and incorporate 'central features of the liberal tradition'. He suggests, furthermore, that 'the most powerful versions of republicanism ... borrow from a significant strand of the liberal tradition'. Along similar lines, Viroli (1999: 6) explicitly challenges the view that 'republicanism is an alternative to liberalism'. Others have also sought to draw areas of commensurability (Patten, 1996; Rawls, 1996; Kymlicka, 1998; Shklar, 1998) between liberalism and republicanism, whilst some have explicitly sought to combine liberal with republican ideas. A particularly strong proponent of the latter is Richard Dagger (1997: 4). He suggests that 'we must find some way to restore a sense of common purpose to civic life ... But restoring a sense of common purpose does not mean abandoning our concern for rights'. Dagger locates this principle as stemming from key liberal thinkers, arguing that '[I]n John Locke, Montesquieu, James Madison, Immanuel Kant, John Stuart Mill, T. H. Green, and others, the "republican"' tendency is interwoven with the "liberal"'. This complexity has to an extent resulted from the fact that whereas the liberal and communitarian writers referred to earlier were fundamentally concerned with theories of justice, contemporary civic republicans have tended to present theories of citizenship, at the very least, as an 'important supplement' to wider theories of justice (Kymlicka, 2002: 287).[6] Integral to republican ideas of citizenship, and in turn conceptions of justice, is the question of what it means for a citizen to be free.

Civic republicanism and freedom

The key defining and organizing concept for republicans today is that of freedom.[7] At first sight, this may appear somewhat surprising. In political discourse freedom is often viewed as synonymous with liberalism, and more specifically with the principle of freedom as non-interference. It was perhaps most famously defined in the 1950s by the political philosopher Isaiah Berlin in his distinction between positive and negative liberty. Recognizing that 'every moralist in human history has praised freedom' but that the word's 'meaning is so porous that there is little interpretation that it seems able to resist', Berlin's (1998: 193) analysis distinguishes between positive and negative liberty (for Berlin, freedom and liberty were the same). Berlin (1998: 203) defines the former in terms of self-mastery, which he expresses in the following passage:

> I wish my life and my decisions to depend on myself, not on external forces of whatever kind. I wish to be the instrument of my own, not of other men's, acts of will. I wish to be a subject, not an object; to be moved by reasons, by conscious purposes, which are my own, not by causes which affect me, as it were, from outside. I wish to be somebody, not nobody; a doer – deciding, not being decided for, self-directed and not acted upon by external nature or by other men as if I were a thing, or an animal, or a slave incapable of playing a human role, that is, of conceiving goals and policies of my own and realising them.

This Berlin compares with negative liberty, which has to do with the 'degree to which no man or body of men interferes with my activity' and is concerned with the 'area within which a man can act unobstructed by others' (1998: 194). It is this latter sense of freedom, the negative sense of freedom as non-interference, which Berlin finds expressed in the work of leading early modern, modern and enlightenment liberal scholars such as Hobbes, Bentham, Mill, de Tocqueville and Montesquieu (cf. Pettit, 1999). Berlin's distinction between negative and positive liberty had also been prefigured in that drawn between different types of liberty drawn by the Swiss born writer and French politician Benjamin Constant in 1816. Constant (1988: 316–7) distinguished between the 'liberty of the ancients' and the 'liberty of the moderns', contending that

> We are no longer able to enjoy the liberty of the ancients which consisted in an active and constant participation in the collective power. Our liberty consists in the peaceful enjoyment of private independence... The purpose of the ancients was the sharing of the social power among all of the citizens of the same fatherland. It is to this that they gave the name liberty. The purpose of the moderns is security in private enjoyment, and they gave the name liberty to the guarantees accorded by the institutions to that enjoyment.

Here, Constant makes the important distinction between freedom as self-government and freedom as the protection of private interests.[8] It is this distinction which has interested those concerned with civic republicanism, as it reminds them of an older and deeper conception of freedom that can be expressed in terms of participation in self-government.

The development and prevalence of the liberal sense of freedom as non-interference – in other words, the liberty of the moderns – during, and since, the Enlightenment period has led to a condition in which freedom has come to be 'separated in theory from civic virtue' (Sullivan, 1995: 188). Civic republicans want to remedy this disjunction and restate the relationship between the two. As Viroli (1999: 103) asserts, once this is accepted, the recent renewal of interest in republicanism can be understood as presenting a 'political vision of a civic ethos that reconnects the words "liberty" and "responsibility"'. A central aspect of recent civic republican writing has been the call to 're-educate the modern political mind' in valuing the politically active life (Duncan, 1995: 148). However, the nature of a politically active life, including its purposes and outcomes, is not agreed upon by republicans. At the heart of such disagreements is the concept of liberty or freedom.

In seeking to categorize civic republican conceptions of freedom, a distinction can be drawn between two strands of republican thought (Skinner, 1986; Held, 1996; Patten, 1996; Rawls, 1996; Sandel, 1996; Maynor, 2003). This distinction is based on a division between those contemporary republicans who value political participation for *intrinsic* reasons and those who identify its value for *instrumental* reasons (cf. Kymlicka, 2002; for a dissenting voice regarding the historical integrity of this distinction, see Dagger, 1997: 187). Drawing on the Aristotelian understanding of the political nature of man, some republicans – like Michael Sandel and Adrian Oldfield – seek to reinvigorate forms of Constant's 'liberty of the ancients' within Western societies today. As such, they appeal to the principle that freedom exists when men and women are able to participate in the exercise of self-government. Moreover, they suggest that this civic engagement relates (at least partially) to a form of the good life. That is, that involvement in public affairs is conducive to a good way of living. Republicans who promote freedom in terms of participation in self-government make specific claims about the essentially intrinsic worth or value of participation in civic affairs. Sandel (1996: 26) explains this position in the following terms: 'given our nature as political beings, we are free only insofar as we exercise our capacity to deliberate about the common good, and participate in the public life of a free city or republic'.

The interpretation of freedom as participation in the exercise of self-government is not the only form of liberty found within republican work. Some republicans have rejected the notion that freedom is commensurate with self-government and have advanced instead a 'negative' conception of freedom, but one which differs from the liberal principle of non-interference. They prioritize the idea of freedom as non-domination, and in doing so appeal to the instrumental value of active civic engagement by citizens. This instrumental approach is expressed clearly by Quentin Skinner in his consideration of the republican tradition which stems from ancient Rome when he conjectures that for many historical republican writers, 'participation (at least by way of representation) constitutes a necessary precondition of maintaining individual liberty' (1997: 75). Whilst at first glance freedom as non-domination bears a resemblance to Berlin's definition of positive liberty in terms of self-mastery cited above, its proponents have been clear to differentiate the two. In making this distinction there is an explicit assertion that neither Berlin's, nor indeed Constant's, characterization of liberty recognizes freedom in the sense that contemporary instrumental republicans hold dear, that is, in the sense of non-domination (Viroli, 1999). The political and legal philosopher, Philip Pettit (1999), a leading proponent of contemporary republicanism, states this in bold terms: 'I believe that the negative-positive distinction has served us ill in political thought, It has sustained the philosophical illusion that, details aside, there are just two ways of understanding liberty' (1999: 18). Drawing on the historical republican work of Quentin Skinner,

Pettit has been the main proponent of the conception of freedom in terms of non-domination. Pettit, and other instrumental republicans like him, counter the idea of only two forms of liberty by suggesting that freedom as non-domination represents a third, which sits outside of the frameworks of both Berlin and Constant. Freedom as non-domination can be defined as the absence of arbitrary dominance or 'an absence of mastery by others' (Pettit, 1999: 22). As Pettit (1999: 22) explains, this idea shares with the liberty of the moderns 'the focus on absence, not presence' and shares with the liberty of the ancients 'the focus on mastery, not interference'. Domination is defined by Pettit (1999: 52) as 'a certain power ... of interference on an arbitrary basis' and he argues that it takes two forms: '*Imperium*' is vertical in nature and refers to the domination of citizens by the state, whilst '*Dominium*' is horizontal in nature and relates to the domination of one citizen, or group of citizens, over another.

For some, the republican formulation of freedom as non-domination that Pettit sets out, and to which others following him have subscribed,[9] is too similar to the liberal notion of freedom as non-interference to warrant the drawing of a line between the two conceptions. For this reason, the distinction that Pettit constructs between the liberal concept of freedom as non-interference and the republican concept of freedom as non-domination is worth unpicking. Both positions are negative in that they hold that the liberty of citizens is transgressed when they are subject to some form of constraint or restriction placed upon them either by the State or by fellow citizens. Their difference lies in the nature and extent of such constraints and restrictions. In his work on republican liberty, Skinner (1997, 1998, 2002) presents freedom as non-interference and as non-domination as fundamentally related. Skinner identifies in the republican tradition on which he draws a sense in which freedom involves the absence of both interference and domination: he argues, in other words, that the liberal account of liberty forms a constituent element of the republican concern for freedom. In contrast to this, Pettit (1999, 2002) has sought to highlight the differences between the liberal and the republican formulations, and in doing so has prioritized non-domination over non-interference. He gives two reasons for this. First, whereas freedom as non-interference is concerned with the specific actions which restrict individual liberty, freedom as non-domination focuses on the *existence* of arbitrary power rather than its exercise. Second, freedom as non-domination allows the lives of citizens to be constrained provided that that constraint has certain checks and does not occur on an arbitrary basis. In this way, the republican appeal to non-domination should be understood, in part, as a critique of liberalism's 'relative indifference to power or domination' (Pettit, 1999: 9). Freedom as non-domination, then, presents a particular form of liberty which values the civic engagement of citizens for *instrumental* reasons. This form of republicanism can be understood as seeking to 'reverse the retreat from republican liberty that occurred in the late eighteenth century and to employ the conception of liberty as non-domination to rethink the form that the state should take as well as the policy agenda that the state should adopt' (Martí and Pettit, 2010: 52; cf. Lovett and Pettit, 2009).

Civic republican conceptions of citizenship, then, have at their core particular conceptions of freedom. As the analysis presented in this book hopes to show, these conceptions of freedom are fundamental in shaping and providing substantive detail to the broad commitments of civic republican thought outlined in the Introduction. This task is taken up in the chapters that follow. Attention here now turns to a second, and of course related, context, within which civic republican ideas have surfaced over the last three decades: the increasingly prominent referencing of civic republicanism within what might generally be defined as 'public philosophy and policy'.

Civic republicanism, public philosophy and policy

A defining feature of recent civic republican writing is that its proponents position their work in terms of public philosophy. As well as making a contribution to political philosophy, republicans are keen to show that their work has importance in terms of critiquing current public policies and of how contemporary Western democracies might increase civic commitment and engagement. The subtitle of Michael Sandel's main civic republican text *Democracy's Discontent: America in Search of a Public Philosophy* affirms this element of the republican project. This turn to the public policy potential and implications of their work generally starts from a characteristic common to all contemporary republican writing, namely its critique of the dominance of liberalism as the main organizing public philosophy within Western democratic societies. Civic republicans point in particular to a number of interrelated tensions caused by the pursuance of liberal politics and policies which relate to the relationship between individuals, their communities and the wider society.

A number of influential and high-profile commentators have raised their concern at what they view as a decline in civic and civil participation. Such a decline is viewed as a result of an increased sense of individualism and private concern in contemporary Western societies. In the United States, two seminal works in this regard are Robert Bellah et al.'s *Habits of the Heart: Individualism and Commitment in American Life* and Robert Putnam's *Bowling Alone: The Collapse and Revival of American Community*. Using the language of communitarianism, Bellah et al. (1985) identify a decline in the social bonds which attached Americans to their social, cultural and political communities. For Bellah and his colleagues (1985: 277), the dominance of liberal individualism has cemented a misplaced fear in Americans that:

> if we give up our dream of private success for a more genuinely integrated societal community, we will be abandoning our separation and individuation, collapsing into dependence and tyranny. What we find hard to see is that it is the extreme fragmentation of the modern world that really threatens our individuation; that what is best in our separation and individuation, our sense of dignity and autonomy as persons, requires a new integration if it is to be sustained.

The highly influential work of Robert Putnam (2000) points to a similar process to that identified by Bellah et al. He suggests that since the 1950s America has witnessed a decline in civic and civil forms of association and action. Putnam cites a range of factors, including lower voter turnout, engagement with political parties, less philanthropy, and declining membership of social organizations as evidence of a general decline in social capital. In 2005, a group of esteemed political scientists, including Putnam and led by Stephen Macedo, published *Democracy at Risk: How Political Choices Undermine Citizen Participation, and What Can We Do About It*. The report grew out of the American Political Science Association's first Standing Committee on Civic Education and Engagement, and in it the authors suggest the problem with civic participation in America has three characteristics: 'questionable legitimacy, high cynicism, and great indifference'. Their response is to call for 'increased participation, more equal participation, and a higher quality of participation' (Macedo, 2005: 16). There are many more sources which could be cited in support of these claims that civic life in American has become somewhat impoverished.

Writing in an Italian context, the republican scholar Maurizio Viroli identifies identical trends within his own country. In an eloquent depiction of contemporary Italy, Viroli (1999: x) depicts two different sections of Italian societies. He suggests that '[O]ne is comprised of people who are concerned only with their families and their own personal successes, the other of people who have a strong civic awareness and are actively engaged in commitments to their community'. The relationship between these two sections of Italian society is complex and intertwined; with some Italians engaging in both the private and civic realms. The problem according to Viroli is that 'uncivic Italy is far stronger than civic Italy, and this is true for many other countries as well'.[10] Writing in the context of the United Kingdom in the 1990s, Dick Atkinson (1994: 1) observes that '[A]cross Britain people are worrying as never before about the state of their streets and communities', adding that '[M]any also feel that the corollary of weak communities is that our beliefs in common values and our sense of responsibility for each other has atrophied'. David Marquand (2004) has expressed similar concerns, and has written about a 'decline of the public' and a resultant 'hollowing-out of citizenship'. Critical of the New Right policies which characterized the Conservative governments in the 1980s led by Margaret Thatcher, Marquand argues that the public domain had been subjected to aggressive state policies aimed at destabilizing the public domain. Expressing his concern in strong terms, Marquand (2004: 2) believes that this process represented a 'relentless *kulturkampf* designed to root out the culture of service and citizenship which had become part of the social fabric'. Similar trends can be identified, though perhaps less pointedly, in relation to other Western democracies.[11] These sentiments are similar to those on which republicans themselves draw in their critique of contemporary societies, which they perceive to have become dominated by liberal individualism and the retraction of public citizens into the private realm. It is perhaps not surprising, therefore, that there has been a degree of interest in the extent to which civic republican ideas can be operationalized into public policy. Whilst such links are somewhat in their infancy, two prominent examples are useful for illustrative purposes.

The first illustration of the application of civic republicanism within public policy is provided in the political approach and ideas of the leader of the ruling Spanish Socialist Workers' Party, José Luis Rodrìguez Zapatero. Zapatero has been vocal about the extent to which he is committed to the form of republicanism advanced by Philip Pettit. References to Pettit's work were made in Zapatero's time in opposition between 2002 and 2004, and have continued to influence his political agenda since his accession to power in 2004. A leading advisor to Zapatero, José Andrés Torres Mora, has explained the relationship in the following way: 'Philip Pettit provided us with the appropriate grammar to furnish our political intuitions, to express the kind of proposals and dreams we had in mind for Spain. Pettit's republicanism has been our north star' (cited in Martí and Pettit, 2010: 1). In a speech made in 2001, Zapatero reinforced the importance of civic republicanism to his socialist political programme:

> The modern political philosophy called republicanism ... is very important to what we want for our country. I think that socialism must make an intellectual effort to think about the politics for the twenty-first century: the varieties of political organization, the structure of the political system, the channels for participation and for fostering something truly republican: the civic virtues manifested in political in political behaviour and public debate, and attitude of great tolerance for individual autonomy, about new ways of living together, about emergent values; and a strong defence of politics as a real instrument for changing people's lives, not to offer them an abstract new world, but to make everyone's world better and better, and to allow them to participate in defining it.

Throughout his first term in office, Zapatero frequently justified his party's policies with reference to republican arguments (for a full analysis of these, see Martí and Pettit, 2010). According to Martí and Pettit, an interesting corollary of Zapatero's attachment to republican principles, and of his explicit talk of these in the discourse of his party's politics, has been an increased interest in republicanism and its central themes within public debate in Spain. As a result, republican ideas have become openly discussed, critiqued and debated in a range of popular media.

Whilst the centrality of Pettit's form of republicanism to Zapatero's policies provides the clearest and most detailed example of the applied relationship between public policy and republican theory, this is not its only instance. A second illustration is provided in the British context by the Labour governments around the turn of the millennium, at which time the phrase 'civic republicanism' featured prominently within the discourse of David Blunkett – a leading member of the Labour government led by then Prime Minister Tony Blair (cf. Annette, 2008). In his time as Secretary of State for Education and Employment, Blunkett oversaw the introduction of statutory classes in citizenship education for all pupils in state schools aged between 11 and 16. During his subsequent time as Secretary of State for the Home Department, Blunkett identified civic republican principles as being of central importance in underpinning the Labour government's policies on communities. These policies were built around the concept of civic renewal. This commitment was spelt out in Blunkett's *Community Service Volunteers Edith Kahn Memorial Lecture* and the resultant pamphlet *Active Citizens, Strong Communities – Progressing Civic Renewal*. In the lecture, Blunkett (2003a: 19) asserted that:

> The 'civic republican' tradition of democratic thought has always been an important influence for me...This tradition offers us a substantive account of the importance of community, in which duty and civic virtues play a strong and formative role. As such, it a tradition of thinking which rejects unfettered individualism and criticises the elevation of individual entitlements above the common values needed to sustain worthwhile and purposeful lives. We do not enter life unencumbered by any community commitments, and we cannot live in isolation from others (Blunkett, 2003: 19).

In the pamphlet, Blunkett (2003b: 2) further invoked the memory of strong communities of the past, suggesting that the challenge for today was to build communities that were similarly strong, and which built a 'sense of belonging', 'shared goals', 'solidarity', 'mutuality' and 'democratic self-determination'. In spelling out these values, Blunkett made clear that they had 'long been associated with what political theorists have referred to as the civic republican tradition' (2003b: 3).

Though these are the two clearest examples of a burgeoning link between civic republican political theory and public policy, there are, perhaps, further examples. Writing in the spring of 2008 in the lead-up to the Presidential elections in the US, Robert Bellah, writing in the *Commonweal*, identified a civic republican element within the writing and rhetoric of Barack Obama. In setting out the case for supporting Obama (the article was entitled *Yes He Can: The Case for Obama*), Bellah praised Obama's understanding of the conditions of American society, in both a historical and a contemporary sense, and his invocation of a sense of hope for change. As Bellah (2008) pointed out, in the process of seeking the nomination to stand as the Democratic Party's Presidential candidate, Obama drew on biblical and theological language, whilst 'in his emphasis on public participation at every level, in his refusal to take money from lobbyists and political action committees, he is reviving the spirit of civic republicanism, of voters as citizens responsible for the common good, not political consumers concerned only with themselves'. What is notable in the vignettes presented here is not so much that politicians and political actors have sought to use a discourse of increased civic engagement and political participation by citizens, but rather that they have openly and explicitly aligned these with civic republican principles (or, in the case of Obama, have at least had these ascribed to them).

Civic republicanism and civic education

Civic republicans do not necessarily present comprehensive or detailed educational theories. However, understood broadly and in both informal and formal senses, they are concerned with education, and more specifically with civic education. This is because all republicans are fundamentally interested in how citizens learn to become active, engaged members of their political communities. As Barber (1998: 229) puts it so eloquently in his exposition of Thomas Jefferson's commitment to education, '...without citizens there could be no republic, and without education there would be no citizens'. In answer to the question as to whether citizens need preparation and formation for the role of citizens, republicans respond with a resounding 'yes'. Indeed, education is a central requirement for the realization and maintenance of republican polities. In this regard, Philip Pettit has cast the need for education in general terms, arguing that '[I]t is essential for the widespread enjoyment of non-domination that citizens understand and are informed about their society and polity, having the know-how required for a full, engaged life' (in Martí and Pettit, 2010: 77). John Maynor (2003: 181) has spoken more directly about the need for civic education in relation to his instrumental republican position, arguing that 'a modern republican state must play an active role in the content of public education by educating citizens in the substance and forms of non-domination, and the necessary values and virtues that accompany it'.

The increase in interest in civic republican thought has coincided with (and at times has been importantly linked to) an increased concern in many Western nations for making provision for the civic education of young people.[12] A feature common to curricular initiatives across a number of nations is that they are shaped in language and terms which, explicitly or implicitly, have a good deal in common with civic republican thought. According to Hughes, Print and Sears (2010: 295), a commitment to a civic republican conception of citizenship can be viewed as common to civic education programmes across the democratic world. This connection is most clearly illustrated in the introduction of statutory lessons in citizenship education for pupils of 11–16 years of age in state schools in England. The statutory Citizenship

Order (QCA, 1999), which set out the Programmes of Study for the new subject for teaching from August 2002, drew heavily upon the reasoning and recommendations of the *Advisory Group for Education and the Teaching of Democracy in Schools* (QCA, 1998; hereafter the 'Report of the Advisory Group') chaired by (later Sir) Bernard Crick. In their report, the Advisory Group (QCA, 1998: 11–13, 2.11) constructed a model of education for citizenship based upon three interdependent themes: social and moral responsibility, community involvement and political literacy. On the basis of these, the Citizenship Order (QCA, 1999: 184–5) established a set of learning outcomes for pupils at Key Stages three and four through which pupils would acquire 'knowledge and understanding about becoming informed citizens', whilst developing 'skills of enquiry and communication' and 'skills of participation and responsible action'. To this end the Report of the Advisory Group and the resultant Citizenship Order contained a number of elements, broadly liberal in nature (Lockyer, 2003: 2) and common to previous curricular initiatives in education for citizenship in England. Critical and independent thinking about topical political and social issues was encouraged, and there was a clear recognition of the controversial form that such issues may take. However, in establishing the broad but clear principles which should underpin the new subject, the Citizenship Order, informed by the Report of the Advisory Group, incorporated an approach to civic education which included certain significant civic republican ideas on citizenship, most notably civic obligations, the common good, civic virtue and deliberative forms of civic engagement (Crick, 2000; Annette, 2003, 2005, 2008; Lockyer, 2003).

As Arthur (2000: 79) argues, 'the view of citizenship education outlined by the government's advisory group…appears to take the view that the citizen must participate in the democratic process in order to be a citizen'. The key aim of this approach to civic education in England is that pupils acquire the values, attitudes and skills necessary for political participation, which are concerned with 'sharing in rule as well as in being ruled' (Lockyer, 2003: 2). This position was established clearly in the Report of the Advisory Group's (QCA, 1998: 1.5, 7–8) most famous statement that '[W]e aim at no less than a change in the political culture of this country both nationally and locally: for people to think of themselves as active citizens, willing, able and equipped to have an influence in public life'. Whilst theoretical understandings of citizenship have been important to citizenship education in England, and have received some attention in the academic discourse on the subject, their place in justifying and shaping curriculum initiatives has largely been *implicit* rather than *explicit*, and has often remained secondary to more expedient justifications (cf. Crick, 2003: 15). Nevertheless, the influence of civic republican ideas upon the aims and nature of citizenship education in England has been attested to by a number of commentators (Crick, 2000, 2002, 2003; Lockyer, 2003; Annette, 2003, 2005). Crick (2002: 114) himself subsequently reflected that:

> I often wonder how many of my group realised that they were signing up to the radical agenda of civic republicanism rather than the less demanding 'good citizen' and 'rule of law' imperatives of liberal democracy.

England is not alone in providing its young people with a formal curriculum of civic education based on the concept of citizenship, nor is it alone in detailing a curriculum for such purposes that chimes with civic republican thought. Particular forms of education for citizenship have also been developed (either by national or by individual state or provincial governments) in a number of Western democratic nations over the last twenty years. The importance of education for citizenship in Europe has been recognized at a supra-national level by the European Union. In October 1997 at a summit of Heads of State and Government of the Council of Europe, a commitment was made to the development of education for democratic citizenship. In 2002 the Council of Europe officially recommended to member states that they 'make education for democratic citizenship a priority objective of educational policy-making and reforms' (Recommendation (2002) 12 of the Council of Europe; CoE, 2002: 3), and supplemented this commitment by designating 2005 as the European Year of Citizenship through Education. A number of nations apart from England took up the call of the Council of Europe, and have introduced or strengthened curricular initiatives for civic education. In 2006 the Spanish government introduced Education for Citizenship and Human Rights as a subject for pupils aged 10–15. Although it should perhaps not be over-played, there is a sense in which these developments had a generative effect across nations. Speaking about the introduction of the subject in Spain, Zapatero (Martí and Pettit, 2010: 121) made clear that the Spanish government were 'not inventing anything new... when we added this subject', but were 'simply following the path laid out by other big democratic countries in which it has been successfully introduced in schools'. Notable developments in civic education framed around the concept of citizenship have also been witnessed in other

European nations, including France,[13] Germany,[14] Ireland,[15] Northern Ireland,[16] Scotland[17] and Wales.[18]

There has also been a good deal of attention and commitment to civic education in Australia. Since the late 1990s there has been progress towards the inclusion of the subject, again framed around the concept of citizenship, in each state or territory 'albeit in different ways' (DeJaeghere and Tudball, 2007: 42). Building on the content of a 1994 report by the Civic Experts Group entitled '*Whereas the People: Civics and Citizenship Education in Australia*', in 1997 the Australian National Government established the *Discovering Democracy* (hereafter DD), a national programme designed to form the focus of civic education in schools (Hughes, Print and Sears, 2009). The DD programme, which ended in 2004 but still promotes its units and materials through its website, allocated a range of resources to schools for the teaching of Australian democracy supported by in-service training for school teachers. In 2006 a set of *National Statements of Learning in Civics and Citizenship* were produced and written by the Ministerial Council on Education, Employment, Training and Youth Affairs (MCEETYA, 2007).[19] These set out the knowledge, skills, understandings and capacities that are expected to be studied by pupils in Year Three (8–9 year olds), Year Five (10–11 year olds), Year Seven (12–13 year olds) and Year Nine (14–15 year olds) based on three 'essential and common aspects': 'Government and Law', 'Citizenship in a Democracy' and 'Historical Perspectives'.

Whilst it is more difficult to delineate trends in civic education in nations where governments at state, provincial or territorial level (rather than at national level) have jurisdictional control over educational curricular policy, in countries such as the United States and Canada there has been a great deal of interest in civic education. In both these countries, civic education is most commonly taught within the wider subject base of social studies. Nevertheless, in the United States, where a number of surveys have attested to the sense that there is 'no real unified policy on civics education' (Scott and Cogan, 2010: 162), a core of important national documents has set out frameworks and standards for civic education. The publication in 1991 of *CIVITAS: A Framework for Civic Education* (Quigley and Bahmueller, 1991: 4) by the Centre for Civic Education established a rationale for civic education which had clear civic republican overtones:

Civic education in a democracy is education in self-government. Self-government means active participation in self-governance, not passive acquiescence in the actions of others ... the ideals of democracy are most completely fulfilled when every member of the political community actively shares in government ... The first and primary reason for civic education in a constitutional democracy is that the health of the body politic requires the widest possible civic participation of its citizens consistent with the common good and the protection of individual rights. The aim of civic education is therefore not just any kind of participation by any kind of citizen; it is the participation of informed and responsible citizens, skilled in the arts of deliberation effective action.

The approach to civic education detailed in CIVITAS provided a theoretical framework for the more detailed account of standards and curricula set out in the *National Standards for Civics and Government*, a document Scott and Cogan (2010: 161) consider to be 'the closest to anything the [US] nation has ever had in terms of a "citizenship education policy"'. Most states continue to have civic standards within the curriculum of their social studies classes, and there are a number of organizations which promote the teaching of civic education in American schools (for example the *Campaign for the Civic Mission of Schools* launched by the Carnegie Corporation of New York and CIRCLE, 2003). Owing to the decentralized nature of educational responsibility in the USA, national policies for civic standards 'remain at the level of recommendations for schools and school systems rather than mandates' (Hughes, Print and Sears, 2009). In other nations, of which Canada is perhaps a good example, the commitment to civic education is more complex and harder to describe, especially because developments in civic education have not been as pronounced as in other nations. Whilst a case has been made by committed supporters for a renewed form of civic education centred on education for citizenship, there is some disparity between the desires of these commentators and the actual policy and curricular provision across provinces. The complexity here is increased further by the fact that educational responsibility falls under the jurisdiction of individual provinces and territories and that 'Canadian goals in social education generally and civic education in particular have been largely borrowed from the USA' (Hughes, Print and Sears, 2009: 300).

It is also worth noting that common to all of the nations considered briefly above is not simply the identification of a need for a clear and, in many cases legislated, form of civic education, but also that education itself has civic aims. In many nations, perhaps most clearly seen in the cases of England and Wales and the United States, the advent of widespread and free mass state or public schooling was influenced by a desire for a better educated citizenry. In contemporary terms, the civic aims of education are often paramount in the general aims of schooling. Two brief examples are sufficient for the purposes of illustration. The revised National Curriculum in England published in 2007 and taught from September 2008, for example, has three interrelated aims, the third of which is that the curriculum should enable all young people to become 'responsible citizens who make a positive contribution to society' (QCDA, 2007). Similarly, the *Melbourne Declaration on Educational Goals for Young Australians* published in December 2008 set out two goals for Australian education.[20] The second of these incorporates the aim that all young Australians become 'active and informed citizens' who, amongst other attributes, 'act with moral and ethical integrity, are committed to national values of democracy, equity and justice, and participate in Australia's civic life', and who 'work for the common good, in particular sustaining and improving natural and social environments' (MCEETYA, 2008). From a political science perspective, Amy Gutmann (1987: 287), in her influential theory of liberal democratic education, contends that it is these political and civic aims which have 'moral primacy over the other purposes of public education in a democratic society'.

This brief overview of curricular initiatives and approaches to civic education across a sample of nations is not to suggest that the process of educating citizens in formal schooling is one with which all are in agreement, much less that it is unproblematic. As Reid, Gill and Sears (2010: 5) make clear, there are likely to be areas of disparity between policy and practice, not least that 'there is never a one-to-one correspondence between the state's agenda and its realization in the classroom'. Such problems notwithstanding, there are sufficient similarities across these approaches to civic education to suggest important commonalities with civic republican thought. First, across a large number of recent civic education programmes and initiatives in Western democratic nations there has been a clear and determined focus on citizenship as the founding and defining concept. The concern is not with producing young people who possess knowledge of key political processes and institutions, but to produce citizens who act in a certain way within their political communities.

Second, there is a common trend to ensure that young people recognize and respect the obligations which they have both to other citizens and to the political communities within which they live. As a result, young people are expected to be able to locate their own ideas, thoughts and interests within the context of the common good of the wider society. Third, there is a common concern that young people are taught a certain set of skills, attributes and dispositions that enable them to play a responsible role in the civic life of their communities. Fourth, there is a desire, given the heterogeneous nature of contemporary Western democracies, to encourage and equip young people to be able to elucidate their ideas with others through a range of public forums, including through discussion and debate. In summary, the aim is for young people to be taught to become active, responsible and morally aware citizens, with a capacity to engage in public life.

Conclusion

For civic republicans the key problem within Western democratic societies is the lack of opportunity for, and recognition of, the civic engagement of citizens. Whilst they may differ as to whether participation in public life is ultimately beneficial for intrinsic or instrumental reasons, civic republicans bemoan the fact that the 'hollowing out of the public realm makes it difficult to cultivate the solidarity and sense of community on which democratic citizenship depends' (Sandel, 1999: 267). Although it is difficult to determine how far civic republican ideas explicitly informed the construction of the aims and content of the various initiatives, curricular documents and practice, there is at the very least a *prima facie* case for the suggestion that civic education initiatives in a number of nations seek to pursue aims in accordance with those argued for by civic republicans. Strikingly, much of the terminology which is employed within republican writing features heavily within the discourse of civic education. This does not mean, though, that this republican emphasis is identified, known or understood. As Crick (2003: 21) recognized in the case of England, the civic republican 'tradition of political thought ... might not have been apparent to the general reader' and furthermore, is 'not yet current in political and public discourse' (Crick, 2000: 120). If we are to understand the educational importance and issues for civic education raised by civic republican models of citizenship, we must be clear as to what the substantive nature of such models is. This is the task of Chapters 3, 4 and 5. In turn, to understand the substantive nature of civic republican models of citizenship it is necessary to comprehend the historical ideas and traditions on which contemporary proponents of the theory draw to inform their ideas. This is the task which is now taken up in the Chapter 2.

2
The Origins of Civic Republican Thought

Present-day ideas of citizenship do not stand in isolation from their historical roots and origins. The origins of recent civic republican thought lie in an extensive and, at times, heterogeneous list of political and moral philosophers, writers and political activists. A civic republican 'tradition' has been identified as running throughout the history of Western political thought by a number of republican scholars since the latter half of the last century (Pocock, 1975; Oldfield, 1990a; Skinner 1990a, 1990b, 1998, 2002; Rahe, 1992; Held, 1996, 1997; Pettit, 1999; Honohan, 2002). Honohan[21] (2002: 4–5), for example, argues that it is appropriate to identify a tradition commencing in Greece and Rome, which developed in the late middle ages and progressed further during the eighteenth century in Europe and America, whilst Oldfield (1990: 4) contends that the 'tradition' is 'at least as resilient a strain in Western thinking as liberal individualism'. The use of the term 'tradition' should, however, be understood broadly, and exactly which scholars should be viewed as contributing to republican ideas is contested. There is a general agreement that civic republican ideas can be traced back to ancient Greek and the work of Aristotle and to the writings of Cicero in ancient Rome, and that these ideas were then borrowed, critiqued, adapted and extended within the writings of Niccolò Machiavelli, James Harrington, Jean-Jacques Rousseau and James Madison.[22] It should be noted, however, that current formulations of the civic republican tradition should not be considered as complete. The contribution of other significant figures, most notably those within a scholastic school of thought, are frequently ignored, and do not feature in contemporary literature on civic republicanism (a point returned to later in this chapter).

It was suggested in the previous chapter that work on the historical basis can be considered as a strand of contemporary civic republican writing. It is this 'renewed interest in the historical origins of the classical republican tradition' (Martí and Pettit, 2010: 53) which forms the focus of this present chapter. There are two reasons why an awareness of the historical derivation of contemporary republican thought is important. First, it helps to establish (or at least to remind us) that the terms employed by contemporary republicans are not new, and that these were often understood quite differently in their historical contexts. Second, this in turn shows that the same concepts can be understood and applied differently today, often depending on how historical ideas are understood and prioritized. With this in mind, this chapter details the basis of the civic republican tradition across four periods of thought: ancient, medieval-scholastic, Renaissance and modern. There is insufficient space here for a full and detailed account of each of the historical writers identified as falling within the republican tradition (for an excellent and more detailed account, see Honohan, 2002). For this reason, this chapter draws on the figures most frequently referenced in recent literature on contemporary republicanism and includes the historical authors who have been the most important in shaping the ideas and arguments of contemporary republicans. It also restricts itself to those elements of each historical writer's thought which have relevance to the focus of this book.

Ancient republican thought

All civic republican writers locate the roots of the theory in the work of Aristotle and Cicero, a fact which has led to the development of two strands of contemporary civic republicanism, one stemming from ancient Greece and the other from ancient Rome. It is important to note that the type of political communities that Aristotle and Cicero have in mind are much smaller than those which developed in the modern period and which comprise nation-states today. The small-scale states of ancient Greece and Rome were intimate in character and permitted forms of direct democracy which were to become considered as impracticable by later proponents of civic republicanism. Nevertheless, Aristotle and Cicero provide the foundations of republican theory and, to some extent, subsequent formulations in the tradition must be understood in the light of the ideas they expressed. It is important, therefore, that any consideration of the civic republican tradition should start by exploring how these two great thinkers understood freedom within the polity and the relationship between citizen and state.

Aristotle

In his two main texts – the *Politics* and the *Nichomachean Ethics* – Aristotle responds to the question of what makes a good person and a good life. In addressing this, he explores the question of how society and the political community can be ordered to achieve this end. His response is to present men as naturally political beings and the *polis* in natural and organic terms, with the good life achievable only through living in common. The claim that what distinguishes 'the citizen proper from all others', is 'his participation in giving judgement and in holding office' is central to Aristotle's understanding of citizenship, and presents a concept of the citizen in active, moral and reflective terms (*The Politics*, 1992: 1275a22: 169). This involves the rejection of solely legalistic, residence-based definitions of citizenship. Indeed, Aristotle (*The Politics*, 1992: 1274b32: 169–170) contends that '... as soon as a man becomes entitled to participate in office, deliberative or judicial, we deem him to be a citizen of that state' (1275a34:171).[23] Aristotle's political work contains both idealistic and realist elements. In defining the nature of political communities, he understands the state as 'an association by kinships and villages which aims at a perfect and self-sufficient life ... The association which is a state exists not for the purpose of living together but for the sake of noble actions' (1992: III, ix, 1280b29–1281a9: 197–98). Here we have a key facet of Aristotle's thought, which has been of interest to contemporary civic republicans who seek to promote a key aspect of civic engagement: namely, the principle that we should have a conception of the good life and then constitute the state so as to achieve this end.

In *The Politics* Aristotle (1992: 1261a22: 104–5; and 1277b7: 182) characterizes freedom in both individual and collective terms. As individuals, citizens are free if they are able to operate and to live free from subordination to, and domination by, the state. To this extent, Aristotle differentiated a free man from those who live under the conditions of slavery (1992: 1261a22: 104–5; and 1277b7: 182). A *polis* consists 'not merely of a plurality of men, but of different kinds of men' (1992. II, ii, 1261a10: 104; see also Oldfield, 1990: 20–23), and one such category of men is that of the citizen. Aristotle contends that since all who are citizens are equal, citizens must rule over each other equally and, therefore, that because it is not possible for all to govern, or to hold administrative or judicial office concurrently, citizens must take turns – and in this sense Aristotle defines a collective sense of freedom as representing self-government or, as he put it, 'ruling, and being ruled in turn'. Because

Aristotle believes that the state is an aggregate of its citizens, he holds that what is ideal and good for the state must be identified with what is ideal and good for the citizen. On this basis, the participation of citizens in the civic life of the community is central to Aristotle's conception of government and governance. It is this sense of freedom, achievable only through collective forms of political organization and activism, which has most interested and shaped subsequent proponents of civic republican ideas. In advocating a positive view of freedom, Aristotle prioritizes a teleological position: participation in self-government by the citizens of a polity creates the conditions within which they (the citizens) can realize their full potential, or *eudaimonia*, as human beings. Aristotle's commitment to the political ends of man can therefore only be understood in relation to his commitment to virtue (*arête*) and to practical or moral wisdom (*phronesis*). Duncan (1995: 147–8) summarizes this relationship in the following way:

> The object of virtuous civic participation for Aristotle... is not to reinvigorate or enshrine the state... but to help individuals fulfil themselves on a multidimensional (and therefore truly human) rather than a unidimensional scale. In other words, it is in the interest of the self, given its social context and 'public' dimension, to participate politically in a virtuous manner.

The commitment to a virtuous citizenry forms a central element of Aristotle's thought, in which the political and the moral were intimately intertwined. Critical of Plato's appeal to other worlds as the basis of our understanding of moral virtues, Aristotle argues for a practical, action-based ethics which citizens learn through habituation. Aristotle (1992, 1323b121: 392, 393) contends that 'there is no such thing as a man's or a state's good action without virtue and practical wisdom'. He argues further that virtues are inherently political, stating that '... the good citizen must have the knowledge and ability both to rule and be ruled. That is what we mean by the virtue of a citizen – understanding the governing of free men from both points of view' (1992, 1277b7: 182).

In *The Politics*, which is primarily concerned with establishing the constitutional rather than the ethical prerequisites for politics, Aristotle (1992, 1276b20: 179; emphasis in the original) pluralizes virtues, asserting that 'there cannot be just one single *and perfect* virtue of the sound citizen', and this is a theme to which he gave more attention in his *Nichomachean Ethics*, in which a list of virtues is proposed as the means between the associated vices of deficiency and excess, these virtues being courage, temperance, liberality, magnificence, magnanimity, proper ambition, good temper, truthfulness, wittiness, friendliness, modesty and right-eous indignation. Although Aristotle's virtues are inherently active, and were postulated in the context of a state which is organized so as to pro-mote ethical action, there is an important distinction within Aristotle's thought regarding the relationship between the politically active life and the more reflective, philosophical life. In *The Politics* Aristotle (1992: 1325b14: 401) presents the notion that '...the active life will be the best *both* for any state as a whole community and for the individual' (empha-sis added), but that:

> the active life need not, as some suppose, be always concerned with our relations with other people, nor is intelligence 'active' only when it is directed towards results that flow from action...thinking and speculation that are their own end and are done for their own sake are *more* 'active' because the aim in such thinking is to do well, and therefore also, in a sense, action.

This intellectual, reflective component of citizen engagement in the virtues is also a central tenet of the *Nicomachean Ethics*, in which Aristotle (1998, Bk. 1, 10: 1101a35, 23) re-affirmed that the happy citi-zen is 'one who is active in accordance with complete virtue'. Happiness as constructed by Aristotle is predominantly understood as 'an activity of the soul in accordance with excellence'. For individuals to flourish in this sense 'requires strenuous, disciplined engagement throughout the course of a person's life in intellectual, moral, and practical pur-suits'. Aristotle also recognizes that participatory civic engagement is not necessarily an inbuilt tendency within citizens, and that educative processes are required in order that a proclivity towards virtuous habits be formed. In this sense, he identifies a formative role for the state in inculcating certain principles within its citizens, a commitment illus-trated in the following passage:

> ...of all the safeguards that we hear spoken of as helping to maintain constitutional stability, the most important, but today universally neglected, is education for the way of living that belongs to the con-stitution in each case. It is useless to have the most beneficial laws, fully agreed upon by all who are members of the constitution, if they are not going to be trained and have their habits formed in the spirit of that constitution – in a democratic spirit, that is, if the laws are democratic. (1992: V, ix, 1310a12: 331)

For Aristotle the education of citizens is a multifaceted process which involves not just formal educational provision, but the laws of a *polis* and the workings of key institutions. He cites the education of the young as the prime duty of lawmakers[24] and suggests that the young study laws and the art of lawmaking in order that the requisite virtues be formed.

Aristotle's work is drawn upon by contemporary civic republicans primarily in relation to their commitments to freedom, civic obligations and civic virtue. Surprisingly few contemporary civic republican commentators reflect directly upon the *deliberative* element of his work. Although he distrusted purely democratic forms of government, Aristotle did see a role for citizen participation within a mixed system of government, and understood such participation to possess a deliberative form. In the *Politics* Aristotle (1992: IV, xiv. 1297b35. 277) highlights deliberation as one of three elements of a constitution, identifying certain public issues suitable for deliberation by citizens, including 'war and peace, the making and dissolving of alliances, legislation, ... the choosing of officials, and the scrutiny of their conduct on expiry of tenure' (1992: IV, xiv. 1298a3. 277).[25] In reflecting upon these topics, Aristotle sets out four different models of deliberative system. The first model involves all citizens taking office in turn. The second involves collective deliberation by citizens, but only on certain matters. The third model restricts citizen deliberation to the allocation and scrutiny of public office, with officials deciding on other matters. In the fourth model, all citizens deliberate on every public matter (1992: IV, xiv. 1298a11). For Aristotle, deliberation is a broad term, and he does not always present it in the same way across the range of his work. Aristotle can thus be understood as assigning a number of features to deliberation, all of which are central to present-day conceptions of the term. Deliberation in *The Politics* is presented in collective terms, and as involving exchanges between citizens in the discharge of their civic role. In this sense, it requires citizens to enter into dialogue with others about 'the expedient and the inexpedient, and therefore also the just and unjust' (Bickford, 1996: 400). Aristotle (1992: IV, xiv. 1298b: 279) identifies reasoned deliberation between different types of citizens as '...beneficial, as it will ensure the presence of the notables as well as of the people, and they will deliberate the better when each side does so with the other'. Second, when Aristotle discusses deliberation within his *Nichomachean Ethics* he is generally referring to an *internal* process of reasoning within the citizen, claiming that '...he who deliberates inquires and calculates' and that 'excellence in deliberation involves reasoning' (VI, 9. 1142a27). Rather than separating thought from actions, practical reasoning conjoins them through *phronesis*. *Phronesis*, or practical reasoning, is an individual capacity and involves citizens in rationally considering the actions that they take in any given circumstance. For Aristotle (VI, 9. 1142a27) '... it is characteristic of men of practical wisdom to have deliberated well'. Third, Aristotle conceived of deliberation as part of the art of rhetoric required by statesmen and public orators. In this sense, rather than being concerned with collective, interactive dialogue or internal reasoning, deliberative rhetoric is a skill employed in public speaking to influence others (cf. Bickford, 1996: 414).

Cicero

A second strand of civic republican thought emanates from the work of the Roman political theorist and statesman, Marcus Tullius Cicero, whom Radford (2002: 27) suggests 'was one of the rare persons in history who combined philosophical wisdom and political power'. The Rome in which Cicero wrote was larger and less intimate than the Greek city-states which interested Aristotle. Cicero's main texts were written between 55BC and 45BC, a time of upheaval and great rivalry in Rome's politics, and in them he celebrated the structure, cohesiveness and virtue of the republican government which had formerly characterized the Roman, republican state.[26] It is from Cicero that many contemporary civic republicans derive their commitment to the concept of freedom as non-domination. In his major work on government and the state, *On The Republic (De Re Publica)*, Cicero argues that a citizen is free only when he is not subjected to conditions of domination or dependence and, moreover, that such freedom should be defined by, and guaranteed through, the protection of the laws and institutions within a state. As Honohan (2002: 36) points out, 'rather than ruling in turns, the citizens were free for Cicero when they enjoyed the legal status of *libertas*', a state which '*was* not the natural possession of individuals but a status acquired politically with citizenship in a republic', and protected through the rule of law. Cicero's political thought is encapsulated in his words '*res publica; res populi*' ('the commonwealth; the people), a standpoint which has been defined as a commitment to society as a 'social reality, constituted by a indefinitely large number of people who jointly agree about what is essential to justice in their dealings with each other, that is, about their laws and rights. They maintain this agreement in pursuit of their common good' (Radford, 2002: 28). According to Cicero, the predilection of citizens to engage in civic affairs is a natural instinct. In this regard Cicero (1998: 3) contends that nature has 'given to mankind...such a desire to defend the well-being of the community, that this force prevails over all the temptations of pleasure and ease'. Like Aristotle, Cicero thus places great importance on the involvement of citizens in political affairs, although he prioritizes this not in terms of human flourishing as Aristotle had suggested, but rather as necessary for the protection of the freedom of individual citizens. In this sense, civic engagement is favoured by Cicero for its instrumental rather than its intrinsic benefits.

This instrumental standpoint is central to other elements of Cicero's thought, including his understanding of virtue. Cicero values virtuous actions largely in terms of service to the state. Reflecting on the Roman republic Cicero observes that '[T]hose...who have adapted themselves to great achievements in the service of the political community, lead lives more profitable to mankind and more suited to grandeur and fame' (1998: 28), and it is from Cicero that Roman republicanism derives its four principal virtues of wisdom (*prudentia*), courage (*fortitudo*), moderation (*decorum*) and justice (*justitia*) (cf. Honohan, 2002: 33–34). Early in *On The Republic* (1998: 4), and perhaps owing to his own engagement in the political system of his time, Cicero establishes that:

> it is not enough to possess moral excellence as a kind of skill, unless you put it into practice. You can have a skill simply by knowing *how* to practise it, even if you never do; whereas moral excellence is entirely a matter of practice. Its most important field of practice, moreover, is in the government of a state, and in the achievement (in reality, not just in words), of those things...For nothing is laid down by philosophers – nothing right and honourable at any rate – which has not been brought into being and established by those who have drawn up laws for states.

For Cicero each of the three main types of government of his time – monarchy, aristocracy and democracy – were stable so long as the prime political vice – corruption – could be avoided.[27] However, Cicero had a fundamental criticism of each type of government. He (1998: 20) argued that in monarchies:

> ...the populace plays too small a part in the community's legislation and debate; in aristocracies the masses can have hardly any share in liberty, since they are deprived of any participation in discussion and decision-making; and when the government is carried on entirely by

the people ... their equality is itself unequal, since it acknowledges no degrees of merit.[28]

On the basis of these thoughts, Cicero (1998: 32–33) identifies a mixed constitution, in which limits could be placed on single interests or factions, as the most suitable for securing republican freedom. Central to this constitution was the rule of law, and it is partly from Cicero that the republican principle of a government, or empire of laws rather than men, is derived (cf. Dagger, 2004: 169).[29] Honohan (2002: 35; emphasis in original) suggests that what Cicero has in mind is not a 'mixture of *forms of government*', but rather an 'equilibrium of *classes*'. Cicero was, however, more sceptical than Aristotle about the extent to which educational processes were necessary, and indeed appropriate, in the formation of an active and virtuous citizenry. In contrast to Aristotle's commitment to formal educational processes, Cicero places less importance on the formative, political role of laws and education and limits the role of the former to the preservation of individual independence and the locus of political power. Cicero also rejects the principle that education is, or indeed should be, inherently political. Honohan (2002: 37) sums up Cicero's belief that 'both universal human qualities and differences of character are given at birth, not developed through habituation, as for Aristotle'.

In summary, whilst Cicero's work is not as extensive as Aristotle's, and his standing in the history of Western political thought less elevated, it is central to the historical development of civic republican ideas. Moreover, it was of central importance to the expression of civic republican ideas within Renaissance thought in the Florentine republics, most notably in the work of Machiavelli, around the fifteenth and sixteenth centuries (a point returned to later).

Medieval scholastic thought and republicanism

To suggest that medieval scholastic thinkers have in some way contributed to the civic republican tradition is not an obvious conclusion, and therefore requires some justification. Writers such as St. Augustine and St. Thomas Aquinas do not feature in historical treatments of republican ideas, and according to David Held's (1997) depiction of the tradition, the period between the fall of the Roman Empire and the Renaissance witnessed the replacement of the active *homo politicus* by the true believer of the Christian faith, the *homo credens*. Similarly, in their accounts of the tradition both Pocock (1975) and Skinner (1978) appear to support the principle that civic republicanism 'developed separately from and in opposition to Christianity' (Black, 1997: 647). Interpretations such as this fail to recognize the contribution of significant theological thinkers and neglect the fact that significant republican themes – including a commitment to man's political nature, to civic virtue and to the common good within a political community – were central to key medieval scholastic thinkers.[30] For this reason, the political thought of Christian theologians, most notably St Augustine and Aquinas, can be understood as to some extent contributing to the civic republican tradition, albeit from a Christian theological perspective.

For St. Augustine, civic participation is founded on the essentially Christian belief that people are bound by a common love. In his *City of God*, St. Augustine distinguished between a spiritual form of citizenship, the *City of God*, and a secular form of citizenship, the *City of Man*. Whilst the former was eternal and spiritual, the latter was transient. The cities St. Augustine had in mind did not stand in isolation from each other. In positing this interdependent relationship between the two cities, St. Augustine 'raised the classic notion of civic citizenship to the level of a religious duty and admonished Christians to assume the obligations of civic citizenship' (Arthur, 2008: 307). In other words, a model of Christian republican citizenship exists within St. Augustine's work, incorporating the idea that the ultimate expression of citizenship occurs in the after-life alongside the principle that citizens should actively participate in the life of their political communities throughout their lives. Although explorations of the civic republican nature (or otherwise) of Aquinas' thought are sparse, Stoner (2007: 9) presents a case that certain elements of the *Summa Theologica* are republican in nature. In support of this claim, Stoner cites Aquinas' description of the true king (as opposed to a tyrant) as one who is devoted to the common good, as well as his commitment to laws and to a role in governance for the people. There is certainly at least a *prima facie* case that Aquinas' work should be of interest to civic republicans. In seeking to incorporate many of Aristotle's ideas within a Christian framework, Aquinas understands the political engagement of citizens in naturalistic terms. Because he conceives humans as essentially political and social beings, Aquinas warrants consideration in any historical analysis of civic republicanism. He addresses many of the themes which had interested Aristotle, and his political philosophy represents a re-emergence of the Aristotelian teleological view of human nature and society, in which political participation and the virtuous life constitute human flourishing. Indeed, it was in the medieval period that Aristotle's works were rediscovered and were used to critically reconsider the dominance of purely theological understandings of human nature and political organization. In this way, ancient ideas of state and citizen were presented as interdependent with (and not as antithetical to) Christian political and theological positions.

In his *The Governance of Rulers* (*De Regimine Principum*), Aquinas argues that '[I]t is natural for a man to be a social and political animal, living in a community' (Aquinas, 2002, Book One, Chapter One: 5–6; cf. Sigmund, 1993: 218). For Aquinas, the good of the citizen and the good of the community are related symbiotically. As Arthur (2000: 82) explains, Aquinas:

> ...held the view that those who seek out the good of society also seek their own good because their own good cannot exist without the common good. However, Aquinas maintained that the common good cannot exist without justice, which in turn demands that the community respect and foster the well-being of all its members equally.

In other words, it does not make sense to talk of the good of the individual citizen as being in conflict with the good of the political community: the two are inherently connected. For this reason citizenship is a co-operative relationship between citizens and their communities. Significantly for understandings of the civic republican tradition, Aquinas rejected Aristotle's view of the *polis* as pertaining solely to small-scale Greek states, widening the extent of the political community to reflect the larger and more wide-ranging political structures of his time. In effect Aquinas considers government to be both a necessary and a positive force, and like others within the civic republican tradition, sees the interests of the individual and the community as indistinguishable (Arthur, 2008: 308).

Aquinas extends the principle of man's inherent rationality, which Aristotle limits to a selected few and which St. Augustine largely restricts to Christians, to all men. The basis for this was Aquinas' core Christian understanding that man was made in God's image. Through rational life and the guidance of natural law, citizens would learn how to act in accordance with a common good, understood in terms of both the general welfare of society and a life conducted in in accordance with the virtues. In his greatest work, the *Summa Theologica*, Aquinas, like Aristotle, conceives of virtues as dispositions or habits which tend to the good, arguing that they have both a rational and an affective component (1981: *ST. I–II*, q. 55, a. 1: 819). Aquinas postulates the existence of four Cardinal virtues of prudence, justice, fortitude and temperance, alongside the three theological virtues of faith, hope and charity (1981: *ST.* I-II, q. 61, a. 2: 846–7).[31] Whilst the four cardinal virtues are not the sum total of 'acquired' human virtues, they are the core virtues from which all others derive. In addition, Aquinas emphasizes other virtues of the Christian faith, most notably, the central virtue of love. The Christianity-informed citizenship within his work therefore includes the principles of loving God, loving thyself, loving thy neighbour and loving the common good. This represents a Christian-based formulation of a commitment found extensively in the civic republican tradition to some form of what Aristotle terms 'concord' or civic friendship.

Central to Aquinas' political philosophy is his contention, based on his teleological standpoint, that the state should adopt a formative role regarding its citizens. In other words, the state has a duty to help citizens fulfil their potential. Aquinas also identifies habituation as a central process through which the acquired virtues become part of the character of citizens (1981: *ST.* I-II, q. 63, a. 2: 87). In this sense he subscribes to the Aristotelian principle that virtues must be learned through a combination of reflective rational thought and practical action. As Ulmann (1988: 117) concludes, Aquinas, 'by absorbing Aristotle's ideas, effected in the public sphere not so much a metamorphosis of the subject as the re-birth of the citizen who since classical times had been hibernating. In doing so, Aquinas' political ideas contain a number of elements which overlap with civic republicanism'. This recognition is important in appreciating that scholastic thought was not blind to republican ideas and that those who suggest that citizenship is by definition secular are mistaken.[32]

Renaissance republican thought

Civic republican ideas were recaptured and extended in the writings of the fourteenth-century Italian republics, most notably Venice and Florence (Lane, 1966; Pocock, 1975; Skinner, 1990; Held, 1996, 1997). It was at this time that the 'first republics without slaves were created' (Viroli, 1999: 1). In simple terms, interest in different forms of government, and indeed in civic republican ideas, at the start of the Renaissance period arose to a large extent out of the tensions between two systems of government prevalent since the medieval age – one based on the election of a *podestà* (an elected official with sole authority) and the other a more traditional system of government based on the rule of hereditary *signori*, (cf. Lane, 1966; Skinner, 1992; Held, 1996).[33] During the Renaissance period, in which republics developed in Florence, Venice,

Sienna, Genoa and Lucca, a number of writers sought to establish a set of ideals which prioritized the election of officials over the hereditary aristocratic and monarchical systems prevalent in Western Europe at the time.

Showing a clear descent from Roman rather than Hellenic roots, freedom was formulated by republican Renaissance writers as obtainable only in a state in which no faction, whether monarchy, aristocracy or the people, became overly powerful or corrupt (Held, 1997; cf. Pocock, 1975; Skinner, 1997). Of the Renaissance writers, it was Machiavelli who did most to shape republican ideas and to whom contemporary republican writers look to inform their own understandings of freedom (Maynor, 2003). It is worth noting briefly, however, that Machiavelli was not the only Italian scholar interested in civic republican ideas. For example, the work of the theologian and political scholar Marsilius of Padua (1275/80 – 1342) has been considered as central to the re-emergence within Italian republics of the Roman republican idea of freedom as non-domination. Combining a number of republican elements in his thinking, Marsilius of Padua conceived the polity in organic terms, with each element defined in terms of its contribution to the community as a whole. The concept of citizen was used by Marsilius to denote those who participated within the community towards the common good. This was supplemented by the belief that government should adopt a regulative role in ensuring the ability of citizens to pursue their own, natural ends (cf. Held, 1996; Viroli, 1999). It was Machiavelli, though, who has been of central and enduring importance to the civic republican tradition. According to Wettergreen (1988: 665), Machiavelli was the 'founder of modern republicanism', and it is partly through his work that freedom 'emerges as the focal concept of republicanism' (Honohan, 2002: 42). The seminal account of Machiavelli's republicanism can be found in John Pocock's *The Machiavellian Moment*. Here, Pocock (1975: viii) encapsulates the Florentine thought of Machiavelli and his contemporaries as fundamentally concerned with the 'confrontation of "virtue" with "fortune" and "corruption" '.[34] Machiavelli's political philosophy is best understood as both a critique of the Italian states of his time, and as a celebration of the ancient Roman republics (cf. Honohan, 2002). This idealizing of ancient Rome is particularly integral to the republican elements of Machiavelli's republican thought, and the conception of the free state contained within his work was fundamentally shaped by the influence of Roman moral philosophers, including Livy, Sallust and Cicero (Skinner, 1990a: 300). It is in Machiavelli's *Discourses (Discorsi)*[35] that the key Roman association between 'living in a republic' and 'living in a free state' was recaptured (Skinner, 1997):

> It is easy to understand whence the love of living under a free constitution springs up in peoples. For experience shows that no cities have ever increased in dominion or riches except when they have been established in liberty ... it is not the pursuit of individual advantage but of the common good that makes cities great, and there is no doubt that it is only under republican regimes that this ideal of the common good is followed out. (Machiavelli, *The Discourses*, Book II. cited in Skinner, 1997: 10)

As Honohan (2002: 54) puts it, for Machiavelli it is through service of 'the common good, rather than their own narrow good' that 'great citizens deserve and gain legitimate honour and glory'. It should be remembered, however, that Machiavelli's prioritization of the common good over individual rights within his ideas on freedom has been interpreted in a number of ways, and as a result is somewhat contested. This is perhaps most clearly shown by the fact that Machiavelli's thought is drawn upon by a number of contemporary republican writers (Oldfield, 1990; Viroli, 1999; Maynor, 2003) who each seek to endorse different forms of republican theory.

Like Cicero, Machiavelli does not deny that individuals within a state have freedom to pursue their own goals; rather, he argued that any such pursuit must be tempered and guided with regard to the freedom and goals of others and with concern for the common good (cf. Maynor, 2003).[36] As Skinner (1990b: 130) argues, Machiavelli's conception of the polity, in which the interests of the individual are outweighed by those of the state as a whole, was clearly influenced by a statement from Cicero in *De Officiis* in which he contends that the quickest way 'to introduce sedition and discord into a city is to look after the interests of only one part of the citizens, while neglecting the rest' (cf. Hulliung, 1984: 32).

> The reason is easy to understand; for it is not the well-being of individuals that makes cities great, but the well-being of the community; and it is beyond question that it is only in republics that the common good is looked to properly in that all that promotes it is carried out; and, however much this or that private person may be the loser on this account, there may be so many who benefit thereby that the common good can be realized in spite of those few who suffer in

consequence (Machiavelli, The Discourses, Book II: cited in Skinner, 1997: 10).

Whilst Machiavelli places importance on citizen participation within the political community, this would be considered extremely restricted in contemporary terms. In part owing to the political and social context in which he wrote (and indeed that of the great Roman republics which he praised), such participation would be 'for many preponderantly a matter of military service, and a commitment to serving the common good more often than active involvement in decision-making' (Honohan, 2002: 73). To achieve this end, Machiavelli contends that it is necessary to place limitations on the rulers so that competing interests are balanced and developed, and domination by particular factions avoided. Machiavelli advocates regular elections and, perhaps more importantly, and showing the clear influence of Cicero, the creation of structures of laws and institutions within a state for this purpose (Skinner, 1997). Following Cicero, Machiavelli also rejects the importance of formal education in the development of an active citizenry, emphasizing instead the educative and regulatory roles of both laws and religious worship (Held, 1996). To this end, it is the stature of great statesmen, of military service in developing the character and order of citizens, and of sound and functional laws and institutions, which support a stable and strong political community (Oldfield, 1990: 36). Here again there is a commitment, common to many within the civic republican tradition, to the educational and functional importance of a polity's laws and institutions. In relation to the former, Machiavelli argues that '[H]unger and poverty make men industrious and the laws make them good' (1974: 112; cited in Honohan, 2002: 57). In addition, Machiavelli allocates fundamental importance to the role of a mass religion, of pagan rather than Christian origin, without which civic virtue would deteriorate (Oldfield, 1990: 35).[37] He presents the state as an autonomous organism and as a 'monopolist of legitimate force'. In the operation of the political community, he saw positive potential in the existence of competing interests and social factions, albeit mediated by laws and the constitution. Machiavelli goes so far as to suggest that, far from eroding the possibility of good and effective laws, such tensions might be 'the condition of them' (Skinner, 1981: 63–6). In this way Machiavelli's work adds an additional element to the principles of self-government and participation in civic life. Held (1996: 52–53) explains that for Machiavelli, '... the basis of liberty ... may also be conflict and disagreement through which citizens can promote and defend their interests'. It should be remembered, though, that such tensions exist as necessary features of a republican state, so Machiavelli considers that citizens should understand them in the context of shared membership of a political community (cf. Oldfield, 1990: 34).

In summary, Machiavelli is ultimately concerned with the 'creation and maintenance of political communities' (Oldfield, 1990: 31). As Pocock (1975: 203) makes clear, for Machiavelli a citizen is 'less a man performing a certain role in a decision-making system than a man trained by civic religion and military discipline to devote himself to the *patria* and carry this spirit over to civic affairs' (cf. Honohan, 2002). This standpoint has important differences from the Aristotelian understanding of the citizen as flourishing and reaching his full human potential through a life in common. In commending the citizens of ancient Rome, Machiavelli elevates them 'as citizens who lived in freedom and therefore served liberty, because they wanted to enjoy their private lives in peace'.

The extension of civic republican thought

Through the development of Western political thought in the seventeenth and eighteenth centuries, civic republican principles were revisited and extended. Early republican writers had formulated their ideas and ideals in small political polities, in which citizen status was largely characterized by patriarchy, material independence and service in the national militia (cf. Held, 1996, 1997; Hess, 2000; Honohan, 2002). These ideas were antithetical to the central principles of the developing liberal tradition, which placed an emphasis on representation and rights. For this reason, those wishing to appeal to elements of civic republican thought had to develop, reformulate and extend the principles of freedom, civic obligation, civic virtue and participation within their modern contexts. Three key historical thinkers – James Harrington, Jean-Jacques Rousseau and James Madison – are central to the extension of civic republican thought in this period, and each features heavily in recent interpretations of the history of civic republicanism. This section considers the republican contribution of each in turn.

James Harrington

Although the work of the English political theorist James Harrington (1611–1677) does not occupy a prominent place in most portrayals of Western political philosophy, it is of great importance to the development of civic republican ideas (Pocock, 1975, 1992; Skinner, 1990a, 1992; Honohan, 2002).[38] Harrington lived through the English Civil War and the resultant flirtation with a republican form of government during the period of the Commonwealth from 1649 to 1660. According to Pocock (1975: viii), it is in Harrington's work that Machiavelli's republicanism became intertwined with the English political and social values of Locke and Burke. Harrington's work is typically understood as a response to Hobbes' critique of the political conception of human nature (Raab, 1964: 195–6; Cotton, 1981: 402).[39] Like Machiavelli, Harrington's concern was with how republican principles, most notably freedom, could be translated into the political practice of his own time (Honohan, 2002: 64). This involved 'the first … theoretical defense of democratically elected, representative government on the large scale of the modern republic as the best regime' (Wettergreen, 1988: 666). In his most famous tract, *The Commonwealth of Oceana*, Harrington views political institutions and states as born out of inherently historical processes, and he prioritizes the importance of laws and the rule of law within a state. In doing so he appeals to the ancient civic republican notion of an 'empire of laws and not men' (Dwight, 1887: 8; cf. Pocock, 1957, 1975; Skinner, 1992) as necessary for securing the freedom of citizens within a political community. A government of laws is defined by Harrington (cited in Cromartie, 1998: 992) as '… an art whereby a civil society of men is instituted and preserved upon', whereas a government of men is '… an art whereby some man, or some few men, subject a city or a nation, and rule it according unto his or their private interest'. In detailing his commitment to the republican principle of a republic of laws, not men, Harrington (cited in Viroli, 1999: 50) cites the example of the citizens of the Italian republic of Lucca. He claims that the citizens of Lucca were free because they were controlled only by laws and because such laws were 'framed by every private man unto no other end … than to protect the liberty of every private man, which by that means comes to be the liberty of the commonwealth'.[40]

According to Harrington, governments gain legitimacy through governance in the common public interest, and he proposes a system of government based on a fully, regularly elected bicameral parliament in which representation and meritocracy are of central importance. As Pocock (1975: 142–144, 343–344) suggests that Harrington believed in 'a scheme of participation for all citizens, based on the frequent assemblies of local communities' (cf. Sunstein, 1988: 1555 *fn*86). For Harrington it is only when citizens participate in shaping the laws of the polity that they can truly be free, and citizens do so through 'self-sacrifice' (Dwight, 1887: 10). Such self-sacrifice involves citizens' concern for the interests of fellow citizens and their prioritizing of the common good of the political community over and above their own interests. To this end Harrington (1992: 20) suggests that '[T]here is a common right, law of nature or interest of the whole which is more excellent and so acknowledged to be by the agents themselves than the right of interests of the parts only' (Harrington, 1992: 21; cf. Honohan, 2002: 20). Pettit (1999: 28–9) suggests, however, that this does not mean that Harrington saw freedom as synonymous with self-government. Instead, Harrington's approach to the importance of political participation is essentially of instrumental value and at times he seems to prioritize the rule of law for the maintenance and effective running of the republic over and above popular participation. This instrumental approach can also be seen in his understanding of civic virtue. Cromartie (1998: 1006–7; italics in the original) points out that for Harrington 'the dispositions of citizens have only secondary significance; virtue is simply action that promotes the common good'. Moreover, as Harrington conceives it, virtue is 'to be understood as action *instrumental* to that good'.

Harrington's political thought 'brings republican argument into the modern world by tracking the issue of establishing a republic in a large-scale territorial state' (Honohan, 2002: 73). In conceiving the goal of the republican state as the protection of the liberty of private men', Harrington (1992: 22) presents an instrumental republican theory which, because it ultimately conceives the role of the state as the protection of individual interests, 'marked a turning point for republicanism' and which, as it was subsequently interpreted, allowed particular forms of republican thought to share certain commonalities with liberal political theory (Wettergreen, 1998: 683). To this end, Harrington's thought was important in shaping the views and actions of early American statesmen (Dwight, 1887: 3).

Jean-Jacques Rousseau

Although his 'concern for individual freedom makes him a precursor of contemporary liberalism as well as republicanism', the political thought of Jean-Jacques Rousseau has formed a central strand of contemporary historical commentaries on civic republicanism (Honohan, 2002: 98; cf. Oldfield, 1990a; Held, 1996, 1997). Rousseau holds a primary place in the canon of Western political ideas, and his thought influenced both the French and American revolutionary periods in the eighteenth centuries. In contrast to Harrington's enlargement of the ideal civic republican state, Rousseau rejected the notion that republican ideals could be applied successfully in the larger and more diverse states which developed in Western Europe and America at the end of the eighteenth century. Instead, Rousseau (1968: 104; cf. Oldfield, 1990: 65) depicts the political community as one in which 'the more the state is enlarged, the more freedom is diminished', and presents an idealized polity structured around a small community.

Freedom is central to Rousseau's conception of the political community and this is presented in two forms. First, and in common with the Roman-derived republican principle of non-domination, liberty is defined as being free from dependence on the will of others. Rousseau's second conception of freedom relates to the sphere of morals and to self-mastery. Here, Rousseau's (1968: 65; cf. Honohan, 2002: 88) concern is with that 'which alone makes man the master of himself; for to be governed by appetite alone is slavery, while obedience to a law one prescribes to oneself is freedom'. In this statement we can see Rousseau's attachment to the rule of law, which he depicts in these terms: '[A] free people obeys, but it does not serve, it has leaders but no masters; it obeys the laws, but obeys only the laws, and it is due to the strength of the laws that it is not forced to obey men' (cited in Viroli, 1999: 9). In his thinking on freedom, Rousseau combines the republican ideals of freedom as non-domination and freedom as self-government. Essentially, however, freedom cannot be divorced from membership of and participation within a political community: 'the power of the state alone makes the freedom of its members' (Rousseau, 1968: 99; cf. Honohan, 2002: 89). In *The Social Contract* Rousseau draws upon and develops a number of republican ideas, showing continuity with both the Aristotelian and the Roman traditions, and it is partly for this reason that appeals to Rousseau's work can be found in the work of contemporary intrinsic as well as instrumental civic republicans (Held, 1996). In his contemporary intrinsic civic republican theory, Oldfield (1990: 54) emphasizes the Aristotelian elements of Rousseau's work, paraphrasing him as follows:

> The right of legislation would be vested in all citizens, 'for who could know better than they what laws would most suit their living together in the same society?'... Citizens would be content with sanctioning laws, 'making decisions in assemblies on proposals from the leaders on the most important public business', and electing 'year by year' the most capable and the most upright of their fellow citizens to administer justice and govern the state.

It is in relation to these sentiments that Rousseau (1968: 141) makes his famous criticism of the English political system: 'The English people believes itself to be free; it is gravely mistaken; it is free only during the election of members of Parliament; as soon as the Members are elected, the people is enslaved; it is nothing'. For Rousseau, citizens enjoy liberty in its fullest form through active participation in developing and maintaining the *general will*. This requires a social contract, the terms of which were 'reducible to a single one, namely the total alienation by each associate of himself and all his rights to the whole community' (cited in Oldfield, 1990a: 58). Here, Rousseau invokes the central civic republican idea of the citizen's obligation to the political community, and he considers the relationship between citizen and state as follows:

> In its passive role it is called the *state*, when it plays an active role it is the *sovereign*...Those who are associated in it take collectively the name of *a people*, and call themselves individually *citizens*, in so far as they share in the sovereign power, and *subjects*, in so far as they put themselves under the laws of the state. (1968: 61–2)

In rejecting the mixed system of government advocated by Cicero and Machiavelli as overly un-democratic, Rousseau sought greater acknowledgement of the 'human need for equal recognition' (Honohan, 2002: 98), in a way which involves the active involvement of the citizenry in the creation and maintenance of laws and the existence of an ongoing deliberative process between citizens. Significantly, Rousseau (1968: 142) rejected appeals in his time to representative (rather than direct) forms of democracy, and he contends that '...the moment a people adopts representatives it is no longer free; it no longer exists'.

Revisiting the themes of his republican predecessors, Rousseau sought to develop an understanding as to how the character of active citizens should be developed. According to Rousseau (1993: 142) '[I]t is not enough to say that citizens "be good"; they must be taught to be so'. Like Aristotle, Rousseau presents us with a model in which the character of citizens is shaped by the laws, through civic education and, departing from Aristotelianism, through civic religion. With regard to the latter, and showing clear descent from Machiavelli, Rousseau was critical of the Christian denominations prevalent in his time, postulating a civic religion through which citizens would congregate in common devotion. Establishing the three dogmas of civil religion as the life to come, the reward of virtue and the punishment of vice, and the exclusion of religious tolerance, Rousseau conceives of civil religion as providing the political community with social cohesion. In fulfilling their religious duties, citizens develop and exhibit central virtues.[41] Significantly, Rousseau understood personal and civic virtues as synonymous. In other words, the good man was the good citizen.

Rousseau's political thought is viewed by contemporary republicans and commentators as representing a continuation from the earlier republican writings of Aristotle, Cicero and Machiavelli. However, for some, the main contribution of Rousseau to contemporary civic republicanism lies in his alignment of the themes of membership and community with a modern, liberal understanding of the social contract (cf. Oldfield, 1990; Honohan, 2002). Rousseau remained committed, however, to a direct form of political engagement within small-scale political communities. Indeed, it was only in the republicanism that grew out of the framing of the Constitution of the United States of America that the comprehensive transition of republican ideas from such small-scale communities to the larger modern political states envisaged by Harrington occurred.

James Madison

The meaning of republicanism was extended in the work of the founding fathers of the Constitution of the United States of America in the late eighteenth century, most prominently in the *Federalist* writings of James Madison, Alexander Hamilton and John Jay. Of these three statesmen it was Madison who did most to promote republican ideas, and who has featured most prominently in commentaries on the history of republican thinking. To some extent, and linking clearly to the contemporary popular usage of the term, the term 'republicanism' in this American sense can be conceived partially as a response to the arbitrary and unchecked monarchist, colonial rule of the English (Appleby, 1985). Its meaning, however, is much deeper and far-reaching than this, and the development of republican thought by the founding fathers witnessed adaptations to the central principles of freedom and active citizenship (Rahe, 1992; Held, 1996).

Rodgers (1992) argues that the identification of republicanism's influence on the work of the founding fathers, which blossomed in the 1960s and 1970s, represented a paradigmatic shift in the historical analysis of the development of the Constitution. He argues that the emphasis on republicanism in the trio of works from Bailyn (1967), Wood (1969) and Pocock (1975) replaced the previously dominant Beardian economic understanding (cf. Lane, 1966) and holds greater resonance than the Hartzean paradigm, in which the Lockean liberal influence on the founding fathers was emphasized (Pangle, 1988). In their attempts to comprehend the development of republicanism, a number of scholars have considered the American contribution to the tradition. Within this field of study, a number of standpoints can be identified (cf. Hess, 2000). In *On Revolution* (1963), Arendt presents American republicanism as an inherently new strand of republican thought, locating Montesquieu as the foremost philosophical influence on the American constitution. Pocock (1975: 524) presents a more complex picture. He considers the tensions over size and the extension of the republic within a nation-state, and argues that the 'American republic proposed from its inception to offer a fresh solution to this ancient problem; the terms of this solution were in some respects dramatically new, but in others a restatement of old'. Pocock (1975) ultimately emphasizes the latter aspects, stating that 'an effect of the recent research has been to display the American Revolution less as the first political act of revolutionary enlightenment than as the last great act of the Renaissance' (1972: 122; cf. Hess, 2000). As a response to the positions of Arendt and Pocock, Judith Shklar offers a further explanation, in which the American contribution is represented more explicitly as both a continuation of, and an innovation within, civic republican thought. Shklar (1998) presents the founding fathers as recognizing both the historical roots of republicanism and the need to add to and adapt key principles in light of the political and social context within which they wrote (cf. Hess, 2000). Like Arendt, Shklar places the influence of Montesquieu at the heart of the renewal of the republican tradition, a fact which recognizes the increasing liberal influence on republican ideas in America at this time. Hess (2000: 36) also highlights the importance of liberalism, and emphasizes that 'republicanism would have to incorporate liberal ideas or else it would not have a future – at least not one on the American continent'.

The development of civic republican political ideas at the time of the founding fathers can most clearly be seen in the work of the politician, political philosopher and future President of the United States, James Madison. In the *Federalist Papers* Madison argued for the acceptance by states of the newly written constitution (which he had largely authored). In *Federalist Paper 10* Madison set out his vision for the application of republican values in a large and pluralist state. Rather than being concerned strictly with self-government and participation in public affairs, Madison appeals to the republican understanding of freedom as non-domination, secured through the separation of powers and a system of checks and balances in order to limit the potential for corrupt factional power. In distinguishing between a democracy and a republic, Madison

(1992a: 45) cites 'first, the delegation of the government, in the latter, to a small number of citizens, elected by the rest; secondly, the greater number of citizens, and greater sphere of country, over which the latter may be extended'. In these statements Madison ties republican government to representative forms of participation and, in addition, to an enlarged polity.[42] In *Federalist Paper 39* (1992b: 191–192) Madison returns to the principle of the republic, which he defines as 'a government which derives all its powers directly or indirectly from the great body of the people; and is administered by persons holding their offices during pleasure, for a limited period, or during good behavior'. Madison's awareness that truly democratic states in their pure forms had, in both theory and practice, been practicable only in small polities is at the heart of the contribution made by his application of republican ideals (Shklar, 1990: 276). In appealing to republican representative, rather than democratic direct, participation, Madison challenged those who were sceptical that republics in the Roman sense could be secured in a state as large as the thirteen colonies (Shklar, 1990). In *Federalist Paper 63*, Madison further differentiates a democracy, in which 'the people exercize the government in person', from a republic, in which the people 'assemble and administer (the government) by their representatives and agents', also arguing that a crucial feature of modern republics is the '*total exclusion of the people in their collective capacity*' from government (1992: 326–7, emphasis in the original; cf. Hess, 2000; Honohan, 2002).[43] For Madison it was the second, republican, form of government which 'corresponded more to the unique American circumstances' (Hess, 2000: 29). In this way, citizen involvement was limited through the – at that time – broadly liberal principle of representative government (Honohan, 2002).

Within this American context, the republican response of Madison combined the historical principle of the separation of powers, the more contemporary theme of federalism, and the liberal restriction of the active involvement of the people in the political process to the selection of representatives. Dagger (2004: 168) suggests that the founding fathers were cognisant that this was a departure 'from the classical conception of self-government as direct participation in rule; yet they saw representation as an improvement within, not an abandonment of, republican practice'. Furthermore, Lane (1992: 586) argues that Madison attributed a deliberative and developmental role to the national government in refining and enlarging the views of the public. It is also clear that the meaning of the republican ideal of the 'active citizen' was reformulated in the work of Madison and the founding fathers (Rahe, 1994;

Held, 1996). Through what he terms the 'end of classical politics', Wood (1969; cited in Pocock, 1975: 523) contends that the active, participatory citizen within a republic became consummated with the liberal citizen, free to pursue his own ends, and involved in politics in order to protect his own particular interests. Held sums up this adaptation (1996: 69):

> Across diverse backgrounds, thinking moved against reliance on virtuous citizens and civic restraint as the basis of political community and shifted towards a greater emphasis on the necessity to define and delimit the sphere of politics carefully, unleash individual energies in civil society, and provide a new balance between the citizen and government underwritten by law and institutions. Over time, the fundamental meaning of liberty as interpreted by the republican tradition changed; and liberty progressively came to evoke less a sense of public or political liberty... and more a sense of personal or private liberty.

In essence, Madison's goal was a form of republicanism which was committed to civic obligation to the common good, to the civic virtue of citizens, and to political participation, but which understood that such principles required different interpretations in the context of late eighteenth-century America. In Rahe's (1992: 601–2) reading, the American Republic which Madison did so much to shape was not a democracy in the ancient sense. Rather, it

> ...occupied an intermediate status between the enlightened despotism of Thomas Hobbes and the classical republicanism of the ancient Greeks, and in assessing the degree to which man could justly be termed a political animal, its advocates tried to strike an appropriate balance.

In shifting the focus of freedom from classical republican ideals of active participation and self-government to the pursuit of individual interests, Madison 'signals the clear interlocking of protective republicanism with liberal preoccupations' (Held, 1996: 93; see also Wood, 1969; Pocock, 1975).

Conclusion

Civic republicanism, as a field and theory of political thought, has a tradition. It is a tradition which is diverse, and which stems from classical foundations found in ancient Greece and Rome. It is a tradition marked by the sharing of common commitments and, perhaps even more critically, by a mutual language. The thinkers explored within this chapter have each contributed to the civic republican tradition in a significant way, and form the basis of the tradition upon which contemporary republicans draw. Contemporary theorists have followed republicans since Aristotle and Cicero in seeking to excavate, adapt and reapply the commitments to civic obligations, the common good, civic virtue and deliberative politics to the context of Western democracies today in order to promote particular versions of republican freedom. Moreover, they have sought to reinvigorate the idea found within parts of the republican tradition considered here that an inclination toward citizenry does not necessarily occur naturally within citizens, but rather has to be developed and inculcated by a complex set of formal and informal processes: in other words, citizens are made and not born. The brief consideration of the historical tradition presented in this chapter acts as a reminder that civic republicanism is not a new political theory and that the central commitments which are at its core permit multiple interpretations. It is to these commitments and their multiple interpretations that the attention of the three following chapters now turns.

3
Civic Obligation and the Common Good

The beliefs that citizens are bound by civic obligation and the concomitant conviction that citizens should have a mind toward the common good are present within all civic republican theories. Furthermore, republicans remind us that these beliefs need to be formed in citizens through a range of educational processes, including those that take place in schools. Whilst these commitments represent a cornerstone of contemporary republican thought, the existence and importance of civic obligation and the common good have also found clear expression within the work of many prominent liberal writers over the last three decades. This does not mean, however, that civic republicans and liberals conceive civic obligation and a concern for the common good in similar terms – nor even that these concepts are understood in the same way throughout contemporary republican thought. In their contemporary theories, civic republicans have looked toward notions of civic obligations and the common good, but have largely furnished them with understandings which, whilst they speak to their roots in classical ideas, have provided them with particular modern meanings. The aim of this chapter is to explore how contemporary republicans have understood civic obligations and notions of the common good, including the role of educational processes in their formation and expression, and how these relate to the various republican conceptions of freedom introduced in Chapter 1. It suggests that recent republican understandings and formulations of these terms permit different interpretations, and starts to point to the integral role that educational processes play in shaping citizens who are cognisant of their ties to others within a common political community.

Civic obligation

Civic obligation is an important term for republicans today, who seek to counter what they perceive as a preoccupation with rights in order to provide a 'substantive notion of the responsibilities of citizenship'. Indeed, it is civic obligations that 'provide a bridge between selfish, rights-bearing individuals and their deliberative republican community' (Sherry, 1995: 132). Civic obligation broadly comprises the duties expected of a citizen within a particular political community. No clear definition of the precise tasks required by civic obligation exists (indeed these are likely to differ according to the particular political community), but they can usually be understood to refer to certain civic, social and economic activities. These may include taking part in community life, voting in elections and participating in other democratic processes, being economically active and responsible, obeying the law and maintaining social conventions, as well as engaging in and supporting the institutions of civil society. There has been a great deal of recent interest in civic obligation from republican political theorists.[44] Civic republican theorists inextricably link the duties and responsibilities which define civic obligation to conceptions of freedom. It is these conceptions of freedom – viewed either in terms of self-government or in terms of non-domination – that furnish civic obligation with its republican meanings. For this reason, the basis of civic obligation is conceived differently within republican theory according to which conception of freedom holds precedence.

The first civic republican conception of the basis of civic obligation derives from Aristotelian thought and has clear similarities with communitarian ideas. The guiding principle for this is the existence of significant moral obligations which citizens, as human beings, have to each other as members of political communities. In this sense, civic obligation is viewed as a fundamental feature of, and as being essentially rooted within, the *polis*. Civic obligation is embedded and, crucially, is prior to the individual. It is in the work of Michael Sandel that this particular republican conception is most clearly set out. Drawing on his depiction of the relationship between the individual and society in *Liberalism and the Limits of Judgement* (1982) and *The Procedural Republic and the Unencumbered Self* (1984), Sandel (1996, 1998) returns to the idea of the embedded citizen in setting out his republican position.[45] Revisiting the arguments of his previous work, Sandel presents civic obligations as founded on the communitarian commitment to an embedded self. Sandel (1996: 12) argues that positions such as his place significance on the obligations humans have to 'fulfil ends we have not chosen – ends given by nature or God... or by our identities as members of families, peoples, cultures, or traditions'. Sandel's position here contrasts with Kantian liberal conceptions of human nature, embodied in contemporary political thought by Rawls, of individuals as essentially unencumbered by moral bonds. Sandel (1996: 13–14) argues that Kantian liberalism cannot 'make sense of our moral experience, because it cannot account for certain moral and political obligations that we commonly recognize, even prize. These include obligations of solidarity, religious duties, and other moral ties that may claim us for reasons unrelated to a choice'. In making this claim, Sandel accepts that the 'moral force' of our 'loyalties and responsibilities' consists partly in the fact that living by them is inseparable from understanding ourselves as the particular persons we are'. Whereas liberals such as Rawls understand the obligations of citizenship to be partial and voluntary, for intrinsic republicans the ties of citizenship are morally bonded. Similarly, whilst liberals view our identity as citizens as simply involving one set of connections amongst many, intrinsic republicans attach special importance to those of citizenship in securing freedom. On the republican reading, citizenship, and the civic obligations which it entails, shapes, protects and nourishes the fulfilment of other forms of identity; without the identity of citizenship others would be impoverished.[46] Indeed, according to Barber (2003: 244), a 'good deal of common bonding goes on in the process of politics itself ... those who practice a common politics may come to feel ties that they never felt before they commenced their common activity'. In fulfilling their obligations, citizens become further integrated into their communities.

This republican conception of civic obligation is inherently different from that which predominates in recent liberal theory. In *A Theory of Justice*, Rawls (1971: 108–117) delineates two senses in which individuals may be obligated to each other. 'Natural duties' are those obligations that are owed by virtue of common humanity, or as a person *qua* person. In contrast, 'voluntary duties' are those based on consent, and can be entered into and, importantly, opted out of. These 'voluntary duties' include the communal ties of citizenship. Although individuals may be *sentimentally* obligated by such communal ties, they are not *morally* obligated. In his later work, *Political Liberalism*, Rawls (1996: 31) recognizes that citizens have certain 'affections, devotions and loyalties' which they cannot 'stand apart from', but he does not include the bonds of citizenship within them (cf. Sandel, 1999: 248). Revising his earlier understanding presented in *A Theory of Justice*, Rawls (1985: 227) considers his account of 'justice as fairness' to embody two related prin- ciples: first, that individuals possess an equal entitlement to basic rights and liberties and second, that any social or economic inequalities are 'attached to offices and positions open to all' and are of benefit to those least advantaged within society'. Rawls (1985: 230–1) contends that this commitment to 'justice as fairness' is not, for this reason, dependent on metaphysical nor epistemological principles: '[T]hat is, it presents itself not as a conception that is true, but one that can serve as a basis of informed and willing political agreement between citizens viewed as free and equal persons...'. The fact that Sandel rejects Rawls' position by viewing obligations in moral terms is important, and means that they cannot be comprehensively adopted, revised or rejected by individual volition alone. Humans are inextricably obligated to others with whom they have communal ties, whether familial, societal, historical or spir- itual. Such obligations are not only common to all, but are an essential aspect of who we are both as citizens and as human beings. In other words, they have an intrinsic nature and worth.

The republican theorist Adrian Oldfield has also been a keen propo- nent of the existence of civic obligations, and uses them to frame his own republican standpoint. Oldfield's position on obligations is interest- ing for the extent to which he views them as of intrinsic importance (in this respect his position is comparable with Sandel's) but derived from agreement within the political community rather than as part of our essential humanity. In *Citizenship and Community: Civil Republicanism and the Modern World*, Oldfield (1990) presents a somewhat ambiguous understanding of the basis for civic obligations. In places, he suggests that humans possess obligations which are embedded, whilst in others he suggests that obligation represents a form of social agreement. Given this, there is a sense in which the ties and obligations of citizenship exist to the extent to which individuals (albeit in common with others) constitute them, adopt them and revise them through common inter- action with other citizens in the political community. These sentiments can be seen in Oldfield's (1990a: 4) argument that 'whilst some of the social identities possessed by humans are conscious choices, others are 'givens' of an individual's existence that remain "often imperishable"'. In a similar vein, he observes that '[I]t is this *choosing* of a political iden- tity that gives rise to the solidarity and cohesion of a political commu- nity' (1990: 7; emphasis added). Oldfield's position here appears to be one in which political obligations are *politically determined* and *optionally chosen* (cf. Honohan, 2002: 157). This is rather different from positions such as that of Sandel which view obligation – including that which relates to citizenship – as deriving from embedded ties, and thus involving the rejection of a metaphysical understanding of the obligations of citizenship. For this reason, Oldfield's republican position, at least as far as civic obligation is concerned, is somewhat unusual. His replacement of the commitment to pre-societal shared ends by an understanding that ends and values are politically chosen has led Kymlicka (2002: 298) to depict Oldfield's standpoint as a 'kind of second-order communitarianism'. Whilst Sandel and Oldfield present different foundations for civic obligation, then, they are both fundamentally concerned not only with its deep-rooted place within political communities but also with its intrinsic worth. Moreover, they are both committed to the view that moral ties between citizens in a political community are unlikely to be generated of their own accord and that they therefore require forming and inculcating through a range of educational processes which act on citizens to ensure that they recognise the affective bonds they share with others and the civic obligations that result.

Not all republicans necessarily share, or at least, not all make explicit, this embedded understanding of civic obligation. Indeed, a notable feature of the work of some republicans, particularly those I present here as advancing instrumental positions, is that civic obligation is valued in terms of the protection of citizens from domination. That is, that civic obligation exists because of, and as a feature of, the political community rather than necessarily because citizens are ontologically embedded in moral bonds. The lack of reference, either in support or critique, to the embedded nature of civic obligation is a notable feature within various republican accounts. Instrumental republicans such as Pettit, Viroli and Maynor, focus on the political basis of obligation rather than on its permanence in the human condition, and therefore put forward a 'weaker' form of community based on reciprocity and a common and regulative understanding of freedom as non-domination rather than embedded bonds.[47] What instrumental republicans do not provide in detail is a substantive picture of the ontological nature of these bonds. Patten (1996: 29; emphasis in the original) draws this point in relation to his categorization of Quentin Skinner's republicanism and his claims about the obligation to be politically active:

> The exact reasoning behind this conclusion is never spelt out explicitly, but it seems to be something like the following. Since we all have reason to live in a free society, and whoever wills the end, wills the necessary means to that end, then, if the republican analysis… is correct, we all have reason to participate actively in politics. To the

extent that the end of living in a free society has priority over our other ends, our reason to participate in politics takes on a similar priority and we can say that it is a *duty*.

Patten questions, however, the extent to which this basis for obligation acts or has the potential to act upon all citizens (a problem which the intrinsic republican notion of embedded ends does not have to answer) on the basis that 'it ignores the familiar problem that no *particular* individual's participation is strictly necessary for the maintenance of liberty'. To some extent the answer lies in the fact that the argument advanced by instrumental republicans is circular. Citizens are encouraged to participate in public life – in short to fulfil their obligations to the republic which acts as a co-operative enterprise[48] – so as to look beyond their narrow self-interests. Their reason for doing so however, is, ultimately, to protect their abilities to pursue their own ends. In other words, it is awareness of this self-interest which motivates citizens to be active in the political life of their communities. Viroli (1999: 77–8) suggests that citizens probably have multiple reasons for honouring their civic obligations:

> For some, the chief motivation for commitment comes from a moral sense, more precisely, from indignation at abuse, discrimination, corruption, arrogance, or vulgarity; for others, from an aesthetic desire for decency and decorum; still others are driven by specific concerns – about safe streets, pleasant parks, well-kept squares, respected monuments, good schools and hospitals; or people become engaged because they want to gain repute and they aspire to public honor, sit at the chairman's table, give speeches, stand in the front row at ceremonies. In many cases these motives work together, reinforcing each other.

What is notable in this reasoning, again, is that there is no real sense in which the obligations which citizens hold are, from an instrumental republican perspective, embedded and prior to individual rights. Instead, they result from sources such as common concern, civic pride, as well as, ultimately, self-interest in living a life free from arbitrary domination.

The common good

Intimately intertwined with civic obligation within republican thought is the concept of the 'common good'. The term is often used by contemporary republicans to distinguish their ideas from liberal political theory. As was stated in Chapter 1, a prime concern of Western political theory over the last four decades has been the relationship between individual rights and the common good, and more specifically the prioritizing of either over the other. Republicans typically respond to this by favouring the common good, but in such a way that individual rights and collective concerns become intertwined. In contemporary societies, the idea that it is through conduct in the public life of political communities that citizens can gain fulfilment is likely to strike many as somewhat old-fashioned and unrealistic. Citizens live diffuse lives where most enjoyment is gained either through private endeavours or through engagement with economic markets and consumerism. However, as Macedo et al. (2005: 5), who are sympathetic to republican ideas, explain:

> ...the benefits of political and civic activity often compete with other good things in life. There can be trade-offs between time spent at a political meeting and the joys of private life, including time spent with family and friends. While acknowledging the existence of important trade-offs and allowing that people frequently lead good and fulfilling lives without engaging in political activity, we maintain that civic engagement is part of the good life and that, under favourable conditions, civic activity complements rather than detracts from other valuable activities.

However, in his consideration of the educational relevance of communitarianism, Arthur (2000: 8) reminds us that 'the term the "common good" is of ancient origin and in contemporary usage it can be amorphous, meaning a variety of things'. This statement is equally true in relation to the way in which the common good is presented and interpreted by civic republicans. Indeed, on closer inspection the idea has not just one meaning, but many. More precisely, so far as contemporary civic republicanism is concerned, it has at least three distinct meanings.

The common good and the good life

The first interpretation of the common good found within recent civic republican literature is better understood in terms of the 'good life'. Aristotelian in derivation, this approach conceives the common good as a particular form of living; that is, a political life lived in accordance with that which is good and just. This valuing of the good in terms of human flourishing lost favour in the discourse of mainstream political theory throughout most of the twentieth century, as theorists became increasingly concerned with the protection of rights and the accommodation of plural interests in heterogeneous societies. More recently, there has been a renewed interest from some civic republicans in the extent to which living in common and the endeavour of citizenship relate to human perfection. In making reference to the common good Sandel (1996: 25; emphasis added), for example, advocates the prioritizing of a *'particular* conception of the good society' over and above the individual rights of citizens. Moreover, he contends that the state cannot be neutral toward the conceptions of the good life that its citizens may wish to favour, and should therefore adopt a formative stance in promoting a particular end. An important question, however, is the extent to which living a political life can be considered as *the* good or as *one* good amongst many. According to Oldfield (1990: 6) the answer is the former, and his republican theory 'holds that political life – the life of a citizen – is not only the most inclusive, but also the highest form of living together that most individuals can aspire to'. In a differentiated form of this republican position, Sandel (1998: 325) also endorses a moral approach to the common good as the best form of living:

> Unless citizens have reason to believe that sharing in self-government is intrinsically important, their willingness to sacrifice individual interests for the common good may be eroded by instrumental calculations about the costs and benefits of political participation.

This intrinsic good is one which is common to all citizens *qua* human beings. However, unlike Oldfield, Sandel does not suggest that political participation is the only, or necessarily the highest, common good available to citizens.[49] As Sandel (1998: 325) puts it '[O]ne need not believe that civic virtue constitutes the whole of virtue in order to view it as an intrinsic good, an essential of human flourishing'. Because the nature of the political life itself is open to some interpretation and refinement, Sandel sees great value in citizens coming together to discuss and deliberate on what the good life may mean. This is a point to which Sandel returns in his book *Justice: What's The Right Thing To Do*. Here Sandel (2009: 261) reaffirms his commitment to the common good as related to the good life, and again suggests that this is something that needs to be reasoned about through public discourse, arguing that 'to achieve a just society we have to reason together about the meaning of the good life, and to create a public culture hospitable to the disagreement which will inevitably arise'. Moreover, because he does not present the political life as the only possible form of the good life (it is rather one form of the good life, common to all), Sandel recognizes that there is likely to be a range of other contexts which hold the possibility of human fulfilment. Again, there is an educational imperative here. Citizens need to learn the capacities and dispositions which will permit the sort of dialogue about the good life that Sandel has in mind.

An important recognition in identifying differences within recent civic republican thought is that not all republicans necessarily support the idea that the state should promote a particular conception of the good, much less that political participation itself constitutes the good life. Indeed, certain republicans are 'explicitly hostile' to this Aristotelian ideal (Barber, 2003: 118). Those republicans who prioritize the instrumental worth of civic engagement – such as Pettit, Viroli and Maynor – support the right of citizens to choose their own ends amongst those available, subject to the constraint of non-domination. This view that citizens should be free to pursue their own goals in life as long as, in doing so, they do not arbitrarily dominate the interests of others, has enough similarities with the liberal ideal for some to question whether the instrumental version of republican theory can truly be differentiated from contemporary liberalism with respect to the relationship between rights and the common good (Patten, 1996; Rawls, 1996; Kymlicka, 1998). A number of commentators have preferred to refer to instrumental republican arguments as encompassing a form of 'liberal republicanism'. Kymlicka (1998: 131) believes that liberalism and instrumental republicanism 'are – or should be – allies' and that 'exaggerating their differences is philosophically suspect and politically counterproductive'. The work of Patten (1996: 27) provides a further, and more critical, illustration of the potential comparability of liberalism and particular forms of republicanism. He argues that 'either... there is no interesting disagreement between liberals and republicans, or there is, but not one which should concern liberals'. What is the validity of such claims?

Procedural liberals understand the relationship between rights and responsibilities as one in which individual rights are 'prior to the good' (Rawls, 1981; Dworkin, 1978a; cf. Kymlicka, 2002). In making this claim, liberals reject the privileging of any conception of the good, and argue that justice lies in the extent to which individuals are free, within certain minimal constraints, to pursue ends of their own choosing. Whilst many influential liberals are concerned with citizens recognizing the need to be active members of their political community, they are not presenting a form of the good. Kymlicka's (1998: 135–6; emphasis in original) reminds us, in relation to civic virtues, that:

> It is clearly not true that promoting a conception of virtue is *by defi-nition* promoting a conception of the good. It all depends on *why* one is promoting a conception of civic virtue. If the state promotes certain virtues on the grounds that possessing these virtues will make someone's life more worthwhile or fulfilling, then clearly it is promoting a particular conception of the good. However, if the state is promoting these virtues on the grounds that possessing them will make someone more likely to fulfil her obligations of justice, then it is not promoting a particular conception of the good.

Kymlicka's argument here is a restatement of Rawls' (1988: 263) contention that political liberalism may 'affirm the superiority of certain forms of moral character and encourage certain moral virtues' whilst avoiding a perfectionist understanding of the good (cf. Rawls, 1993: 194). The relationship between such values and the common good, or social justice, promoted by Kymlicka and Rawls, is both instrumental and causal: procedural liberals promote the virtues of liberal citizenship for the social and political goods which they generate, not because they are goods in themselves. These 'secondary values', as Kymlicka termed them, are aimed at improving and protecting the possibility of individuals choosing their own final ends. As a result, they do not prioritize such ends, and liberal neutrality remains intact. In his account of the similarities between liberalism and republican theories which reject the privileging of a particular form of the good life, Patten focuses his critical reflection on the influential republican work of Quentin Skinner. According to Skinner (1990a: 301–2), a 'free state' is one in which individuals are free from arbitrary constraint. In possessing negative liberties, individuals are thus 'unconstrained from pursuing whatever goals we may happen to set ourselves'. In itself this claim is commensurate with liberalism, and Skinner's (1990a) main point of differentiation between the two approaches is that republicanism places greater value on political participation. In outlining the republican attachment to civic virtues, Skinner (1990a: 307) observes that:

> to insist on rights as trumps...is simply to proclaim our corruption as citizens. It is also to embrace a self-destructive form of irrationality. Rather we must take our duties seriously, and instead of trying to evade anything more than 'the minimum demands of social life'

we must seek to discharge our public obligations as whole-heartedly as possible.

Patten (1996) views Skinner's distinction between liberalism and his version of republicanism with scepticism. As Patten (1996: 32) observes, and as I have suggested previously, the liberal view 'allows that we may have social duties, so long as they are rights-based, that is, are ultimately justified not by goals or duties, but by the preservation and protection of rights' (see also Dworkin, 1986; Kymlicka, 1989, 1998; Rawls, 1996; Dagger, 1999, 2004; Mason, 2000). As such, Patten suggests, the position of liberalism is not very different from that of Skinner's republicanism in that both positions adopt instrumental arguments for the existence of duties, and he limits differences to questions of the scale of obligation for civic duty and the political arrangements necessary for securing negative liberty. As Patten (1996: 36) concludes, 'Skinner's formulation of instrumental republicanism... fails to identify any philosophically interesting disagreement between the two positions'.

The idea was considered in Chapter 1 that the essential difference between Pettit's particular form of republicanism and liberalism lies in their respective conceptions of freedom as non-domination and non-interference. Although he recognizes his debt to Skinner's historical republican insight, Pettit (1999) critiques his understanding of freedom as non-domination. In part, Skinner's aim in his early texts had been to challenge the common understanding of republicanism as concerned with a positive conception of freedom. In doing so, Skinner (1983, 1984) sought to distinguish instrumental forms of republicanism from its populist strand, which privileges a form of the good life for intrinsic reasons. Pettit's instrumental republican theory is more detailed and comprehensive than Skinner's essentially historical analysis. In identifying a non-perfectionist role for the state, under which individuals are deemed free to pursue their own goals within the constraints of freedom as non-domination, Pettit makes a philosophical claim compatible with procedural liberalism: that in republican political communities the state should seek to protect freedom as non-domination, through strong institutions, laws and active citizenship. Such institutions and laws are essential because they enable individuals to act free of arbitrary domination, and in doing so protect the ability of individuals to pursue their own conceptions of the good. Pettit (1999: 120; see also 297–8) argues, for example, that 'in seeking a relatively neutral brief for the state – a brief that is not tied to any particular conception of the good – republicanism joins with liberalism against communitarianism', and he dismisses the notion that political communities should involve a 'cooperative pursuit of certain common goods' (1999: 4). Pettit (1999: 120–121) makes clear, however, that in promoting freedom as non-domination his republican theory involves advocating 'particular, sectarian conceptions of how people should live'. Pettit (1999: 121; cf. 1993a) understands these to be social goods rather than common goods, as suggested in the republicanism of Sandel and Oldfield. Pettit (1999: 121–4) argues that a social good is one whose 'realization presupposes the existence of a number of people who display intentional attitudes and perhaps intentional activities'. Because freedom as non-domination is achievable only in a social grouping, it constitutes a social good.

A further attempt to differentiate instrumental republicanism from liberalism is provided by John Maynor. Although his theory draws heavily on Pettit's work, Maynor (2003: 43) seeks to extend his republican theory and charges Pettit with denying 'republicanism a robust account...that helps us to differentiate it from rival liberal approaches'. Maynor makes a number of seemingly conflicting contentions. He argues on the one hand that instrumental republicanism adopts a more substantive approach to virtues and values, and that in doing so it 'abandons liberal neutrality', whilst at the same time suggesting that instrumental republicanism 'does not endorse a robust singular version of the good' (Maynor, 2003: 63). Central to ,Maynor's thesis is the argument (2003: 69; emphasis added) that freedom as non-domination involves the isolation and favouring of 'only *one* strand in individuals' conception of the good', leaving citizens free to follow their own conceptions in a non-dominating manner. Ultimately, Maynor's (2003: 81) argument is for what he terms a 'quasi-perfectionist' state. Whilst this is stronger than the liberal position, it remains 'not as strict as some perfectionist accounts in that a wide range of final ends is available to individuals as long as those final ends cannot be said to dominate others'.[50] Maynor's claim concerning liberal neutrality is somewhat disjointed, and his argument that his republican theory is different from liberalism in relation to foundationalism fails for important reasons. Liberal neutrality would need to be abandoned only if Maynor's republicanism was promoting a view based on a particular, privileged conception of the good, which it clearly was not. Akin to procedural liberalism, it posits a principle to guide the values, actions and institutions of the political community, without founding this on metaphysical principles. In reality it presents freedom as non-domination and thus as a social good as Pettit defines it, rather than as a form of the good life. In essence, Maynor's republicanism is therefore rooted in the same instrumental arguments as Pettit's: civic engagement is valued for what it enables, not in and for itself. Freedom as non-domination is a pre-requisite for individuals' pursuit of their own conceptions of the good, and is not a form of the good life itself. Like liberalism, instrumental republicanism remains neutral toward ends, but not necessarily towards the means to such ends. In other words and, crucially, because they 'do not have fixed or unchanging conceptions of the good', individuals are left free to pursue their own ends (Maynor, 2003: 69).

The common good and general welfare of the political community

A second, and more frequent, republican understanding of the common good presents it in terms of *the general welfare of the political community*. Expressed in this way, a commitment to the common good can be seen as the belief that citizens should look beyond their own individual private self-interests and toward those of the wider community in their thoughts and actions. As Maynor (2003: 75) says, '[T]he republican state, through its institutions, seeks to accommodate the private interests that individuals express in a manner that channels them into the common good'. In effect this interpretation of the common good might be better understood as the 'public interest', that is, the good that exists over and above individual or private interests. An important corollary of conceiving the common good in these terms is that it can be less demanding of citizens in requiring a commitment to participation and interdependence rather than necessarily to a virtuous way of living. This can be illustrated in relation to the work of the American political theorist Benjamin Barber and his theory of 'Strong Democracy'. Barber (2003: 117) suggests that his theory 'rests on the idea of a self-governing community of citizens who are united less by homogeneous interests than by civic education and who are made capable of common purpose and mutual action by virtue of their civic attitudes and participatory institutions rather than their altruism or their good nature'.

Viewing the common good as the general welfare of society furnishes the concept with a particular feature. Implicitly rejecting correspondence theories of truth and objectivity, the common good is presented as something to be forged within the political community, rather than as an entity which exists independently of particular societies. In this sense the understanding is pragmatic in nature, and results from the consensus which may emerge from deliberation between citizens (Peterson, 2009). This is what Sandel (1996: 274) has in mind when he argues that that republican self-government requires 'deliberating with fellow citizens about the common good and helping to shape the destiny of the political community' and 'political communities that control their destinies, and citizens who identify with those communities to think and act with a view to the common good'. Sandel (1999: 263) argues for a 'politics of the common good', at the heart of which is a commitment to finding 'a way to cultivate in citizens a concern for the whole, a dedication to the common good'. Though he only outlines the processes though which this could be achieved, Sandel points toward military and public service, as well as public education and schooling. In her commentary on civic republicanism Honohan (2002: 156) contends that '[T]he model of the common good central to republican politics is that of inter-subjective recognition in the joint practice of self-government by citizens who share certain common concerns'. Understood in this way there are likely to be not just many but competing versions of the common good. A further consequence of considering the common good in terms of the general welfare of the political community is that the common good is fluid and dynamic. What might be in the interests of the political community at one time may not be so at another. This requires processes through which citizens can regularly deliberate on and engage with issues of public concern (presumably with a basis for prioritizing competing conceptions of the good) and public institutions which are able to take such interests into account (this is explored in detail in Chapter 5).

The common good and non-excludability

A third conception of the common good which finds some expression within recent republican work, most notably within Philip Pettit's (1999: 121–4) republican work, views the common good as a property that 'cannot be increased (or decreased) for any member of a relevant group without it at the same time being increased (or decreased) for other members of the group'. This notion is essentially of economic abstraction and is explained as follows by Honohan (2002: 149): '...common goods that people in Western societies have tended to take for granted are now under threat, for example, clean air and fresh water'. In essence what Honohan is referring to is public goods. This economic definition in terms of 'non-excludability' is of liberal origin, and as Honohan (2002: 151–3) proceeds to note, when common *goods* are defined in this way they are again pluralized; there are a number of common goods 'from which everyone benefits' as 'separate individuals with our own priorities'. This largely economic sense of common goods has parallels with Charles Taylor's notion of 'convergent' goods, and his distinction between such convergent goods and 'common' or 'irreducibly social goods' is useful to our focus on civic republicanism. Taylor (1995: 190–1) defines convergent goods as those with which society is concerned only by their provision for all, asserting that '[I]n the unlikely event that an individual could secure it [the good] for himself, he would be getting the same valued provision that we all get now from social provision'. The sorts of goods which Taylor has in mind include national defence and police forces. In contrast, common or irreducibly social goods are premised on the belief that 'the bonds of solidarity with my compatriots in a functioning republic are based on a sense of shared fate' (1995: 192). This deep embedding of goods in social practices is very different in nature from the pursuit of convergent goods which seeks instead to 'satisfy[ing] an aggregate set of desires of a discrete group of individuals', and which are ultimately provided for all, for the benefit of individuals. In contrast, social goods are fundamentally rooted within social practice and communities. Social goods gain their value from, and result from, co-operative endeavour.

The common good, pluralism and coercion

Republican conceptions of the common good are open to two main criticisms, one of which relates to what has become known as the 'fact of pluralism' and the other to the charge of coercion. The basic premise of the 'fact of pluralism' is that contemporary Western democratic societies are too heterogeneous and have such diversity that it is no longer possible or desirable for one conception of the good life to be prioritized and promoted by the state. Members of the political community have a range of private, religious, historical, political, social and familial interests, which involve different conceptions of the best way to live a life. For this reason, and for most liberals, any attempt by the state to favour a single conception of a common end or to shape citizens toward a particular conception of the good undermines individual freedom and fails to fully recognize plurality. In other words, individual bearers of rights in a pluralist society should be free to develop their own understandings of their ends, and should be free within the construct of the laws to follow, within given boundaries, whatever end they deem desirable. In terms of citizenship, this liberal view permits citizens to hold different conceptions of what it means to be a citizen and leaves as largely voluntary the decision as to whether to engage civically or otherwise. The view that republicanism undermines the fact of pluralism is particularly problematic to those who, like Oldfield and Sandel, believe that the state should promote the political way of living as a form of the good life. Kymlicka (2002: 298–9) believes that any attempt by republicans to 'privilege a single conception of the good life' is untenable in modern societies, given that societies are too diverse and cosmopolitan for one view of the good life to ever achieve a 'consensus on the intrinsic value of political activities' (cf. Rawls, 1996: 4).

The question of plurality is an important one. Contemporary society is increasingly heterogeneous, and agreement on values and goals is hard to reach in Western societies in which individuals possess various, and sometimes incompatible, religious, social, political and moral standpoints. So how do republicans respond to this tension? The answer is that civic republicans have devoted surprisingly little attention to how republican politics can respond to plurality. What they do have to say comprises three interrelated strands. First, with the exception of Oldfield, they do not deny the possibility of a range of interests and final ends for individuals and simply point to the idea that the identity of citizenship is a necessary and important one. Plural group interests do not negate the existence and importance of the common good, rather they are encouraged to shape it jointly through participation in public life. As Maynor (2003: 133) suggests, republican positions 'must not only accept the inevitability of pluralism, but also seek to harness and utilize the dynamic energy created by difference and diversity'. Second, republicans suggest that this participation takes place in civic and civil institutions, which act to fill the space between different groups of citizens. This is in essence a civic approach to plurality, which identifies for the state and civil society a role in ensuring that the interests of individuals and groups become known in public life through engagement and discourse (this point is returned to in Chapter 5). In this way, the republican state '…nurtures the distinctive expressions of community' (Sandel, 1996: 117) and seeks not merely to tolerate different interests, but to engender their commitment to the sort of civic engagement which republican models of citizenship require. Third, and this is also a related point, it is only through the participation of different voices in public life that a wide range of interests, not just those of small factions, can act to shape decisions in a fair and open way. Because different groups within society are able to 'articulate and effectively publicize their interests' (Maynor, 2003: 135), including in deliberating about the common good, a more meaningful response to heterogeneous societies than the pluralism of procedural liberalism emerges.

It is not just the existence of heterogeneous and plural interests which challenges contemporary civic republican positions. An equally cogent problem is that of coercion. This can be understood as the claim that because civic republicans are concerned with the common good of the political community this results in, and even requires, the subjugation of individual interests (Honohan, 2002: 148). In response to this charge, republicans suggest that rather than involving the subordination of self-interest, the prioritizing of the common weal is in fact an enterprise in self-enlightenment. That republicans are not blind to the rigour and demands of a life lived in common by citizens is an important recognition. As Sandel (1999: 221) accepts, '[C]ommunal encumbrances can be oppressive'. Indeed, most civic republicans would accept that a certain 'spirit of sacrifice is needed to place the common good above one's individual interest' (Viroli, 1999: 71). They would suggest that, as thinkers in the republican tradition such as Aristotle and Aquinas make clear, individual interests are best met not through a life lived solely in private, but through one which is conducted in part publicly and with a concern for the public interest. Viroli (1999: 103) suggests that 'the best republican politics is, precisely, a politics that can speak to self-interest in the best sense'. In other words, properly constituted, the relationship between citizens and the state in a republican system of government is not one of conflict but of co-operation (aided of course by the involvement of citizens in that system). Barber (2003: 155) provides an interesting perspective on this argument. He suggests that it is the alternative to the type of civic engagement promoted by republicans that is most likely to lead to coercion: 'community without participation first breeds unreflected consensus and uniformity, then nourishes coercive conformity, and finally engenders unitary collectivism of a kind that stifles citizenship and the autonomy on which political activity depends'. It is the civic republican commitment to public deliberation by citizens that prevents the common interest from being singular, marginal and pervasive. Macedo et al. (2005: 175–6) extend this argument further, suggesting that it 'is hard to believe what is objectionable about this kind of "social engineering" or "manipulation", given that it has certain important features, such as that it is open to the attention and scrutiny of public judgement and as such is not only critical but better protects basic liberties'. These sentiments are important and help to clarify the fact that civic republicans are interested in a critical and enlightened approach to the common good, rather than one which is fixed, uncritical and dogmatic.

Republicans prefer to view the formative process operating within their proposed political communities as involving habituation, persuasion and education rather than coercion. This is most clearly illustrated by Sandel (1996) who is concerned that republicanism is able to provide a valid and clear response to this tension. Drawing on the work of Alexis de Tocqueville, Sandel (1996: 320) illustrates the desirable approach to the inculcation of citizen civic engagement in republican society as one that involves a 'gentle[r] kind of tutelage'. In effect, Sandel is arguing for republicanism to be viewed as desiring a more refined approach to cultivating 'independence and judgement to deliberate well about the common good'. In order to demonstrate this distinction Sandel draws contrasts between his Tocquevillian position and Rousseau's understanding of the general will.[51] Rousseau understands the common good as a single entity. Such unity is total to such an extent that political discord within a body of citizens becomes obsolete. Rousseau encapsulates this unity in his view that '[T]he first to propose [a new law] merely says what everybody has already felt' (cited in Sandel, 1996: 320). Sandel rejects this on the grounds that it serves to exclude, rather than celebrate, public discourse about the general welfare of the political community. Sandel therefore suggests that differences between individuals should be 'filled' by political institutions, through which issues of public concern can be debated. For Sandel (1996: 321), political institutions act as 'agencies of civic education' that 'inculcate the habit of attending to public things', but yet 'given their multiplicity ... prevent public life from dissolving into an undifferentiated whole'. Sandel's republicanism is committed explicitly to an understanding of the common good as something about which citizens come together and deliberate within political institutions. Rather than subordinating their interests for the common good, citizens accept that such interests are protected and maintained through public co-operation within political communities. In other words, civic participation represents a form of enlightened self-interest. According to Barber and Battistoni (1993: 237) in their consideration of service-learning in higher education institutions in the US, it is the focus on the 'mutual responsibility and the interdependence of rights and responsibilities' and 'not on altruism but on enlightened self-interest' which distinguishes the type of civic obligation and service that republicans have in mind from forms of philanthropic service based on the more conservative principle of *noblesse oblige*. Honohan (2002: 160) provides the summary that for republicans 'there is a difference between enforcing obligations and fostering the capacities which dispose citizens to fulfil these special obligations' (cf. Mason, 2000: 112–113).

The position adopted by Oldfield (1990: 161–167) concerning coercion is similar to the Tocquevillian approach of Sandel, and he would agree that citizens require some form of persuasion if they are to become active members of the political community. In fact, Oldfield states this in stronger terms than Sandel. According to Oldfield (1990: 164) the character required for citizenship, which would presumably include concern for the common good, 'has to be authoritatively inculcated'. Moreover, 'minds must be manipulated'. This idea is strong, and is likely to concern many in contemporary society as involving of a lack of critical capacity on the part of the citizenry. Oldfield denies, however, that performing the citizen's role would result in a loss of autonomy for individuals who 'find their interests changing'. Drawing on de Tocqueville's reference to the 'habits of the heart', Oldfield (1990: 172) suggests that:

> No amount of political participation and economic democracy, no level of civic education or national service, will suffice for the practice of citizenship in a political community – unless and until the external covenant becomes an internal one.

In making this statement, Oldfield (1990: 165) appeals to Gutmann's theory of 'conscious social reproduction'. Gutmann's theory presupposes that *all* democratic states, whether liberal or republican, consciously shape the character of citizens, including through their education systems. Once this recognition is accepted, Gutmann contends, attention can shift to the content and methods by means of which citizen virtues are inculcated. Significantly, 'deliberate instruction', in which citizens play a role in shaping the educational methods and content experienced by future citizens, replaces covert political socialization. This reminds us that any educational process (whether through societal processes or through a nation's schools) is likely to seek to shape citizens in a particular way and that, as such, education, even in a liberal state, is not a neutral process.

Conclusion

Intrinsic republicans question how people can be active in their communities in a truly meaningful way without a clear and sustained sense, both rational and emotional, of their attachments to those communities and their other members. Drawing on communitarian themes, for intrinsic republicans, civic obligations are the result of fundamental bonds of community, which involve a common and shared sense of history and endeavour. Such bonds have to be developed in citizens through a range of formative processes which act upon citizens in a way conducive to common concerns. This requires citizens to learn not only how to participate, but to actively engage in discussions about the good life and the common good of the political community. Moreover, it is a process which involves citizens coming to learn about the shared historical basis of community. As Oldfield (1990: 162) explains '[O]ne of the duties of citizenship is to take responsibility for the intergenerational continuity of the community'. Instrumental republicans share this concern with civic obligation, but largely understand it in liberal terms, and as deriving from a sense of reciprocity and civic pride. The common good is no more than the general interest of the political community which, on closer inspection, is ultimately aimed at the protection of individuals' ability to follow their own conceptions of the good life in a non-dominating and non-dominated way. An understanding of these accounts helps us to conceptualize differences within the field of civic republicanism and reminds us that, in terms of their operationalization into civic education, civic obligations and the common good are not easily defined nor readily agreed upon terms.

4
Civic Virtue

One of the chief features of republican positions, both historical and contemporary, are the beliefs that participation within the political community is central to the protection and maintenance of freedom and the related belief that such active civic involvement requires citizens to develop and possess certain attitudes and dispositions – that is, civic virtue. As Pocock (1975: 184) puts it, for republicans '[T]he freedom of each depends on the virtue of all'. In this sense, civic republicans are not neutral toward the preferential behaviour and attitudes of citizens within the political community. The need for such civic virtue raises the question as to whether these occur naturally within individual citizens, or require cultivation and inculcation by the state. The purpose of this chapter is to consider the place and nature of civic virtue within contemporary republican conceptions of citizenship. The idea that civic virtue is meaningful to contemporary Western societies represents a central feature of recent civic republican ideas and serves to remind us that citizenship, both as a practice and as an educational endeavour, contains a central moral component. According to both Michelman (1988) and Sunstein (1988), civic virtue is the 'animating principle of civic republicanism', for Gey (1993: 806) it represents the 'leitmotif of all civic republican theory', whilst for Viroli (1999: 69), civic virtue is the 'foundation' of republican government. Despite the centrality of the notion, appeals to civic virtue within contemporary republican thought are nebulous. For this reason, the 'concept is both the theoretical core and the Achilles heel of civic republican theory' (Gey, 1993: 806). In her analysis of civic republicanism, Honohan (2002: 160) has gone so far as to suggest that the 'idea of civic virtue' is 'as currently advanced ... too vague to give any understanding of its practical implications, and therefore may have very diverse political implications'. This chapter has two parts. In the first, the nature of republican civic virtue is considered. It is suggested that whilst the idea of civic virtue is clearly central to republican theories today, the term is not always used to mean the same thing. The second part focuses upon the extent to which republicans have identified a formative role for the state in the inculcation of civic virtue. Educative processes outside formal schooling are considered first, before attention is paid to the extent to which, in referencing civic virtue and identifying a role for the education system in cultivating it, civic republicans can be understood as subscribing to some form of character education.

What is republican civic virtue?

As Kymlicka (2002: 288) remarks '[T]he first task for theorists of citizenship' is 'to specify...the sort of civic virtues required for a flourishing democracy'. This prompts the question as to how civic republican theorists conceptualize civic virtue and the specific virtues that comprise it. Although it is difficult to define precisely, civic virtue can be described as a particular public role and denotes, ultimately, the 'disposition to further public over private good in action and deliberation' (Burtt, 1990: 24). The concept of civic virtue is not, however, always understood the same way within republican thought, and Sunstein (1988: 1541*fn*8) suggests that '[S]ome of those who value civic virtue emphasize the improvement of individual character – as in the classical formulation – while others understand it as a precondition for the achievement of social justice' (Sunstein, 1988: 1541fn8). Because the terms civic virtue and civic virtues are used in this vague sense within civic republican theories, it is difficult to define them in anything other than broad terms. That, at least, is the task here.

Central to the civic republican project is an attempt to engender civic virtue in part as a protective endeavour against liberal atomism and the power of economic free markets and in part in order to advance republican aims. In order to understand recent republican work in this area, it is necessary to once more draw on the distinction between forms of republicanism that understand freedom in terms of self-government and value civic engagement for intrinsic reasons, and forms of republicanism that understand freedom in terms of non-domination and that value civic engagement for instrumental reasons. The differences between these two positions make it possible, and for that matter necessary, to identify two different approaches to civic virtue within recent work on civic republicanism.

For intrinsic republicans, civic virtue is understood largely in a classical sense, and as relating to the development of the individual character of citizens. The intrinsic republican position outlined by Sandel in *Democracy's Discontent* is illustrative of this approach. For Sandel, civic virtue can be understood as those dispositions and character traits which, in their social expression, enable citizens to participate effectively in the government and public affairs of their communities. Sandel (1996: 5) argues that '[T]o share in self-rule...requires that citizens possess, or come to acquire, certain qualities of character, or civic virtues'. In establishing this commitment, Sandel traces what he terms 'republican' virtues through the economic and socio-political history of America. It is through this narrative that we gain some understanding of the specific civic virtues central to self-government and political engagement. For example, Sandel considers the conditions necessary for the development of republican virtues in his analysis of the political economy of America in the late 1700s and early 1800s. At this time, politicians influenced by republicanism advocated and admired the principally agrarian form of economic production in America. In considering the reaction to Alexander Hamilton's economic policies, Sandel (1996: 135–6) contends that:

The argument that brought the Republican Party into being was that Hamilton's political economy would corrupt the morality of citizens and undermine the social conditions essential to republican government...Civic virtue required the capacity for independent disinterested judgement. But poverty bred dependence, and great wealth traditionally bred luxury and distraction from public concern.

In this quotation, Sandel refers to two conditions necessary for civic virtue, 'material independence' and 'disinterested judgement'. The conditions conducive to civic virtue are further alluded to when Sandel (1996: 130–1) argues that '[D]espite their revision of classical republican assumptions, the framers of the Constitution...continued to believe that the virtuous should govern and that government should aim at a public good beyond the sum of private interests'. In his narrative Sandel stops short, however, of explicitly developing the specific set of civic virtues which relate to these conditions in either a historical or contemporary context. Sandel (1998: 324) defends this ambiguity by viewing it as reflecting the 'different conceptions of civic virtue and the formative project' to be found throughout the discourse of American political history. Sandel (1998: 324–5) explains that whilst '[S]ome emphasized conservative virtues such as obedience, discipline, and reverence for tradition; others stressed the democratic virtues of active, critically-minded citizens who possessed sufficient economic independence and equality of condition to exercise political judgement and engage in public affairs'. Whilst this may be true, it does little to clarify (at least in an explicit sense) the precise civic virtues that are necessary for the republican project in contemporary society.[52] In his critique of Sandel's position, Pangle (1998: 21) perceptively wonders 'whether a more systematic, direct, specific, and argumentative presentation and analysis of the virtues, and thus of the human good, is not essential, if we are to have clarity as to what it is we are seeking to encourage'. Like Sandel, Oldfield's republican theory focuses on broad conceptions rather than on specific civic virtues. Oldfield (1990: 147–51) lists a set of broad requirements that citizens would need to embody, including 'devotion to the community', a commitment to the 'defence of the republic', and 'the exercise of judgement on common affairs'.

The fact that republicans such as Sandel and Oldfield have not provided details of the specific virtues, civic or otherwise, which are required by their republican theories is somewhat puzzling. In describing republican citizenship in broad terms, and through a set of general commitments which citizens share, we are left very much to infer the sorts of virtues which are inimical to the effective civic life of a political community founded on republican principles. Indeed, a consequence of the lack of clearly specified civic virtues within republican arguments has been the tendency for commentators less sympathetic to the republican position to extract a list of such virtues. A prominent example of this can be found in the work of Pangle (1998: 22–26) who, within his critique of Sandel's work, infers the following list of virtues: 'virtues of the family', 'marital fidelity', 'honesty', 'frugality', 'industry', 'craftsmanship', 'simplicity of manners', 'economic independence', 'discipline', 'moderation', 'temperance', 'obedience', 'respect for authority', 'orderliness', 'courage', 'passion for the common good', 'honour' and 'power'. These are the same sort of largely conservative virtues central to the ideas of public communitarians like Amitai Etzioni, and we would have to question whether republicans like Sandel would embrace them in full. Unfortunately, republicans leave us with little clarity as to whether they would.

More significantly, there are a number of elements in the classical formulation of virtues that are either rejected or ignored in republican accounts that seek to reconstitute republican civic virtue in contemporary society (here I am talking largely about the work of Sandel and

Oldfield), and our understanding of republican conceptions of civic virtue is helped through considering two such omissions. First, it was suggested in Chapter 2 that the classical conception of virtues found within the work of both Aristotle and Aquinas limited the number of virtues to a central core. Moreover, virtues were understood as relating to the totality of an individual's actions. As such, the classical conception did not distinguish specifically 'civic' virtues as necessarily separate from more general virtues. In other words, as they were understood by Aristotle, the possession of the requisite general virtues directly related to and enhanced the civic dispositions of citizens. There is a tendency within contemporary republican theoretical discourse to separate out civic virtues as distinct from the other dispositions and character traits that a citizen may possess. To some extent this reflects the belief of republicans like Sandel that the goals of the political community, which include the virtues necessary within the citizenry, are determined and agreed by that community, and are thus 'created' rather than 'discovered' (cf. Gey, 1993: 809; Sustein, 1988). Sandel (1996: 212) argues that '[O]nce character formation for the sake of substantive moral and civic ideals is accorded legitimacy, citizens can debate which virtues their political community should cultivate and prize'. Here Sandel is suggesting that it is the forum of public deliberation through which the content of civic virtues can be defined. Unlike many of the historical scholars upon whom they draw, contemporary republicans typically reject the possibility of *a priori* definitions of virtues (cf. Gey, 1993: 801). Second, it was also considered in Chapter 2 that according to the classical conception, the possession of virtues related to the good life and to human flourishing. Through living the good life, and through exercizing virtue, citizens are able to secure happiness. For Aristotle, whilst other virtues, such as honour or intelligence, could be considered either as a means, or as an end, happiness alone could represent an end in itself. In the *Ethics*, Aristotle (1998: 1097b, 16–19) argued that happiness is a good in itself and that it is the most desirable good for the human being. The relationship between virtue and human excellence is much stronger in Aristotle's thought than it is in contemporary republicanism. For Aristotle, living in accordance with the virtues led to happiness and the good life. This conception of the good life, whilst containing constituent parts, was unified in nature. Furthermore, for Aristotle, the good life ultimately involved what Norman (1983: 54–5) has termed 'the rational emotional life' and 'the activity of intellectual contemplation'. The former means to a life in accordance with the virtues, the latter, a life in pursuit of reasoned wisdom. It is noteworthy, though, that contemporary intrinsic republicans, who in broad terms make a meaningful commitment to virtues in the Aristotelian sense, have a tendency to down-play the link between civic virtue and human excellence or flourishing. We are told, instead, that civic virtue is of political value and of worth in terms of the good life, but not that this relates in any way to particular standards of human excellence.

There is a second republican formulation which, in contrast to the viewing of civic virtues in terms of internalized dispositions inimical for citizenship, conceptualize them in terms of preconditions of citizen behaviour conducive to a well functioning political community. This formulation is less demanding of citizens and does not seek the deep internalization of positive character traits suggested by the intrinsic republican account. Rather than being constitutive of human flourishing, civic virtue – or civility as its proponents prefer to term it – represents a set of principles for citizen behaviour which are valued because they permit active citizenship within the political community and as such protect and promote freedom as non-domination (Selznick, 1992: 389–90).[53] Pettit (1999: 245–260) employs the concept of 'civility' to refer to the behaviour required by citizens, arguing that 'republican laws must be supported by habits of civic virtue, or good citizenship – by habits, as we may say, of civility – if they are to have any chance of prospering' (see also Pettit, 1990). Although he employs the language of civic virtue, Pettit's concept of civility is rather different from the classical understanding of civic virtue, and can be understood in terms of 'decency' (Kymlicka, 2002: 300). There is no requirement that citizens internalize certain civic virtues within their character, nor that such dispositions be replicated in the private realm. Whilst the language of internalization is used, this 'represents fidelity to civil norms' (Pettit, 1999: 258) and not the incorporation of such virtues and values within one's own character. On this republican account, norms themselves are agreed standards or ways of doing things, determined by and within the political community. This standpoint is illustrated by Pettit (1993a: 313) in his earlier work, *The Common Mind*, in which he asserts that '[R]epublicans are sometimes accused of requiring people to be spontaneously good: requiring them to be lovers of the common weal. But it is worth emphasizing that all freedom as citizenship requires is reliably beneficial behaviour, whether the result of character or circumstance'. I suspect that what instrumental republicans like Pettit are really referring to is character defined as a cognitive willingness to act and behave in a certain way, rather than character defined as internalized dispositions which relate to being a certain sort of person.

Drawing on Pettit's work, Maynor (2003) also suggests that civic virtue is required by an informed and active citizenry if they are to act, and in turn be treated, in a non-dominating manner. Here again the language of civic virtue is used, but in reference to something which remains outside a citizen's sense of being. Maynor's (2003: 182) approach to civic virtues is similar to Pettit's, and he contends that '... civic virtue is understood as individuals' ability to cast their ends in a manner that does not interfere arbitrarily with others and an appreciation of how their actions impact on the whole of society'; in other words, that citizens conform to certain regulatory requirements in terms of their behaviour and actions in public life. From this viewpoint, civic virtue is, as Galston (1995: 42) puts it, 'socially functional' but not 'individually advantageous'. For this reason, the instrumental republican account is better understood as one of civic principles than of civic virtues. When civic virtue is understood in its less demanding form of civility – or as civic principles – it involves a causal and mutually beneficial relationship between profitable citizen behaviour and the institutions and laws of the republican political community. It is the values and actions which support behaviour conducive to freedom as non-domination that the 'republican state legitimately promotes' (Maynor, 2003: 182), whilst, in turn, citizens 'enjoy a higher degree of non-domination' under a regime where there are norms to support republican laws' (Pettit, 1999: 244).

There are noticeable similarities between this instrumental republican conception of civility and the work of a number of liberal theorists who appeal to the idea of civic virtue, but do so on instrumental grounds. Seeking to reject the idea that the liberal state is neutral regarding the behaviour required of citizens, liberals including Galston (1995), Patten (1996), Rawls (1996), Callan, (1997), Dagger (1997) and Kymlicka (1998), have each advanced the principle that certain types of behaviour within the citizenry are necessary for the effective functioning of liberal political states. For example, in his 'republican-liberal' theory, Dagger (1997: 195) has contended that a republican-liberal promotes civic virtues because they '... enhance the individual's ability to lead a self-governed life as a co-operating member of a political society', whilst Callan (1997: 3) suggests that 'creating virtuous citizens is as necessary an undertaking in a liberal democracy as it is under any other constitution'. Crucially, such civic virtues are promoted without a particular conception of the good. Citizens learn certain capacities and to follow certain rules (those that I have termed here 'civic principles') because they strengthen the republican community. There is no real sense that learning these capacities and following certain rules makes citizens better humans, only that it makes them better citizens, able to operate effectively in public life in a non-dominating manner. Further similarities between the instrumental republican and liberal positions can be identified in regard to the question as to whether the republican state should seek to maximize civic virtue or civility within its citizenry. Because they do not believe that the behaviour and attitudes required for effective engagement in political life must be internalized character dispositions, republicans such as Pettit and Maynor need not be concerned with developing maximal civility within citizens. Instead, there may be a sufficient level, short of the maximum, at which citizens are able to fulfil their obligations to track the interests of others and to cast their own ends in a non-dominating manner. From a liberal perspective Kymlicka (2002: 293) has made reference to a 'critical threshold' of citizens who possess 'virtues to a sufficient degree', whilst Dahl (1995) has made reference to the 'adequate citizen'. Along similar lines Galston (1995: 42) explains that:

> When I speak of certain virtues as instrumental to the preservation of liberal communities, I do not mean that every citizen must possess these virtues, but rather that most citizens must. The broad hypothesis is that the proportion of non-virtuous citizens increases significantly, the ability of liberal societies to function successfully will progressively diminish.

In addition to critical and important differences within republican thought, there are significant issues relating to civic virtue which cut across contemporary republican arguments. This tension centres on the type of virtues which republicans (whether intrinsic or instrumental in outlook) emphasize. Whilst the classical conception emphasized a range of virtues, contemporary republicans typically advocate only *civic* virtues. The classical understanding provided by Aristotle, for example, was concerned with the virtuous conduct of the whole person, not just the conduct of the virtuous citizen. Although the concept of 'virtue' is itself contested, Aristotle (1998, II 6, 15) defines a virtue as 'a deliberated and permanent disposition, based on a standard applied to ourselves and defined by the reason displayed by the man of good sense'. A virtue is a disposition, or a way of living, that relates to the cognitive, affective and behavioural domains of the individual. In proposing his set of twelve virtues, Aristotle is suggesting that virtues relate simultaneously to both personal and civic conduct. Conceptualized in this way, the dispositions necessary for political participation have their basis within more personal virtues. Furthermore, virtues are themselves inherently social qualities. Therefore, although virtues are conceived as an individual property, they relate to, and should be understood within, their social context and expression (Pence, 1984: 281). In classical terms any formulation of republican civic virtue which seeks to separate the good of the citizen from that of the individual is problematic. When Honohan (2002: 163) describes republican civic virtue as establishing requirements which are 'not for saints but for "good enough" citizens', and asserts that in 'the modern world there will be a difference between the requirements for the good citizen and the good person', the disjunction between the civic and the personal is clear.

It is not clear that such a disjunction is useful, nor even psychologically possible, at least as far as virtue is concerned. When an action is described as 'virtuous' a claim is made about the nature and personal qualities of the individual character, and not simply about the act itself. In this sense ethical theories based on virtues fundamentally differ from rule- or act-based deontological or consequentialist theories. The distinction between civic and personal realms may be possible as far as the rules which guide citizen actions are concerned (one can, for example, conform to certain rules in the civic world which are different from the rules that shape one's personal behaviour), but this is not true of virtues. If a citizen is truly virtuous, they will act in accordance with such virtues in the variety of contexts in which they are involved. As Arthur (2003: 34) puts it:

> Being virtuous is not a matter of following a set of prescribed rules, but rather of expressing one's moral character in attitudes, feelings and deeds. Virtuous people are disposed not simply to do the right thing, but to become the right sort of person.

The specific focus on the virtues of the citizen, and not on the totality of virtues central to the character of persons, separates republicans from a number of 'public service' communitarians who focus on the whole character of the individual (Etzioni, 1995; Sacks, 1997; Selbourne, 1997; cf. Honohan, 2002). Because they focus strictly on *civic* virtues, republicans typically have 'nothing to say about the accounts of family values, marital fidelity, religious belief, punctuality, industry or self-sufficiency' (Honohan, 2002: 164), which form the focus of the communitarian agenda. Whilst a strength of contemporary republicanism is the fact that it draws our attention to public responsibilities and the civic virtues necessary to fulfil them, a limitation is that it offers relatively little regarding the character of citizens outside their public role. This separation of civic virtues from what might be termed personal virtues is strange, given that (as is explored in Chapter 5) republicans are generally sceptical of any attempt to separate 'our identity as citizens from our moral and religious convictions... when engaging in public discourse about justice and rights' (Viroli, 1999: 69). This demarcation of specific types of virtues can be viewed as part of a process within contemporary political science which has resulted in the proliferation of virtues and the subsequent division of these into certain adjectival categories. This tendency is exemplified in the work of William Galston (1995: 42–45), who sets out a range of different types of virtues. These include 'general' virtues, such as courage, law-abidingness and loyalty; the virtues of 'liberal society' such as 'independence', 'fidelity', 'self-restraint', 'self-transcendence', 'tolerance'; the virtues of 'liberal economy' which are divided into 'entrepreneurial', 'organizational' and 'generic'; and the virtues of 'liberal politics', which are divided into 'citizenship', 'leadership' and 'general political virtues'. Importantly for our focus here, in this exposition of liberal virtues Galston (1995: 46) differentiates between the liberal citizen and the civic republican citizen, citing the duties 'to participate actively in politics', 'to place the public above the private' and 'to systematically subordinate personal interest to the common good' as all falling within the civic republican domain.

To distinguish between different *types* of virtues has important implications in terms of the depth, permanence and practice of such virtues. As Galston (1995: 42) explains, the 'liberal virtues demand less self-discipline and sacrifice than do the virtues of classical antiquity, of civic republicanism, or of Christianity'. In effect, Galston widens the meaning of what constitutes a virtue in order to facilitate the distinction he is making between the liberal conception of state and citizenship and the civic republican conception of state and citizen. What is not clear is that the attitudes and behaviour he describes as falling within the liberal and civic republican conceptions respectively are in fact virtues at all, as opposed to useful skills and attributes, and there is a danger that there becomes no limit to what can be called a virtue. If 'virtue' is defined as moral excellence and as denoting a quality of character which is good in and of itself we can see that certain virtues, such as courage and loyalty, are virtues *per se*. Many of the 'virtues' which Galston cites are better understood as moral values; that is, as positive guiding principles for human action. To some, the distinction I am drawing between values and virtues may be purely a matter of semantics. However, there are substantive differences between what might be considered as the classical virtues, and the sorts of capacities which many republicans appear to designate as civic virtues. Dagger's republican-liberal approach illustrates my point well. He (1999: 195–196) recognizes that it 'is tempting to suggest that all virtues contribute to republican-liberal citizenship...These and other qualities do indeed help to nourish personal autonomy or the sense of community – or both'. Here Dagger seemingly accepts that civic virtues are, in essence, the classical virtues writ large and enacted in public life. However, rather than citing the importance of classical virtues, Dagger presents a set of six civic virtues, namely, the respect for individual rights, the valuing of autonomy, the toleration of different opinions and beliefs, playing fair, the cherishing of civic memory, and the taking of an active part in the life of the community. To raise the status of the capacities Dagger cites to the level of virtues runs the risk of separating virtues from *human* character. Such capacities are certainly important and are fundamental to the effective operation of a republican political community. They do not in themselves, though, constitute virtues properly understood. As I have written elsewhere, the particular 'virtues' being promoted, and how they are defined and understood in practice, holds important implications for the focus of civic education programmes aimed at the formation and expression of character and civic behaviours (Peterson, 2010). The republican tradition makes clear that the capacities of the citizen are not generated through innate ability alone, but need to be educated and formed. This is a theme to which recent republicans have returned and have sought to re-emphasize in the context of Western democracies. But to what extent do they advance what might broadly be considered as a form of character education?

Forming civic virtue

For republicans the citizen is an interdependent agent furnished with the skills and dispositions necessary to engage fruitfully in civic life. The civic republican tradition makes clear, however, that the capacities required by citizens do not necessarily occur naturally – civic virtue must be developed and inculcated in citizens. All republicans posit a developmental view of human nature, which understands that processes of socialization need to occur if citizens are to possess the civic virtue required for the protection of various forms of republican freedom. Typically, contemporary republicans view humans as complex beings often with diverse and sometimes competing interests who, without some degree of tutoring and persuasion, would not necessarily possess the knowledge, skills and attributes to participate in public life. In its contemporary form this republican conception of human nature is most clear in the work of Oldfield (1990: 151–152), who contends that '[I]t is a consistent theme of civic republicanism that human beings are weak and short-sighted'. As the desire and character necessary for the practice of citizenship may not be inherent within humans, it has to be 'inculcated and maintained', and, '[I]n some sense citizens are *in statu pupillarii* for the whole of their lives'. Similarly Sandel (1996: 319) cites the importance of the formative state 'when the natural bent of persons to be citizens can no longer be assumed'. If the conception of human political interaction as inherently complex is accepted, as a number of republicans have argued it should be, it is not simply advisable that the state adopt a formative role, rather it becomes a necessity, for without a formative state to cultivate civic virtues, citizens may or may not choose to participate in public affairs. The instability of this 'choice' would undermine the whole republican project. For most republicans it is, therefore, necessary to inculcate civic virtue in the citizenry. There are two central mechanisms to which republicans typically point for their formative project. First, the laws, institutions and political processes which feature in public life, and second, the formal education system.

The formative role of republican laws and institutions

Drawing on the historical precedents of the republican tradition explored in Chapter 2, contemporary republicans identify processes of formation as acting upon citizens through republican laws, institutions and practices. Within republican states, laws and institutions are furnished with an important role in cultivating and sustaining effective active citizen engagement in public affairs. To some extent this reflects a more widespread interest in the processes within the contemporary political communities that support civic action and engagement. Such increased interest comes in the context of Macedo et al.'s (2005: 6) assertion that 'modern political scientists and those engaged in crafting public policy too often neglect the formative dimension of politics as a whole'. Notwithstanding this recognition, the formative nature of political systems and processes has been attested to by a number of theorists. For Sandel (1996: 321), for example, political institutions act as 'agencies of civic education' that 'inculcate the habit of attending to public things'. Maynor (2003: 191) supports this position, similarly citing the importance of 'informal sources of civic education' within the political community. In other words, as they act in public life though democratic institutions and in accordance with the law, citizens are (both explicitly and implicitly) subject to educational processes which further sustain their ability to undertake such practices. For this reason, in their constitution and operation, the institutions of the republican state are founded on, and in turn generate, specific republican aims and goals. According to Barber's theory of Strong Democracy, the process involved is one in which '[T]he taste for participation is whetted by participation: democracy breeds democracy' (Barber, 1984: 265); for a critique of positions such as this see Kymlicka (2002: 303). Oldfield (1990: 155) describes this in comparable terms:

> Not only is the process educative in itself – the more one participates, the more one develops the attitudes appropriate to a citizen: largeness of mind and an appreciation that the interests of the community are one's own – but the example set by the initial participators will draw ever-widening groups of individuals into the political arena.

In his republican theory, Pettit appeals to the concept of an 'intangible hand' as central to the inculcation of civility within the citizenry. Pettit (1999: 253) is conscious that the process of inculcating civility is one which is largely undetermined in Western democracies, and he suggests that '[W]e know little or nothing about how to generate widespread civility where it has more or less ceased to exist'. Indeed, Pettit (1999: 253) is somewhat sceptical as to whether the state is always justified in terms of interventions to develop civility. From this perspective, the state must be careful 'not to get in the way of the marvels which the intangible hand can facilitate in the supply of civic virtue'. Furthermore, the formative and socializing function of laws, which themselves must be predicated on republican norms and values, provide many of the necessary conditions for facilitating 'those habits of civility on the presence of which the very success of law depends'. Pettit's emphasis on the intangible hand is similar to the conception within a number of democratic theorists' work that civic engagement within a political community has a self-perpetuating effect. There is, however, a significant addition in Pettit's analysis, as he supplements the educative function of civic engagement itself with the development of one's *esteem with others*. It is this esteem which underpins civility and which 'helps to nurture a pattern of behaviour by holding out the prospect that its manifestation will earn the good opinion of others and/or failure to manifest it will earn the bad' (Pettit, 1999: 254). Republicans also extend the educative function of democratic engagement to the institutions of civil society. In his formulation of civic republicanism, Sunstein (1988: 1573) recognizes the centrality of non-state organizations and processes in preparing citizens for citizenship, suggesting that '[M]any organisations serve as outlets for some of the principal functions of republican systems ... These functions include the achievement of critical scrutiny of existing practices, the provision of an opportunity for deliberation within collectivities, the chance to exercise citizenship and to obtain a sense of community and the exercise of civic virtue'. For republicans, the relationship between the civic organizations of the state and those that operate within the space of civil society is of mutual benefit, with citizens engaging in democratic processes in both spheres.

The formation of republican civic virtue through education

A further element of republican socialization in civic virtue (and one which is of central importance to this book) is a state's formal education system. In citing the importance of formal education in inculcating the dispositions and behaviours necessary to promote and sustain active citizenship in contemporary political communities, republicans identify an essential moral component within the education of young people as citizens. But what form does this moral component take? For our purposes, it is important to determine precisely how republican models of citizenship understand the nature of the dispositions and behaviours to be inculcated. Crucially, and to reintroduce the distinction made earlier in this chapter, this question centres on the extent to which republicans require (or at least imply) a form of character education or, alternatively, a form of cognitive moral education centred on the learning of certain civic principles or values. In other words, are republicans concerned with educating young people to become certain sorts of people or just to rationally behave in certain ways?

It is clear that some republicans, particularly intrinsic republicans who view freedom in terms of self-government, imply a form of character development through schooling. In this sense, schooling is used in a broad sense to refer not simply to taught lessons, but to other socializing processes deriving from school structures, organization and ethoses. Oldfield's argument is for an extended educative programme, at the heart of which is citizenship understood as active participation, and in which there is a clear focus on social morals. This is based on his understanding of civic republicanism as a theory in which human frailties are recognized and addressed in order to produce a participative citizenry. For Oldfield (1990: 164), an education in moral character is of central significance as '[T]he moral character which is appropriate for genuine citizenship does not generate itself; it has to be authoritatively incul-cated'. In advocating this, Oldfield's (1990: 172) theory addresses the concern later raised by both Mulgan (1991: 40–1) and Kymlicka (2002: 303) that citizens learn to participate 'in a public-spirited, rather than self-interested or prejudiced, way' and he argues furthermore that:

> No amount of political participation and economic democracy, no level of civic education or national service, will suffice for the prac-tice of citizenship in a political community – unless and until the external covenant becomes an internal one.

Oldfield is suggesting here that it is not sufficient that citizens be able to follow certain rules or patterns of behaviour, but that instead civic virtues must be internalized within the character of the citizen. That is, that citizens must become certain types of people and that the formal education system has an important role to play in achieving this end. Similarly for Sandel (1996: 6) '[T]he republican conception of freedom, unlike the liberal conception, requires a formative politics that culti-vates in citizens the qualities of character self-government requires'. These statements are suggestive of a clear and important role for school-ing and education in developing citizens with the requisite civic virtue for the republican project. Intrinsic republicans state their educational objectives, however, in broad terms, and have surprisingly little to say directly about what goes on in schools and classrooms. Nevertheless, it is not overly speculative to draw links between the type of education for civic character to which Oldfield and Sandel make reference and the field of what has become known as 'character education'. This compari-son is useful, given our educational focus, and helps to clarify certain aspects of the intrinsic republican position regarding the education of civic virtue.

What is character education? Whilst it should be remembered that character education is a diverse field, it can be generally defined as incorporating the ideas of those who have an interest in the relation-ship between education and virtues and who advocate an approach to moral education which centres on the teaching of particular virtues (cf. McLaughlin and Halstead, 1999: 132). A range of commentators in the US – Bennett and Delattre, 1978; Wynne (1982, 1985, 1986, 1988, 1988. 1997); Ryan, (1989); Lickona (1991); Kilpatrick, (1992); Bennett, (1993); Brooks and Kann (1993) – and subsequently in Britain – Carr (1995, 1996); Skillen (1997); Steutal (1997); Wringe (1998a, 1998b, 2000) and Arthur (2003) – have contended that virtues should form the basis of school-based moral education and that education should be concerned with the development of the character of pupils (for critiques of character education, see Nash, 1997; Kohn, 1997a, 1997b; Yu, 2004).

Although they are distinct fields of thought, there are certain similarities between the work of character educators and the arguments made in relation to the development of civic virtue through education found in the ideas of republicans such as Oldfield and Sandel. Both character educators and intrinsic republicans are interested in the development of the virtues and dispositions of pupils. As McLaughlin and Halstead (1999: 134) affirm in relation to character education, 'what is important in education (and specifically moral education) is the sort of person one is or becomes, and not merely the nature of the thinking one engages in'. If we replace 'person' in this sentence with 'citizen' this view is very similar to those expressed by Sandel and Oldfield. From this republican position, pupils must be educated to be a particular *type* of citizen: one able to act and participate effectively in public affairs, precisely because he possesses the necessary dispositions within his character. This similarity between intrinsic republicans and character educators rests on the relationship between virtues and the individual. Both character educators and intrinsic republicans have appealed to the idea that virtues should be *internalized* and that the educational process is an important mechanism for this. It is not enough for individuals to know how to act in accordance with a particular virtue. Rather, the virtue should become an integral part of one's moral conduct. This internalization is essential if MacIntyre's (1999: 131) critique of contemporary understandings of virtues is to be addressed:

> What the morality of the virtues articulated in and defended by the moral rhetoric of our political culture provides is, it turns out, not an education in the virtues but, rather, an education in how to seem virtuous, without actually being so.

It is not sufficient that citizens act in a virtuous manner. Rather, they must themselves *be* virtuous, and to be so requires intellectual and practical activity. As Lickona (1991: 51; emphasis in the original) has argued:

> Character so conceived has three interrelated parts: moral knowing, moral feeling, and moral behaviour. *Good character consists of knowing the good, desiring the good, and doing the good* – habits of the mind,

habits of the heart, and habits of the action. All three are necessary for leading a moral life; all three make up moral maturity.

Republicans who posit the need for the development of civic character, such as Oldfield and Sandel, would find much to agree with in this categorization and it is noticeable that they use language similar to that of Lickona in relation to the character which needs to be inculcated in citizens. For Oldfield, for example, civic virtues must be internalized by citizens through educational processes: that is they must become habits of the heart. Indeed, Oldfield claims that it is the prerequisite that citizens internalize virtues that is the 'central teaching of the civic republican tradition'.

There are, however, important differences between the views of intrinsic republicans and character educators, which serve to highlight certain limitations of intrinsic republican thought in the area of inculcating civic virtue. The first such difference relates to the clarity with which each field of thought has categorized the virtues central to their position. It was suggested earlier in this chapter that intrinsic republicans have largely failed to produce a specific set, or list, of virtues. This is not true of character educators, who have set out a range of virtues which should be learned by pupils throughout their education. A consideration of the virtues prioritized by character educators is helpful in elucidating the virtues which, we might confidently presume, would be at the heart of the republican state intrinsic republicans support, including its goals for civic education. As one of the main proponents of character education in the US, Lickona (1999: 23), has argued, '[V]irtues are objectively good human qualities, such as a commitment to truth, wisdom, honesty, compassion, courage, diligence, perseverance, and self-control'. Several schemes, initiatives and associations have implemented programmes of character education in the US based on such virtues. Founded on the philosophical work of character educators, these have included the work of a number of groups, including the Character Education Partnership (CEP) and the Center for the 4th and 5th Rs. Although differences in the precise focus of each programme make it difficult to generalize key themes (cf. Noddings, 1995; Yu, 2004), there is a sense that these specific programmes, and indeed the character education movement in general, seek to generate and inculcate certain virtues, many of a civic nature, within pupils. Leming's (1997) comparative research across ten 'representative' character education programmes in the US highlights this focus on virtues. According to Leming, each of the ten programmes focused on the development of 'character traits' which are claimed to be universal. Leming (1997: 16–21) found that the programmes each prioritized specific character traits to be promoted. A number of the programmes could be considered as focusing on *broad* character traits. The AEGIS programme, for example, valued 'worth and dignity', 'rights and responsibilities', 'fairness and justice', 'effort and excellence', 'care and consideration' and 'personal integrity and social responsibility', whilst the Child Development Project promoted 'fairness', 'concern and respect for others', 'helpfulness' and 'responsibility'. Other programmes placed greater focus on more *specific* character traits. The Character Education Curriculum sought to encourage 'honour', 'courage', 'conviction', 'honesty', 'truthfulness', 'generosity', 'kindness', 'helpfulness', 'justice', 'respect', 'freedom', and 'equality', and the Heartwood Curriculum 'courage', 'loyalty', 'justice', 'respect', 'hope', 'honesty', and 'love'. Within the virtues found by Leming are a number of classical virtues such as 'courage', 'truthfulness', 'generosity', 'justice' and 'honour' (cf. Peterson, 2010). This suggests that character education is not only virtue-centred; it also focuses on many classical virtues drawn from the writings of the scholars that intrinsic republicans such as Oldfield and Sandel cite as lying within their own tradition.

A second notable distinction between character education and the intrinsic republicanism of both Oldfield and Sandel, which serves to highlight a tension in the work of the latter, is more critical. Unlike republicans, character educators have typically focused on a holistic conception of the individual; that is, they consider the virtues necessary to sustain effective public and private relationships. In other words, the virtues associated with citizenship become one strand of character education amongst others. In his consideration of the lists of values and virtues which underpin character education programmes in the United States, Yu (2004: 136) identifies 'citizenship' as being a common theme. The Character Counts programme the largest character education programme in the United States recognizes citizenship as one of its six pillars of citizenship. Likewise, of eight strengths of character expounded by Lickona and Davidson (2005) in their report *Smart and Good High Schools: Integrating Excellence and Ethics for Success in School, Work and Beyond*, one is being a 'contributing community member and democratic citizen' (cf. Peterson, 2010). In contrast, and as was considered earlier in this chapter, intrinsic republicans have almost exclusively focused on specifically civic virtues and therefore seek only to promote a conception of the virtuous citizen, not necessarily the virtuous person. As a result, there is little recognition within intrinsic republican theories (and I would extend this to non-intrinsic forms of republicanism) of the personal virtues and dispositions required by citizens to sustain effective private relationships.

In considering the role and nature of the education system in developing civic virtue I have focused so far on the work of intrinsic republicans, largely in terms of drawing educational inferences from their wider political arguments and from a comparison with the field of character education. It should be noted, however, that instrumental republicans are not silent on the potential of a nation's schooling for supporting the development of the moral capacities required by citizens. The sort of moral development that instrumental republicans have in mind is, I would argue, largely cognitive and based on the development of a rational commitment to adhere to the civic principles associated with civility. Although in his republican theory Maynor (2003: 174) invokes the terminology that '... if republicanism is to breathe and live as a real force, its ideals and institutions must become resident in the habits and the hearts of the citizenry', his position does not involve the type of internalization of virtues required in the republicanism of others. The 'internalization' instrumental republicans such as Maynor have in mind should be considered as aiming to produce in pupils attitudes more akin to what Nash (1997: 163) has termed 'democratic dispositions', such as 'self-discipline, obligation, tolerance, fairness, and generosity', rather than deep-rooted character virtues. According to Nash, these democratic dispositions are sufficient to enable 'us to work with others who are different from us, to compromise when necessary, and to realize that no single person or group can get everything they want all the time'. An illustration of the difference I am seeking to draw between instrumental and intrinsic republicans is provided by Dagger (1997: 131) in his exposition of a republican liberal position which, he claims, 'does not advocate "the education of desire" characteristic of a stringent form of republicanism'. Maynor (2003: 182) argues that the state school curriculum should educate pupils 'to learn how to tolerate and respect others', and he prioritizes the goal that citizens possess the requisite capacities to engage with others to understand, track and monitor their interests. This involves citizens coming to learn and accept certain agreed principles in accordance with which they commit to act. Notably, Maynor (2003: 186) cites the approach to civic education adopted in England as a 'robust form of citizenship education that is consistent with the theoretical goals of modern republicanism'. For Maynor (2003: 187):

Asking them [pupils] to consider both moral and spiritual issues and in effect asking them to go well beyond the liberal focus on political issues. Moreover, by asking them to consider other people's experiences and to be able to recognise another's interests, it moves in the direction that any modern republican approach to civic education should take.

Significantly, Maynor here praises the requirement that pupils consider and reflect on moral and spritual issues, but makes no recommendation that the moral component of education for citizenship go any deeper than this in terms of developing the character of pupils as citizens. Although he does not link his republican theory to a particular form of moral education, Maynor's position resonates with a cognitive development approach to moral development and learning. Based on the cognitive developmental writings of Laurence Kohlberg, such an approach rejects the relativistic individualism of values clarification models of moral education, but rejects the need for virtues to become internalized dispositions within citizens.[54] Kohlberg's argument is that moral education could, and should, be centred on universal values. Central to this view is that it is the reasoning behind moral judgements which should provide the focus of moral education. In other words, students should be prepared to reflect on their moral positions, to take perspectives and to make rational and reasoned autonomous decisions (Yu, 2004: 50–51). The critical reasoning regarding moral behaviour central to Kolhberg's theory appears similar to the learning and acceptance of social norms advocated by Maynor. This position understands the values central to civility to include a range of cognitive skills such as listening to others, analysing evidence and critically evaluating decisions made. If citizens are to be able to engage with others from an informed position it is necessary that endeavouring 'to find common ground and solve problems in a conversational manner, dialogue and compromise must be a part of any civic education curriculum' (Maynor, 2003: 183; cf. Skinner, 1996: 15–16; Pettit, 1999). The shaping of citizens suggested by Maynor is similar to a number of liberal understandings of civic education which recognize that *all* democratic polities, whether liberal or republican, consciously shape the character of citizens (Gutmann, 1987; Macedo, 1990: 53–4; Callan, 1997: 3; Kymlicka, 2002: 307–8; cf. Rawls, 1996). Amy Gutmann's theory of 'conscious social reproduction' referred to previously illustrates this point. Gutmann presupposes that once it is recognized that states are concerned with social reproduction, attention can shift to the content and methods through which citizen virtues are inculcated. According to Gutmann, 'deliberate instruction', in which citizens play a role in shaping the educational methods and content experienced by future citizens, should replace covert political socialization.

Conclusion

Republicans are, then, seemingly committed to the formation in citizens of what is described in broad terms as civic virtue. This formation involves a range of complex and interrelated mechanisms, only one of which is a nation's system of education and schooling. This chapter started by noting that whilst civic virtue is a defining concept for civic republicans it is a term characterized by ambiguity. It is a concept resonant of ancient and classical republican thought, but which, in contemporary usage, has developed a range of meanings. Its use in contemporary republican discourse, has, to some extent, resulted in a thinning out of the concept of virtue. Whilst intrinsic republicans are committed to civic virtue as a set of internalized dispositions, they are largely silent on the relationship between virtue and human excellence. Instrumental republicans go even further, employing the concept not in the sense of a citizen's internalized character, but in terms of a set of principles, rationally ascribed to, which maintain the functioning of a republican state so as to protect its citizens from being dominated on a arbitrary basis. All civic republicans depict virtue solely in the civic sphere, to the neglect of more holistic conceptualizations such as that provided by Aristotle, which see civic virtues predominantly as personal virtues expressed in public life. That republicans conceive civic virtue in these terms raises particular questions, and suggests different foci, for the development and formation of civic virtue through educational processes, a point returned to in more detail in relation to civic education in Chapter 6.

5
Civic Republican Deliberative Democracy

Deliberative democracy is a central commitment within the civic republican political agenda and as such it represents a 'characteristically republican belief' (Sunstein, 1988: 1539). It is the assertion 'that government is a public matter to be directed by the members of the public themselves' (Dagger, 2006: 153) and the strong commitment to deliberative practices, which form the core elements of republican approaches to politics and which, furthermore, hold particular resonance for civic education. In their critique of liberal democratic societies, republicans point to the lack of citizen political participation as evidence of a lack of civic commitment (or at least appropriate outlets for this) and, as a result, a lack of freedom. In order to remedy this situation, republicans typically look to deliberative forms of politics, which require citizens to actively participate in public dialogue with other citizens about matters of public concern, not only as a solution to the problem but also as the optimum form of democratic system. This position is exemplified in the work of Sandel (1996: 202), who suggests that the growth of liberalism in the USA has 'coincided...with a growing sense of disempowerment'. Citing the view of John Dewey, Sandel (1996: 204) further argues that the expansion of mass suffrage:

> reenforced the voluntarist self-image by making it appear as if citizens hold the power 'to shape social relations on the basis of individual volition. Popular franchise and majority rule afforded the imagination a picture of individuals in their untrammeled individual sovereignty making the state'.

Republicans challenge this 'voluntarist' understanding of citizen engagement by emphasizing the fundamental benefits which citizens, and indeed the state, gain from participation in the political realm. This chapter starts with a brief consideration of the meaning and field of deliberative democracy. It then explores deliberation as a central theme of recent republican writing, before considering the central issue of consensus as a goal (although not always a necessary one) of civic dialogue. It suggests that a distinction can be drawn between those republicans who see deliberative consensus as involving shared values and those who view it as a mechanism to secure political agreements, and assesses the importance of this difference.

What is republican deliberative democracy?

The focus upon deliberation within contemporary civic republican thinking has coincided with what has been termed the 'deliberative turn' in democratic theory (Dryzek, 2000:1). The concept of deliberative democracy is itself contested, and we should be careful not to think of it as having just one meaning. Pettit (2001: 268), for example, has suggested that deliberative democracy should be considered 'inherently ambiguous', whilst Stephen Macedo (1999: 4) reminds us that deliberative democrats 'do not altogether agree about what the democratic ideal is or how it should be fostered'. A working definition would broadly understand deliberative democracy as a commitment to developing mechanisms within the decision-making process which permit, and take into account, the reasoned dialogical interaction of citizens. In common with republican ideas, the work of deliberative democrats can be considered as a reaction to a perceived democratic deficit within Western political societies; that is, that deliberative arrangements facilitate more frequent and more effective citizen involvement in the political process and that this in turn leads to more effective and reflexive governance. In its contemporary form, the concept of deliberative democracy has been developed within the work of a number of theorists (see, for example, Bessette, 1980, 1994; Manin, 1987; Cohen, 1989; Elster, 1989; Fishkin, 1991; Dryzek, 2000; Gutmann and Thompson, 2003, 2004), but was most clearly defined by Joshua Cohen (1989) who outlined five key principles of deliberative democracy, namely: the existence of an ongoing association; the organization of institutions which permit and recognize deliberation; respect for plural aims; respect for the legitimacy of decisions taken deliberatively; and the mutual recognition of the deliberative capacities of citizens. Given the concentration on active, reasoned political interaction, it is not surprising that republican theorists have sought to make links between their own work and deliberative forms of political engagement.

A central theme across the work of deliberative democrats is the principle of 'democratic legitimacy' (see, for example, Benhabib, 1996; Gutmann and Thompson, 1996; Cohen, 1997). This can be understood as the view that particular policies gain greater democratic legitimacy when they are subjected to, or are the result of, deliberative consideration by members of the public. For some advocates of deliberative democracy the extent of such democratic legitimacy is far-reaching. As Barber (1998: 24–25) explains, 'democratic rules, the definition of citizenship, the character of rights – however they originate – become legitimate only when subjected to reflexive scrutiny, democratic deliberation and decision'. The application of ideas of deliberative democracy is increasingly finding expression in public policy in many Western nations.[55] These are too multifarious to explore in any real depth here, but include initiatives such as citizen panels, the recall of representatives through petition, deliberative polling, local town or neighbourhood meetings and forums, as well as local and national referenda on public issues.[56] Notwithstanding their view that 'the idea of deliberation draws far more attention than its actual practice', recent extensive research conducted in the United States by Jacobs et al. (2009: 20) suggests that '[D]iscursive participation is more common than assumed' and 'encompasses the most taxing forms of citizen engagement – face-to-face deliberation' (p. 13). However, for republicans there is both the scope and a need for even greater deliberative participation.

It is clear that all contemporary republicans are committed to a form of deliberative democratic politics. Those republicans who are interested in a conception of freedom as self-government value deliberation for the extent to which it permits citizens to truly govern and affect the decision-making process in their political communities. Those republicans who are interested in a conception of freedom as non-domination value deliberation for the extent to which it permits both government and citizens to publicize their interests as well as each learning those of the other. However, republican writers vary in the depth of attention they pay to this commitment within their work. This has led Honohan (2002: 235) to suggest that rather than setting out detailed structures, some republicans (particularly those which I have referred to here as intrinsic republicans) simply offer 'guidelines...for designing participative deliberative institutions'. This recognition notwithstanding, instrumental republicans have furnished their commitment to dialogical interaction between citizens with a good deal of detail and have presented a clear republican programme for deliberative democracy.

We will consider first the work of those intrinsic republicans who present a broad commitment to deliberative democracy, but who do not specify a clear set of processes involved in the achievement of this aim. Fundamentally, the attachment which republicans have to deliberation in public life results from the possibilities it extends for the greater facilitation of citizen involvement in the civic sphere through open, discursive and democratic forums. Central to this process is that citizens are able to use good 'judgement' about the efficacy and outcomes of public policies and other matters of civic concern (Oldfield, 1990: 25). In his historical narrative on public philosophy in the USA, Sandel (1996: 208–9) emphasizes the importance of 'various projects for urban reform' which enabled citizens to take control of an important area of public concern, and we can understand him as using this example to illustrate effective public deliberation. In his consideration of the importance of different interpretations of the Bill of Rights we find additional references to deliberative politics in Sandel's republicanism. Citing the First Amendment to the American constitution, Sandel (1996: 290; emphasis added) argues that rights do not have to be defended on liberal terms, observing significantly that a 'right to free speech might be defended, for example, on the grounds that it makes possible the *political debate* and *deliberation* on which self-government depends'. Sandel (1996: 348) portrays the potential for citizens to engage in public debate in expansive terms. He suggests that 'proliferating sites of civic activity and political power can serve self-government by cultivating virtues, equipping citizens for self-rule, and generating loyalties to larger political wholes'. The proliferation of sites for civic dialogue between citizens which Sandel has in mind, and which republicans in general desire, is not limited to the civic sphere and extends to the institutions of civil society – the voluntary institutions present within society, including the family, community groups and religion-based organizations, that exist in the space between the public and private sphere.[57]

There is, then, a general commitment within intrinsic forms of civic republicanism to deliberative democracy. But what makes this a specifically republican approach to civic dialogue? Intrinsic republicans leave this question unanswered, though they do believe that deliberation can further republican ends in building civic obligation and civic virtue. For example, though forceful in his contention that deliberative forums should exist 'where potentially everyone can take part', Oldfield (1990: 28) offers nothing more precise than the belief that 'self-government can refer to any public tasks and activities that a community wishes to engage in'. We should remember, however, that the type of institutions and processes that intrinsic republicans would support are likely to be rather conventional. Practical deliberative structures have been delineated in the wider field of deliberative democracy and many of these are likely to be attractive to civic republican projects. James Fishkin (1991), for example, has established the process of the deliberative opinion poll, whilst Ackerman and Fishkin (2005) have written of a need for a *Deliberation Day* national holiday in presidential election years in the United States. Work emanating from the writing of Ned Crosby at the Jefferson Centre for New Democratic Processes established the principle of 'citizen juries' – panels of citizens who come together to critically investigate issues of public concern.[58] In his theory of Strong Democracy, Barber (2003: 261–2) sets out a number of institutions for strong democratic talk. These include 'neighbourhood assemblies', 'a national initiative and referendum process', 'universal citizen service' and increased 'democracy in the workplace'. Rather than representing a fundamental change in current political systems, the intrinsic republican commitment to deliberative politics requires the maintenance and extension of current practices such as these, within both the public sphere and civil society, in order to permit citizens to deliberate on matters of common concern instead of retreating into a private world of self-interest.

In contrast to the general commitment to deliberation found in intrinsic republican accounts, instrumental republicans have been much clearer about the potential for a specifically republican form of deliberative democracy. Pettit's instrumental form of republicanism identifies the primary aim of the political process as the permitting of the interests of citizens to be publicized and tracked in order that arbitrary domination be minimized. It was suggested in Chapter 2 that domination within a political state can take two main forms – *imperium* and *dominium*. The former refers to instances when the state arbitrarily dominates the lives of citizens, whilst the latter involves citizens arbitrarily dominating the lives of other citizens. The desire to reduce arbitrary domination within the state has led instrumental republicans to advocate a form of politics in which the interests of all groups in society can be publicized through deliberative means. Pettit understands freedom as non-domination, as something worthy of promotion within and amongst the citizenry, rather than as something which should necessarily be honoured by the state. As such, freedom as non-domination is of instrumental worth rather than of intrinsic value and government is presented as encompassing a large number of responsibilities, but a small number of independent powers. Here Pettit is suggesting that republican government should be both big and small, and that it should be subject to a system of checks and balances which limit the dominance of any one element – including the citizenry – within the republican state.

To understand the form of republican deliberation which Pettit has theorized it is necessary to grasp his principle of 'contestation'. Contestation can be understood as the ability of citizens to challenge – or contest – public decisions and policies which affect them. It is through participation in contestatory practices that citizens are able to both publicize their own interests and come to learn about and understand the interests of others. This process permits a variety of causes to be articulated in public discourse and it is in this way that plural interests find expression in public discourse (Pettit, 1999: 132–3). Moreover, contestation can be understood as a specific kind of deliberative politics. According to the American political scientist Ian Shapiro (1990: 266), who also supports the kind of contestatory politics Pettit has in mind, 'a government will be democratic, a government will represent a form of rule that is controlled by the people, to the extent that people individually and collectively enjoy a permanent possibility of contesting what government decides'.

Drawing on a range of literature, most notably the work of Cass Sunstein (1988, 1993a, 1993b, 1993c), Pettit (1999: 174–183) contends that the means through which a modern nation-state can 'advance republican aims' whilst avoiding 'assuming an arbitrary, dominating form' can be seen as dependent upon three necessary conditions (each of which has a clear lineage from the Roman republican tradition). These are: 'the empire-of-laws', the 'dispersion of power', and 'counter-majoritarianism'. Underpinning these three conditions is the principle that, if arbitrary sectional interests are to be avoided in the decisions of a republic, government must be based not on the consent of citizens, but on the extent to which citizens are able to contest the political decisions taken by those in office. It is through the principle of contestability, Pettit (1999: 184) argues, that 'public decision making tracks the interests and the ideas of those citizens whom it affects', a position Pettit contrasts sharply with the interest-group pluralism prevalent in Western political systems and which, he argues, pays greater attention to minority interests in policy formulation and evaluation than is often the case in liberal democracies. According to John Maynor, certain practical structures need to be in place in order to achieve the type of contestatory deliberation that Pettit has in mind. Maynor

(2003: 159–166) therefore provides five practical steps in the policy-making process which he believes 'represent a way to bolster the processes of today's polities in light of the democratic contestatory nature of modern republicanism to ensure that domination is minimized'. The five steps are: the identification of 'legitimate issues for the state to address'; the 'formulation of a reasonable and measured legislative or executive response to the identified and legitimate issue'; that proposed policies be 'subjected to a public review period'; 'that policies, once in operation, be subjected to periodic reviews'; and that 'periodic, meaningful, fair, and open' elections occur through which 'officials and their performances are subjected to the ultimate democratic contestatory exercise'. In effect, Maynor is simply connecting many of the practical forums and systems for civic dialogue advocated by proponents of deliberative democracy in the wider field and turning them toward republican ends. Nevertheless, his work is useful in illustrating the types of practical structures which might help to realise the contestation that Pettit's republicanism promotes.

Attaching importance to the principle of contestation promotes citizen involvement at a number of stages in the political process. Significantly, contestatory deliberation focuses attention on the opportunity citizens have to contest policies following their instigation. This confers a specific set of obligations upon citizens, who must consider and understand the effect of public policies on the interests of others, and not just from a position of narrow self-interest. Pettit (1999: 295) has explained that, in important ways, citizens should be considered as representing the 'editors' of public policies rather than acting as 'joint authors' (cf. Honohan, 2002: 236). In this way public bodies and institutions can be kept informed about how, following their implementation, specific policies and practices are understood and experienced by a range of groups and sections within society. For republicans interested in the absence of domination, a strong civil society also works to limit domination, and in doing so reduces this role for the state (Braithwaite and Pettit, 1990; Pettit, 1999: 148).[59] However, for some commentators this editorial role for citizens within the deliberative process raises an important tension. Honohan (2002: 237) argues, for example, that it is 'harder (and sometimes too late) to challenge what has already been determined': that is, once the main elements of the policy in question have already been decided. It should be remembered, however, that contestatory deliberation includes this 'editorial' form of deliberation in addition to, and not instead of, other procedural and consultative processes. Indeed, according to Pettit (1999: 296) these three aspects of deliberation – procedural, consultative and '*ex post* appellate' – comprise the 'three sides of a contestatory democracy'.

The contestatory procedures advocated by Pettit, and indeed by Maynor, place particular demands on citizens. It was considered in Chapter 4 that republicans understand it to be imperative that citizens possess (and be educated for) sufficient levels of civic virtue – or civility as Pettit calls it – in order to play an effective role in public life. Active citizenship requires citizens to participate, and to remain constantly vigilant in relation to the political decision-making process in order that domination is reduced. This approach places particular burdens on citizens not only to publicize their own interests, but also to track those of others within public forums in order to protect freedom as non-domination. In effect, this calls for a public relationship between the state and citizens, and indeed between citizens themselves, which is contractual and which requires that citizens have the knowledge, skills and attributes that will allow them to participate meaningfully in civic discourse. Many are likely to be sceptical that citizens either can or would want to undertake what may be considered a burdensome role. Sherry (1995: 137–8), who is sympathetic to civic republican ideals, raises the following concerns: '...the republican ideal of deliberative democracy borders on the utopian. The vast majority of Americans are neither inclined nor equipped to engage in the kind of sustained, reasoned deliberation contemplated by the republicans'. There are two potential responses to perspectives such as this. First, whilst most literature in the field bemoans the lack of civic engagement of citizens, there is some evidence that citizens are not quite as apathetic as Sherry's characterization suggests. In addition to reporting higher than expected levels of citizen deliberation, Jacobs et al. (2009: 72) point to a sense in which deliberators in the United States are motivated more by collective concerns than by purely personal interests. Second, Sherry's concerns serve only to increase the educational imperative at the heart of civic republicanism. If Sherry is correct that citizens in America (or indeed in other nations) have neither the desire nor the capacities to engage in civic dialogue, then the need for education and formation for this becomes of paramount importance.

In detailing the deliberative elements of their republicanism Pettit and Maynor present freedom as non-domination as a *non-normative* principle (cf. Christman, 1998; MacMahon, 2005). According to Pettit (1999: 80), freedom as non-domination should be understood as representing the 'supreme political value' for society. In this sense freedom as non-domination is viewed as a first principle about which citizens agree. Seen in this way, freedom as non-domination takes on the form of a regulative ideal, rather than a normative judgement; its nature and importance is given rather than dependent on further contentious principles. The state enacts certain policies to limit the extent to which citizens, or groups of citizens, arbitrarily dominate the lives of others. However, because it will be the government's role to judge the means of determining which actions, in respect of citizen-to-citizen interaction, should be considered as arbitrarily dominating and which should not, the idea that freedom as non-domination can be understood in non-normative terms has been questioned. As MacMahon (2005: 68) points out, the principle of non-domination does not, in and of itself, provide a clear agenda for the sorts of 'policies that a society ought to adopt'. Therefore, if 'determinate con-clusions about policy are to be obtained, freedom as non-domination must be supplemented with other political values'. Instrumental republi-cans like Pettit and Maynor assume that it will be clear to all which acts are arbitrarily dominating. This, however, is not necessarily the case. As one of the leading republican proponents accepts, '[D]etermining what constitutes an arbitrary will of an individual... cannot help being par-tisan and questionable' (Viroli, 1999: 55). Furthermore, in determining why an act should or should not count as arbitrarily dominating, gov-ernment will inevitably draw on other moral or political values in their reasoning (cf. MacMahon, 2005). Such values would presumably include respect, tolerance and reciprocity. But these are, themselves, normative concepts, the meanings of which are likely to be contested in contem-porary Western societies. For this reason, freedom as non-domination is properly understood in normative terms. In response to this charge, Pettit (2006: 278) suggests that '[A]s the facts of the matter, including facts about local culture and context, determine whether a certain act counts as interference, so the facts of the matter determine whether a certain act of interference counts as arbitrary'. It is difficult to accept however, that citizens will necessarily agree on a single understanding of such arbitrariness, nor whether the 'facts' to which Pettit refers represent facts at all or will be easily arrived at without recourse to further, norma-tive principles of justice. Put simply, whether an act of domination is understood as arbitrary involves an evaluative commitment on behalf of the individual, group or state exercising that judgement.

Republican deliberation and consensus

The issue of consensus is a pertinent one for deliberative democrats, and so too for civic republicans. The term is used here to denote a state of concord reached by a community of deliberating citizens in free, open and non-dominating discourse within either (or both) the public sphere and the institutions of civil society. As the exploration of Chapter 2 indicates, the republican tradition offers various perspectives on the possibility, potential extent, and value of consensus in contemporary political communities. One need only contrast the differences between the value placed upon disagreement by Machiavelli and that central to Rousseau's principle of the general will for such complexities to be highlighted. This raises the question of the extent to which recent republican writing has sought to value the consensus which may result from deliberative processes, as well as the particular nature – or status – of such consensus.[60] The issue of consensus is of central importance for republicans, given their concern that citizen deliberation involves the public delineation of common interests. However, I believe there to be two distinct forms of consensus to be achieved through republican deliberative processes. The first form of consensus, found largely within the work of intrinsic republicans, is communitarian in nature and is based on shared values that are discussed, clarified and understood through deliberative practices. Shared values are inherently deep bonds of association and belonging which are dependent for their meaning on certain historical and social understandings. The second form of consensus, which finds expression more commonly in the thought of instrumental republicans, is liberal in nature and is based on political agreement, or what Benhabib (1996: 68–70) has usefully termed 'episodic' agreement.[61]

Before considering republican conceptions of consensus, it is useful to outline briefly the value placed by republicans on disagreement. A general concern within political theory, raised commonly by critics of deliberative forms of politics, is that despite the operation of discursive or contestatory processes, citizens will irrevocably disagree with each other over key public issues (see, for example, Sunstein, 1988; Moon, 1993; Benhabib, 1996; Gutmann and Thompson, 1996, 2003; cf. Honohan, 2002: 227; Larmore, 1996; Mouffe 2000). That is, given the heterogeneous nature of contemporary Western democracies citizens will, on certain matters, hold incompatible opinions about political values despite participating in public deliberation. Whilst some commentators have wrongly viewed contemporary republicans as asserting that a successful outcome of deliberation will always be consensus (see, for example, Gey, 1993: 834), republicans typically follow Machiavelli in highlighting the positive role which divergence and disagreement play in progressive democratic political communities. Indeed, conflict and disagreement are viewed as fundamental to republican politics (cf. Honohan, 2002: 230). Sunstein (1999: 145), for example, has viewed disagreement as a potentially 'productive and creative force, revealing error, showing gaps, moving discussion and results in good directions', whilst Sandel (1996a: 337–8) suggests that a 'successful revival of republican politics would not resolve [all of] our political disputes'. Although Blattberg (2000) suggests that such disagreement creates unnecessary and unhelpful tensions between citizens, as Honohan (2002: 230) reminds us, conflict is part of being a republican citizen and permits 'richer dialogue', where 'working compromises' cannot be found. In his instrumental republican theory Viroli (1999: 54–55) suggests that:

> Precisely because republican theorists do not believe that the common good is the good of each and all, they do not fear social and political conflicts, as long as those conflicts remain within the boundaries of civil life, and they appreciate the value of the clashes of rhetoric that occur in public councils. They do not foster the notion of an organic community where individuals work toward a common good, nor do they waste time fantasising about republics where laws aspiring to the common good are approved unanimously by virtuous citizens.

It is worth pointing out, though, that whilst conflict can be considered as an important feature of republican politics, the position of contemporary republican theorists should be distinguished from what have been called 'agonistic democrats', who typically argue for a more open political life in which citizens discuss, and disagree about, a wider range of issues including 'the conditions of their political association' (Schaap, 2006: 256). Agnostic democrats are less hopeful than republicans about the role of consensus within contemporary Western states. Mouffe (1999: 756; 2000: xi–xii) illustrates this position well when she speaks of the 'inherently conflictual aspect of pluralism', and the 'ineradicability of antagonism'.

So what of consensus? Referencing both historical thought and recent communitarian writing, intrinsic republicans highlight the centrality of human bonds to meaningful communities and view deliberative processes and forums as civic spaces within which shared values can be derived. Whilst Sandel (1996) uses the term 'solidarity' to describe such bonds, Oldfield (1990: 20–4) prefers the term 'friendship', central to which is Aristotle's principle of 'concord' (*harmonia*). Living is, we are told, 'a shared venture'. These statements hold resonance for the types of consensus which exist between citizens, and provide a basis for the development and maintenance of shared values within political communities. Shared values are inherently deep bonds of association which are dependent for their meaning on certain historical and social understandings. The consensus founded on shared values which some republicans have in mind derives from the bonds of solidarity or friendship which exist between citizens as members of a particular political community. Furthermore, shared values suggest a common sense of shared history and culture. Crucially, shared values are internalized by citizens and, where deeply internalized, cannot be discarded or replaced at will. This affords them a sense of permanence which may not be available in political agreements. It was outlined in Chapter 1 that a commitment to shared values formed an important element of the critique of liberalism within Sandel's earlier work (see, for example, *Liberalism and the Limits of Justice*, 1982). In his more recent, explicitly republican, writing, Sandel (1996: 15) returns to this theme, emphasizing the 'obligations of membership' and 'moral ties antecedent to choice' that exist within and between citizens and their communities. For Sandel, citizens in a republican state share important values, which have a deeper and more meaningful basis than the forms of political agreement to which both liberals and instrumental republicans are attached. Moreover, the deliberative process is one which brings together citizens to explore, define and realize those virtues which they share, and to deliberate about the common good. Like Sandel, Oldfield makes few explicit references to shared values, although this seems to be what he has in mind throughout his work. Oldfield stresses the importance of the shared social identities and obligations which exist between citizens as members of particular political communities. Furthermore, it is these identities, which presumably would include shared values, that help to define those communities. Ultimately, Oldfield (1990: 145) suggests that his republican theory is communitarian in that it 'stresses not that which differentiates individuals from each other and from the community, but rather what they share with other individuals, and what integrates them into the community'. Once again, we can assume that amongst those things that citizens share within a community are a certain set of common values which are ultimately tied to membership of that group.

There is a significant relationship between deliberation and shared values, as intrinsic republicans understand them. In Chapter 3 it was stated that Sandel understands shared values as deriving both from pre-political obligations and from deliberative processes and that it is in the latter that these values should become verbalized, mediated and understood. Oldfield's position contrasts slightly with Sandel's in that it makes less reference to pre-existing values and contends that 'no set of public purposes may exist waiting to be discovered, democratic procedures are necessary for creating such purposes' (Oldfield, 1990: 23). Instead, shared values must be constituted by, and inculcated within, the deliberative republican community. Such a process involves both the cognitive and affective domains, with citizens – as members of a shared political community – coming to both know and feel common attachments and bonds. The deliberation intrinsic republicans have in mind is similar to that proposed by the communitarian writer Amitai Etzioni (1998). In his critique of procedural approaches to deliberation, Eztioni (1998: 183) questions the complexity of issues likely to be under discussion, and suggests that, given this, 'participants...must rely on much humbler processes than the ones of the rational decision-making school'. Importantly, Etzioni reminds us that those issues being discussed will not simply be empirical or logical; rather they will involve normative issues about which citizens feel passionately. Instead, Etzioni suggests that citizens engage in 'moral dialogues', at the heart of which is an appeal to either a single value or a set of values which citizens share. It is such 'moral dialogues' which I understand to be advocated within intrinsic republican accounts of deliberation.

In contrast to the intrinsic commitment to shared values as a basis for consensus, instrumental republicans identify the arrival at *political agreements* between citizens as a central outcome of deliberative practices. This approach is based on the liberal notion that, given the range of deeply held moral convictions within plural societies, it will be difficult (if not impossible) for citizens to arrive at deeply held shared values. In his consideration of civic and moral education in America, Bull (2006: 23; emphasis in the original) makes this point in relation to the work of Rawls when he suggests that the

> difficulties and contradictions [between citizens' deeply held moral convictions] illustrate some of the apparent problems in rendering civic ideals consistent with this assumption about a liberal society: civic ideals, it seems, will have to be merely facts about what citizens of a liberal society happen to agree about politics at a particular time; otherwise those ideals will make moral claims that compete with or displace citizens' existing moral commitments. Nevertheless, Rawls suggests, it may still be possible to create a *political* agreement about the principles that are to govern their larger association by seeking what he calls an 'overlapping consensus'.

It is such political agreements that instrumental republicans believe will result from deliberative processes, starting with the idea that the first and foremost political value is freedom as non-domination. The instrumental republican understanding of consensus as political agreement is found in the work of Pettit and Maynor, but is summarized best by Sunstein (1988: 1550), who believes that '[T]he requirement of deliberation is designed to ensure that political outcomes will be supported by reference to consensus (or at least broad agreement) among political equals'. Significantly, such agreements are not necessarily the result of deeper shared values but, rather, involve citizens with different interests reaching common positions as a result of free and open dialogue. Such political agreements can be understood as temporary and revisable. This does not mean, however, that a rich form of dialogue does not find expression in instrumental republican accounts of deliberation. It does suggest, however, that subject to the operation of non-domination, instrumental republicans typically prioritize the *process* of deliberation over and above its substantive outcomes, although both Pettit and Maynor stop short of complete acceptance of a position which Gutmann and Thompson (2003: 31) term 'pure proceduralism'. Maynor (2003; 156–7), for example, prioritizes the equality of input into public matters over and above any consensus when he asserts that citizens are less likely to suffer from arbitrary domination if they have been able to contest the decision through a deliberative process. Indeed, according to Maynor, citizens are more likely to accept public decisions which are against their own interests if they are content that the process of deliberation has been fair. A similar point is made by Pettit (1999: 198), who claims that in the case of certain disputes, where, for example, personal interests or notions of the common interest conflict, citizens 'should be able to recognize that reasonable people differ on the matter in question' given that correct procedures have been followed. Pettit (1999: 199) cites evidence from Tyler and Mitchell (1994: 746; emphasis added) which found that 'research indicates that the key factor affecting the perceived legitimacy of authorities is *procedural* fairness'. However, despite the evidence that Pettit cites to support this procedural claim, and particularly where highly contentious issues are concerned, this element of instrumental republican thought represents somewhat of a leap of faith. Both Pettit and Maynor fail to address fully those issues where the parties involved, as MacMahon (2005: 75) puts it, cannot accept 'that, ultimately, it is more important that the society makes a decision in the matter than that the decision go their way'.

This focus on process serves, in part, to bifurcate instrumental republican aims for deliberation, and we should be careful not discount the importance placed on reasoning as a means through which consensus within the political community can be derived. Sunstein (1993a; 1993b; 1993c) refers to a deliberative endeavour in terms of a 'republic of reasons', whilst Pettit (1999: 187) contends that it is through deliberation that 'people recognize certain relevant considerations in common, and they move towards an agreed outcome by interrogating one another about the nature and import of those considerations and by converging on an answer to the question of which decision the considerations support'. This understanding represents an explicit rejection of ancient and medieval understandings of reason as a process through which citizens come to know certain independently existing truths, and is built around the modern idea of common interests. Throughout his work Pettit employs a number of terms for such common interests, including 'interests and ideas held in common' (1997), 'common recognizable interests' (1999) and most recently, 'common avowable interests' (2001; 2006). We can understand these to refer to interests concerning which citizens 'will all benefit from jointly seeking to cooperate with one another' (Pettit, 1999: 287). Common avowable interests importantly rest on a form of political agreement. The process is one in which 'different parties try to agree on which arrangements answer best to considerations that they can all recognize as relevant', where importantly, 'one of the relevant considerations is that they should reach an agreement' (Pettit, 1999: 187; cf. Scanlon, 1982; Sunstein, 1993a; Barry, 1995). Moreover, once interests have been agreed upon by citizens, political institutions and practices are expected to account for them within of their work. In this sense, agreement 'serves as a *regulative* ideal', guiding and shaping the work of political institutions (Pettit, 1999: 189; cf. Cohen, 1989; Habermas, 1994, 1995).[62] Through this process, the state is able to track the interests of its citizens. Agreement, then, represents an important term within Pettit's principle of common avowable interests. Through active deliberative processes, citizens come to understand the interests they have in common with others. The agreement reached is based on rational dialogue, and is not dependent on shared, internalized values. As long as they do not arbitrarily dominate other citizens, either collectively or individually, they are free to revise their assent to common agreements. In this way the political agreement envisaged by Pettit is, as suggested previously, inherently temporary and revisable.

The approach to arriving at consensus provided by Cass Sunstein (1999) in his article *Agreement without Theory* provides a further example of an instrumental republican commitment to political agreement and also serves to illustrate tensions with the location of consensus in agreement. Sunstein (1999) extends Gutmann and Thompson's (1996) principle of 'economizing on moral disagreement', according to which citizens should mutually restrain from challenging deep-held moral and religious convictions. Sunstein's (1999: 126; emphasis in the original) commitment is based on what he considers to be a 'major goal of hetero-geneous society: *to make it possible to obtain agreement where agreement is necessary, and to make it unnecessary to obtain agreement where agreement is impossible'*. Crucially, with regard to consensus, Sunstein (1999: 123) suggests that citizens may be able to arrive at a broad agreement on issues 'without achieving agreement on the theoretical commitments that underlie' them. The principle that valid agreement may be reached without theoretical commitments underlines the instrumental republi-can focus on political agreement. Significantly, the agreement between citizens conceptualized by Sunstein does not necessarily depend on shared values within a political community (thus marking a distinction with intrinsic republicans). Furthermore, Sunstein's principle of agree-ment without theory raises a particular tension which has educational resonance. It is not clear that citizens would, or indeed should, want to enter into agreement with those with whom they possess common political commitments but not shared values. In certain cases, such agreement can only be based on either self-interest or on factional inter-ests, and may undermine the common interests of society as a whole. This concern can be explained by way of two educational examples which I have drawn elsewhere (Peterson, 2009). Let us consider firstly, that both pupil A and pupil B are in favour of re-instating capital pun-ishment for certain crimes. Pupil A's support is based on the belief that capital punishment will act as a deterrent for potential criminals. Pupil B does not particularly support this notion, and instead justifies capital punishment on the principle of just deserts. In this example, pupils A and B disagree on general principles, but agree on a particular outcome, that capital punishment be re-instated for certain crimes. It would seem likely that despite their areas of divergence, pupils A and B would be content, should they so determine, to work together to support the reinstatement of the practice in question. However, if we consider a second example, Sunstein's hope for agreement without a shared theo-retical basis becomes more problematic. In this example, both pupil C and pupil D are opposed to the United Kingdom's increasingly politi-cal commitment to the European Union. Pupil C's opposition centres on his concern for meaningful democratic accountability within the institutions of the EU. In contrast, pupil D's opposition stems from his support of a nationalist political party and is driven by particular chauvinistic views which pupil C considers to be abhorrent. Whilst pupil D may be happy to work with pupil C in promoting their general commitment, it would appear unlikely that pupil C would reciprocate this. In such cases the principle of incompletely theorized arguments, and indeed political agreements, becomes heavily compromised by the absence of shared values between the two pupils. This reminds us that, when deeper values and motivations are concerned, forms of consensus which are not entrenched in something stronger than political agreement become problematic.

This reference to deeper values and motivations reminds us that the focus on consensus as an important outcome of deliberation within republican thought raises a question about what types of argument are relevant and appropriate in the dialogical interaction undertaken by citizens. The types of arguments deemed permissible – or reasonable – in public deliberation is an important concern within contemporary democratic theory. This question is often considered with reference to Rawls' political thought. For Rawls (1996) the position is clear: only arguments that are based on, and can be justified through, reason should be considered acceptable in public discourse. Rawls contends that certain philosophical questions are unanswerable and, for this reason, should not form the basis of arguments advanced by citizens within public, that is, political, debate. In other words, arguments should be based not on metaphysically derived comprehensive doctrines, but on the basis of public reason. Rawls suggests that positions held by citizens derived from comprehensive moral or religious doctrines should remain in the *private* realm. This effectively requires citizens to 'bracket off' certain viewpoints – most notably those based on a particular faith or religious foundation – in their civic deliberations, and renders public deliberation an inherently secular process.

There are a number of problems with Rawls' position, and several republicans have taken issue with his standpoint. Not least, the 'bracketing-off' of religious views and beliefs requires a separation of self-identity which is neither possible nor beneficial to inclusive deliberation. Maynor (2003) is forthright in his rejection of Rawls' belief that citizens should rely only on certain *types* of arguments in publicizing their interests. In recognizing that the denial of faith within public discourse is problematic, Maynor (2003) identifies religious-based arguments as integral to the political process (cf. Miller, 1995; Burtt, 1992). To be forced to 'bracket off' moral and religious beliefs would fundamentally undermine the republican effort to track citizens' interests. As the British theorist David Miller (1995: 447) has explained, the deliberative process 'requires of citizens a willingness to give reasons for what they are claiming, but not that they should divest themselves of everything that is particular to them before setting foot in the arena of politics'. A similar criticism is made by the democratic theorist John Dryzek (2000: 1), who criticizes the absence of 'argument, rhetoric, humour, emotion, testimony or story-telling, and gossip' within Rawls' theory of public reasonableness. In recognizing that for many citizens it would be both unsatisfactory and indeed, impossible, to separate their political position from other moral and religious beliefs, Maynor, Miller and Dryzek are all committed to a wider understanding of legitimate public reasoning. Michael Sandel (1996: 66) supports these views from his republican position. He points to the content, rather than the basis, of the viewpoints which citizens bring to public dialogue: '[W]hat makes a religious belief worthy of respect is not its mode of acquisition... but its place in the good life or, from a political point of view, its tendency to promote the habits and dispositions that make good citizens'. More recently, Sandel (1999: 243) has suggested that to require citizens to 'leave their moral and religious convictions behind them when they enter the public realm' runs the risk of suppressing free and open dialogue. For Sandel, it is 'an open invitation to narrow, intolerant moralisms. Fundamentalists rush in where liberals fear to tread'. The point being made by Sandel is important. Without full recognition within public discourse, deeply held moral and religious convictions will be ignored or, worse still, suppressed. This has important implications for public discourse. If they are not subjected to the rigours of public critique and challenge, such beliefs will operate outside public forums, leading to their non-representation and marginalization. In other words, if we accept Gutmann and Thompson's (2004: 9) premise that the 'democratic element in deliberative democracy should turn on how fully inclusive the process is', without the inclusion of a plurality of voices and interests the democratic basis of deliberation is undermined.[63] There are also important educational implications here. Kenneth Strike (1993: 178) has identified, deriving the idea from Rawlsian liberal conceptions of public reasonableness, a 'liberal silence' in certain schools where moral questions are tactically avoided (cf. Victoria Costa, 2004: 8). In these schools 'the voices of particular moral communities are silenced because they are not shared', leading to a condition in which because we 'fear our individual differences and the controversy they invite... we create schools that extol mutual respect and tolerance but resist any real exploration of competing moral visions' (cf. Arthur, Sears and Gearon, 2010).

In his instrumental republican theory Maurizio Viroli provides an interesting addition to these criticisms of Rawlsian 'public reason'. Viroli joins others in rejecting the principle that comprehensive religious and moral doctrines should (and could) be absent from public discourse. He questions, however, the nature of the reasoning that should take place within public forums. Typically within republican theories, public discourse is expected to centre on inherently rational processes, a fact which in turn reflects the predominant standpoint in the wider field of deliberative democratic theory. In their dialogical interactions, citizens reflect on evidence placed before them, subject their thoughts and ideas to the critical attention of debate, and explore different ideas within an unforced and uncoerced environment.[64] Viroli (1999: 18–19), however, points us towards a deeper and more affective domain of public dialogue found within classical republicanism:

> Unlike contemporary political theorists who presume that legislative deliberations offer the give-and-take of reasoned arguments in a public forum that aims at justifying a mutually binding decision, classical republicans believed that what in fact occurs in deliberative councils is the give-and-take of partisan arguments couched rhetorically... aimed at moving the listeners' passions.

On this basis, Viroli argues for greater recognition of the role and place of rhetoric and the stirring of the emotions within the discourse of public life. Whilst Sunstein and Pettit cast their approach to deliberation in terms of a republic of reason, Viroli encapsulates his preference in terms of a republic of eloquence. Whilst the former is concerned with the mind, the latter is concerned, as an important addition, with the role of deliberation in stirring affective feelings. As such, republican thinking on deliberation also serves to remind us that dialogical engagement involves processes that occur internally within citizens. This is what Goodin (2003a; 2003b) refers to as 'internal-reflection', or the cognitive and emotional faculties within citizens which are necessarily stimulated through dialogical interaction with other citizens. Internal reflection is likely to take place at various stages of dialogical interaction and places an obligation on citizens to internally consider their own position and, importantly, the effect that views advanced by others have upon one's own standpoint. It is best understood as a necessary counterpart of external-collective deliberation, and it is unlikely that effective external deliberation can occur without prior and con-current internal reflection taking place. Indeed, external and internal reflection are in an interdependent relationship. As Benhabib (1996: 71–2) has argued:

> the very procedure of articulating a view in public imposes a certain reflexivity on individual preferences and opinions... The process of *articulating good reasons in public* forces the individual to think of what would count as a good reasons for all others involved.

Similarly, Goodin (2003a: 55) reminds us that external-collective and internal-reflective deliberation are 'inextricably intertwined'. From an explicitly republican perspective, Sunstein (1988: 1555) implicitly references internal reflective processes when he highlights the impor-tance of citizens demonstrating 'political empathy' within their delib-eration. He defines political empathy as 'the requirement that political actors attempt to assume the position of those who disagree'. Political empathy inherently calls upon citizens to internally reflect not only on their own standpoint, but on the relationship between this and the views of others. Whilst this is part of an external process, it requires internal reflection. Similarly when Pettit (1999: 146) suggests that as 'people interact, and organize, and affirm certain identities... they are always liable to see what had been unquestioned' internal reflective processes, involving a form of civic empathy, are at play. Although it is an underdeveloped aspect of deliberative theory, internal reflection represents an integral, and therefore crucial, element of the deliberative process. Moreover, it has importance for civic education. Recognition of the internal-reflective component of deliberation places an obliga-tion on schools and teachers to help pupils develop the thinking skills necessary to manage one's own thoughts and deliberations on matters at various stages of dialogical interactions with fellow pupils. As Barber (1984: 179) reminds us, 'talk as communication involves receiving as well as expressing, hearing as well as speaking, and empathizing as well as uttering'. If the deliberative process is understood in cyclical terms, internal reflection can be viewed as operating before, during and after engagement in external-collective deliberation.

Conclusion

Republicans perceive deliberation as a having an important function within republican democratic states. It is through deliberation that citizens come to share their interests and learn the interests of others. In participating in common dialogue, citizens are able to discuss, amongst other things, notions of the common good and the content and extent of civic virtue. Republican deliberation, particularly when framed around the notion of contestation, furnishes decisions and public policies with a heightened claim to legitimacy. This legitimacy is gained not just from popular sovereignty, but from the reflexive nature of public discourse. Whether deliberation aims at consensus in terms of deeply held shared values or in terms of political agreements remains a difference of opinion between republicans. Nevertheless, by coming together to discuss matters of public concern in a wide variety of forums, republican citizens are able to demonstrate, and in turn strengthen, their commitment to the political community, conferring on them a sense of empowerment and, indeed, civic consciousness. Once more the educational imperative of republican thinking is clear. Not only do citizens need to learn the capacities and skills required for effective deliberation, but deliberation itself plays an educative function in the republican state.

6
The Expression of Civic Republicanism in Civic Education

In the foregoing chapters the ideas and principles which form the substantive nature of civic republicanism have been explored. I have suggested that running through these republican commitments, at times explicitly and at others implicitly, is an interest in and an attachment to civic education. The type of political engagement within public life that is central to republican models of freedom requires cultivation and habituation. Such cultivation and habituation requires formation through education, starting at a young age. For this reason, it is not too strong to suggest that without civic education, civic republican projects are seriously undermined. The purpose of this chapter is to draw out and analyse the central issues for civic education which result from recent republican work. It is suggested that the differences and tensions within contemporary republican discourse prompt significant questions for the aims, purposes and curricular approaches of civic education. It takes as its framework the four broad republican commitments which have provided the structure for the analysis so far, namely civic obligations, the common good, civic virtue and deliberation in public life. The analysis provided in this chapter is premised on my views, stated previously, that curriculum models of civic education derive from certain sets of beliefs (for this reason no curriculum can be considered a neutral document) and that whilst connections have been made between civic republican models of citizenship and civic education there is great benefit in exploring the substantive nature of the former in order to better understand the latter. It considers each of the four republican commitments depicted throughout this book in turn, for the purpose of highlighting the issues that differences within republicanism raise for civic education. To this end, and where appropriate, references are made to initiatives and programmes in civic education in a number of Western democracies, in an attempt to illuminate these issues.

Before commencing this task, a few points by way of establishing the focus of this chapter are necessary. First, as has been suggested throughout the proceeding chapters, civic republicans allocate an educational and formative role to a number of civic institutions, not just to schooling in the formal education system. Education for civic engagement in public life can be created and shaped through a nation's system of laws, through the constitution of institutions and, indeed, through the generative effects of civic participation itself. The focus of this chapter and the one that follows is, however, on formal systems of education and schooling, and more specifically, those that relate to pupils broadly in the 11–16 age range. Second, in drawing parallels between particular policies and curricula for civic education in different nations I do not pretend that the influence of civic republican principles has always been unequivocally acknowledged and recognized by those involved. There are nations, such as England and Spain, where this acknowledgement has to some extent been made, whilst there are others where the link remains inferred. Nevertheless, and as stated in Chapter 1, I concur with Hughes, Sears and Print (2009) in their identification of civic republican models of citizenship as heavily informing recent initiatives in civic education. Third, and this is an important recognition, whilst they do not form the focus here, I am cognisant of the disparity there may be between, on the one hand, policy intentions and curricular provision and, on the other, actual practice within schools and classrooms. As Reid, Gill and Sears (2010: 5) remind us, across nations, '...no matter how tightly the state seeks to prescribe educational practice to conform with the educational settlement, there is always 'wiggle room' for educators, creating possibilities for contestation and resistance. That is, there is never a one-to-one correspondence between the state's agenda and its realisation in the classroom'.[65] Fourth, and perhaps most importantly, is the fact that whilst this chapter separates out the four commitments that underpin civic republican models of citizenship, it does so for purposes of analytical clarity. These ideas are, in fact, heavily intertwined, and any form of civic education that seeks to respond to republican concerns but that fails to take into account this interconnectedness is likely to suffer as a result.

Civic obligation, the common good and civic education

The republican focus on civic obligations has provided a broad model for initiatives in civic education. Such education, framed around the concept of the citizen, is perceived to be an essential mechanism in developing within pupils the knowledge, skills and proclivities they need to understand and fulfil their responsibility to participate as citizens in civic life. Important here is the republican understanding of citizenship as *practice*, and in employing this idea, recent curricula across a number of nations have sought to establish approaches to civic education which transcend purely liberal, rights-based constructs. As has been stated previously, in many Western democracies, this call for a more developed sense of obligation to communities within civic education has formed part of a wider concern for a more active and participatory citizenship across public life. The idea that civic education should develop in pupils a sense of their responsibilities to other citizens and to the state is one of the fundamental and defining features of recent curricular programmes in this area. This development of pupils' understanding and commitment to their civic obligations involves both the cognitive and affective domain. As Richard Battistoni (1985: 159) warns in his perceptive exploration of civic education in the United States, we should not forget the latter because:

> Only by building in students the affective feeling towards their fellow citizens can the foundation for a democratic political community be established. In fact, as the life of the political community progresses and becomes more complex over time, and as common goals and purposes are needed and sought more often by citizens, the importance of a basic affection between and encouragement among citizens grow. If they are not cultivated in the civic education of the young the affective bonds necessary to the continued success of democratic politics will not develop.

But, even if this civic affection is accepted and developed, how do civic educators conceive the basis for one's obligations to other citizens and to the political community? Typically, the sense of civic commitment in civic education is expressed and framed in terms of 'responsibilities', 'responsible action' and 'duties' rather than 'obligations'. Reflecting on the changing focus and conceptions of responsibility in Canada, where civic education is defined at a provincial level largely through its inclusion within social studies, Hébert (2009: 7) considers practice in Alberta, which has witnessed a shift from passive accounts of responsibility based on simple knowledge and understanding to a more collective sense of responsibility based on action. Such a trend finds expression in a number of other nations.[66] Eschewing the liberal notion that citizenship is solely a voluntary activity, a core purpose of the statutory curriculum for citizenship education in England, for example, has been to develop within pupils a knowledge and understanding of specifically *civic* responsibilities and duties (Crick, 2002; Annette, 2003, 2005; Lockyer, 2003). The *Report of the Advisory Group on Education for Democracy and the Teaching of Citizenship in Schools* (QCA, 1998: 6.6, 40), which preceded and informed the development of citizenship education in England, included as part of its stated aim and purpose for citizenship education the requirement that the subject should enhance 'the awareness of rights and duties, and the sense of responsibilities needed for the development of pupils into active citizens'. The report also established social and moral responsible behaviour as one of its three strands of citizenship education, alongside community involvement and political literacy. When this sentiment was translated into curricular provision in the resultant Citizenship Order (1999), which set out Programmes of Study for pupils in Key Stages Three (11–14 year olds) and Four (14–16 year olds), the focus was slightly different. Pupils were to be taught skills of participation and *responsible* action in the context of knowledge and understanding about becoming informed citizens. The terms 'obligation' and 'duties' were, however, missing. The language of the revised curriculum for citizenship produced in 2007 and taught since 2008 incorporates the term 'obligations', at least as an adjunct to greater references to responsibilities.

Is the use of the terms 'responsibilities' and 'responsible' rather than 'obligations' educationally significant? I believe that it is, and that this importance relates to the derivation and depth of civic bonds explored in Chapter 3. There are significant differences between the terms, which are to do with action and depth. A citizen (or indeed a pupil) can have civic responsibilities, and may be aware of these civic responsibilities, but this does not in and of itself mean that that citizen will act or behave in a responsible way. Just as a parent has certain responsibilities for their children, but may not act in a responsible manner in respect of these, so too a citizen may have a responsibility to vote or to engage in other forms of civic action but may opt not to do so. As we have seen, central to civic republican theory is the idea that citizens take up their civic responsibilities and do so in a responsible way. This is echoed clearly in curricular approaches to civic education that centre on the concept of citizenship. Young people are not only taught about their responsibilities, but (and here the link to citizenship as practice is clear) are provided with opportunities to take responsibility in an informed way. The problem with forms of civic education which focus on *only* these two understandings of the responsibilities between citizens and their communities is that they do not necessarily provide pupils with a clear, and perhaps substantive, basis for their connections with fellow citizens. Neither the focus on responsibilities nor the desire that citizens act in a responsible manner necessarily involve the deep and embedded bonds of moral obligation and duties that are central to intrinsic republican ideas. It is this deeper sense of embedded obligation that intrinsic republicans like Sandel and Oldfield promote, but that is largely absent from recent civic education curricula.

This recognition raises a tension for civic education which is worthy of further thought and reflection. In Chapter 3 the basis of civic obligation within republican thought was considered, and it was suggested that instrumental and intrinsic republicans understand the basis of civic obligations differently. It was argued that instrumental republicans understand civic obligations to result from voluntarily chosen associations made by citizens in order to further non-domination within the political community. Obligation results from reciprocity and a commitment to protecting freedom as non-domination (and for this reason is ultimately linked to self-interest). In terms of reciprocity the claim is often two-fold. First, that obligations (or responsibilities at least) are reciprocated by rights and, second, that citizens have obligations in a reciprocal relationship with other citizens. This position contrasts sharply with the intrinsic republican positions that understand civic obligations as 'inseparable from understanding ourselves as the particular persons we are (Sandel, 1996: 14) and as 'givens of an individual's experiences' (Oldfield, 1990: 7). Understood properly, civic obligations, or duties, involve deeply held bonds with fellow citizens within a shared political community. They involve, and in part are derived from, a sense of shared history which entails that citizens of particular political communities have a sense of obligation not simply to their communities today, but to the historical ideas, actions and values of that community. In this sense they eschew the moral individualism of purely voluntary obligations (cf. Sandel, 1999). Recognition of such histories and obligations is particularly important given the plural nature of contemporary Western democracies. This deeper concern for civic obligation would involve the notion that the communities in which pupils live and participate are shared collective enterprises, which often involve a shared sense of history and include a common sense of belonging and responsibility. The role of the formal civic curriculum, operating alongside more informal practices, would be to develop in pupils a sense of belonging and to integrate them into the social histories and narratives of their communities – including that of the school. Understood in this sense, the development of a respect for civic obligation would form part of the socializing role of schools. In her analysis of different curricular programmes for civic education in Canada, Hébert (2007: 7) makes clear that 'In Canada, young people may wonder if they are responsible for the prejudices and discriminations of previous historical times. Although present-day citizens may not be legally liable, they are nonetheless responsible for righting the wrongs of previous centuries'.

Whilst seemingly interested in notions of civic obligations, current civic education curricula have a tendency to simply assert that these exist without their basis being entirely clear. In other words, there is a danger that pupils are taught to understand their civic responsibilities and obligations, and how to enact these in an appropriate way, but without a clear sense as to why such responsibilities exist. It is also interesting to note that, at least in the case of England, despite the influence of republican ideas, neither the instrumental republican language of non-domination nor the intrinsic language of self-government are explicitly used to justify the basis of civic obligations within civic education. Instead, the curriculum adopts a pragmatic stance, typically with an implicit suggestion that civic responsibilities result from the existence of certain civic rights.

A further issue for civic education concerns the spheres in which civic responsibilities and obligation may be recognized and played out. In relation to this, the discourse around citizenship education in England provides a useful case-study. Civic republican thought reminds us that civic obligations do not stand in isolation from other aspects of citizens', and therefore pupils', lives. Recent republican work has called for a re-awakening of the civic spirit and engagement in the political life of our communities but, as the exploration of such work presented here suggests, this involves the deliberative institutions of civil society as well as those of the civic sphere. The term 'public' is not just political, but can also refer to citizen engagement within *civil society* (cf. Jochum et al., 2005). In other words, active citizenship in its fullest sense involves *both* political participation and engagement in civil society. This area of republican thinking builds on Tocqueville's understanding of a mutual relationship between engagement in civil society and participation by citizens in the political affairs of their communities. The case of citizenship education in England illustrates the extent to which a misrepresentation of civic republican models of citizenship can lead to an overly narrow approach to civic education. A key question for citizenship educators in England has been the extent to which participation in *civil* activities by pupils will help them to develop the skills and capacities for specifically *civic* engagement. The Report of the Advisory Group (QCA, 1998: 11, 2.8) made clear that 'freedom and full citizenship in the political arena itself depends on a society with a rich variety of non-political associations and voluntary groups – what some have called civil society'. The Report (1998: 11, 2.8) makes the related claim, however, that 'voluntary and community activity cannot be the full meaning of active citizenship'. Statements such as this have provided citizenship education in England with an essentially *political* concept of active citizenship as a supplement to, but not as a replacement for, voluntary and community engagement. However, since the inclusion of citizenship education in the statutory curriculum for schools in England, some commentators have sought, in both theoretical and practical terms, to separate voluntary and community activity from political engagement in a way which downgrades the former in favour of the latter (Crick, 2002; Nelson and Kerr, 2005). In other words, they seek to separate direct political and civic engagement from social acts deriving, for example, from charity and philanthropy. In the process they prioritize the former as by far the more valuable function of civic education. Nelson and Kerr (2005: 14), for example, have been critical of the elision of active citizenship and volunteering, arguing that '[A]lthough citizenship education, volunteering and participation all involve degrees of action or activity, as stand-alone entities they do not necessarily equate to "active citizenship"'. With reference to *A National Framework for Youth Action and Engagement* (Russell Commission, 2005), Nelson and Kerr criticize the focus on volunteering given 'the current confusion between active citizenship and volunteering, and the desire of those in policy circles to distance active citizenship from purely altruistic acts'.

Whilst it is useful to distinguish between civic and civil activities, the basis for this distinction requires further reflection, particularly as it relates to the nature and expression of civic obligation. There is a danger that it produces a disjointed understanding of the relationship between civil society and political engagement. Data produced by the extensive ten-year longitudinal study of citizenship education in England conducted by the National Foundation for Educational Research (NFER) found that, in practice, pupil engagement in active citizenship opportunities has included participation in *both* civil and civic society (Ireland et al., 2006; Nelson and Kerr, 2006). Further evidence from a national study of character and education has found that pupils' engagement in public life takes a number of forms, and is often facilitated through their membership of particular communities which operate outside schooling, such as faith and religious-based groups. Recognition of the engagement of young people in civil society increases the necessity that civic education programmes in schools take into account pupils' activity outside their formal schooling. Young people are likely to be involved in a range of community-based groups through which they acknowledge (sometimes consciously, sometime unconsciously), cement and play out their civic ties. As the NFER's study found, 'a number of the key underlying factors, which foster and sustain active citizenship, were already evident to, and supported by, young people in their daily lives' including those activities which occurred 'beyond schools' (Ireland et al., 2006: 72–73). As Bentley (1998: 66) reflects:

> Schools are the institutions which contain a young person's activity for most of their first two decades, but they also live in the wider world; they are members of numerous communities, and their expectations and sources of learning are far richer and more diverse than school-based learning opportunities, however good these might be.

Barber (1998: 6) argues that a robust civil society can help strengthen democratic practices and should be seen as 'the free space in which democratic attitudes are cultivated and democratic behaviour is conditioned'. Importantly, Barber's position places participation in civil society within a public context. As such, participation in civil society is essential for any meaningful sense of active citizenship. This position has been supported by a number of theorists, including Jochum et al. (2005: 10; emphasis in the original) who argue that participation in civil society is '*equally* valuable because it frequently stimulates or reinforces' democratic, political engagement (cf. Hirst, 1993; Putnam, 2000). Any form of civic education which fails to appreciate this connectivity is likely to be disjointed. The theoretical and pedagogical responsibility of civic education lies not in distinguishing civic engagement from civil society, but in a careful exposition of the links between them. The elucidation of such links is likely to be stronger when the civic and the civil are understood as distinct, but mutually interdependent realms which work together toward a 'double process of democratisation' (Held, 1989). We can add to this that it is through engagement in civil society – in addition to the civic sphere – that republican citizens respect their civic obligations.

Of central importance for pupils in this regard is likely to be a clarification of different learning outcomes in relation to specific public spaces and domains. A distinction provided by Annette (2003: 140) is useful here. Activities concerned with civil society are likely to involve 'learning through volunteering with social capital as a learning outcome', whilst civic engagement will incorporate 'learning through community involvement with democratic citizenship … as a learning outcome'. I would argue that most policy and curriculum documents for civic education framed around the principle of citizenship speak to both of these outcomes, despite the fact that the interdependent relationship may become confused in the discourse surrounding civic education. This is certainly the case in recent initiatives in England and Australia, and is exemplified in the approach to education for citizenship taken in Scotland, which is described by Biesta (2008: 44) as one 'based on what we might call a social rather than an exclusively political conception of citizenship, one which understands citizenship in terms of membership of and concern for the many communities that make up people's lives. This includes the more narrowly political domain of citizenship, but extends to civil society and potentially includes any community'. The nature of civic education programmes which combine knowledge and experiential learning and which can develop both social capital and active citizenship remains a necessary research focus for civic educators (Campbell, 2000; Annette, 2003: 145–6; cf. Kahne et al., 2000; Print and Coleman, 2003). As Annette (2008: 390) suggests, this might usefully 'be informed by the recent work on the "politics of everyday life" which can broaden our understanding of what "the political" could mean in the lives of students' (Boyte, 2004; Bentley, 2005; Crick, 2005; Ginsborg, 2005; Stoker, 2006). If meaningful, this is likely to involve a critical consideration by educators concerning what form the political can, does and should take. We are still left, however, with the question as to what is the basis for civic obligation which is to be promoted within civic education. In short, whether civic obligation is the result of deeply held and embedded moral bonds or the result of other connections, such as reciprocity and civic consciousness, that result from the operation of the political community.

These reflections on the place and nature of civic obligation within civic education are interrelated with notions of the common good. To be civically and communally obligated is to a large extent to be an integral and active part of a political unit or community. As such, citizens, and for that matter pupils, must consider how their own individual interests relate to those of the wider community. Whilst the common good forms a central idea for civic education, its meaning and implications remain largely under-determined, and there has been very limited exploration of what an education for the common good may comprise (for an exception, see Barton and Levstik, 2004 and Peterson, 2011). Contemporary civic republicanism incorporates at its heart the understanding that citizens are essentially 'participants in a co-operative enterprise' (Dagger, 1997: 79). A key feature of recent civic education curricula that have centred on the idea of citizenship has been the perception that such education should foster within pupils a sense of, and a commitment to, the common good. It was suggested in Chapter 3 that the common good is a somewhat vague term, which can have a number of different meanings – the good life, the general welfare of society, and, in economic terms, non-excludability. Of these three understandings of the common good, it is the second which has clear prominence in recent approaches to civic education. Usually, this is expressed in terms of developing within pupils a disposition to have a mind or a concern for the common good.[67] But what does this mean and entail? In simplistic terms it is to suggest that pupils, in their civic actions and thoughts, should seek to take into account the interests of others and the community as a whole in their civic deliberations and interactions. In this sense, the desire is for pupils to transcend their own narrow self-interest. This approach to the common good also incorporates the notion that through civic engagement with others, pupils can broaden those interests that are shared. Through deliberative civic interactions in school and beyond, pupils come to play a part in forging the common good within their own communities, rather than having the common good formed within them. Arthur (2000: 90–91) describes this in the following way:

> An education for citizenship, or the promotion of the common good, needs... to encourage practices of cooperation, friendship, openness and active participation in society. Schools do not impose their definition of the common good but provide opportunities for pupils to experience the reality of these practices. Pupils do not know the common good innately but must learn how subtle a concept is and to realize that the material content of the common good at one point in time is the most disputatious of subjects. It should set off a number of discussions, not settle the argument.

This analysis is surely correct – schools must be wary of not invoking a narrow and partial understanding of a common good which is uncritical and dogmatic. Moreover, there is a need for pupils to be active co-constructors of the common good. However, a problem with such an approach is that it requires pupils to consider what may be in the interests of other citizens and their political communities without necessarily having the breadth of knowledge and understanding required to do this. In addition, this requirement may be in place without a corresponding appreciation as to why pupils should be concerned for the common good, beyond a vague notion of a social conscience. Co-operation is likely to result but this may not always be with a common and shared purpose. Taught uncritically, this would involve pupils in learning about, advocating for, and representing others at local, national and global levels, without necessarily comprehending the links and associations they share (cf. Peterson, 2011). For this reason, there is some benefit in questioning, as certain civic republican positions prompt us to, whether pupils are able to undertake such activity without a fuller and more substantive comprehension of what the common good could mean.

Here the republican notion of the common good as the good life may provide a beneficial adjunct to conceptions framed in terms of the public interest. It was suggested in Chapter 3 that intrinsic republican theorists, such as Oldfield and Sandel, look to supplement the understanding of the common good as the general welfare of society, with a further, differentiated, use of the term. This relates to what might be understood as a neo-Aristotelian understanding of the good life. In short, this sense of the common good refers to the good way of living common to humans. In order to live the good life, and in order to flourish, humans must live a civic life, achieved through individual participation within a collective endeavour. In recent civic republican work, this political life can be viewed as either *a* version of the good life common to humans (Sandel, 1996; 1998) or as *the* version of the good life (Oldfield, 1990). To suggest that pupils should, as part of their civic education, explore such notions of the common good is to claim that deep moral questions about what represents the good life, and how citizens *qua* humans are connected, are pertinent and relevant for young citizens and, as a result, that educational practices for civic education should run deeper than presenting the common good solely in terms of deliberation on what is in the public interest. In essence, this would aim at engaging pupils in considering the extent to which their own interests and those of the political community are interconnected. In other words, it would, at the very least, require that pupils dialogically explore how civic participation may represent enlightened forms of community living and self-interest. These ideas are not completely alien to discussions on civic education, but they are rarely expressed in curricular documentation, which tend to focus instead on notions of reciprocity, civic pride, and altruism as a basis for citizen obligation and the common good.

Civic virtue, moral learning and civic education

Civic education contains a moral component. In making provision for civic education centred on the principle of citizenship, national and regional governments in a number of Western democratic nations have, in effect, adopted the moral position that pupils should recognize and understand their civic obligations and rights and that, more specifically, they should learn to fulfil such obligations in a certain way. There is some variation, though, in how this moral component may be understood. Distinct approaches within recent civic republican work point to such differences, and provide a useful framework for distinguishing between two specific approaches to the development of civic virtue through civic education, namely, approaches that view civic virtue as relating to the development of internalized character dispositions, and approaches that seek instead to educate pupils to act in accordance with certain civic principles necessary for a functioning political community.

It was suggested in Chapter 4 that a commitment to civic virtue represents a central contribution of contemporary republican thinking, but that civic virtue is a broad term, which beyond certain broad pronouncements, can have substantively different meanings according to which particular republican position is being expounded. The distinction drawn in that chapter was between two forms of civic virtue. The first, ancient in origin and found within intrinsic republican approaches, conceives civic virtue as internalized dispositions of character. The second, modern and liberal in origin, understands civic virtue in terms of civility. Understood in this way, civic virtue denotes preferential patterns of behaviour which are valued to the extent to which they are conducive to effective citizen engagement within society. In other words, these 'virtues' are not strictly virtues, but are better conceived as numerous civic *principles* that serve to guide citizens' action, and which do not necessarily require internalization within the character of citizens. As Dagger (1997: 194) reminds us from his liberal-republican position, in this second formulation, virtues are promoted and cultivated, but there is no real appeal for them to be maximized either within or across the citizenry. In educational terms, Dagger (1997: 131) makes clear, this rejects 'the "education of desire" characteristic of a stringent forms of republicanism [and the] "moulding" of citizens' and calls instead for 'a way of linking individual rights to public responsibilities'. Some instrumental republicans claim to support precisely the sort of approach to the education of virtue dismissed by Dagger. Maynor is the clearest example of this. In his consideration of the centrality of formal civic education in schools, Maynor (2003: 180) draws on Berlin's (1981: 43–4; emphasis in the original) assertion that republican forms of civic education seek to inculcate virtues and look to form 'certain faculties... of inner moral strength, magnanimity, vigor, vitality, generosity, loyalty, above all public spirit, civic sense' and a 'dedication to the security, power, glory, [and] expansion of the *patria*'. Although Maynor agrees with Berlin's assertion, he goes on to talk, not of Berlin's classical virtues, but of what are better understood as values and principles, such as tolerance, respect and the commitment to attend to the interests of others. A similar position is adopted by Freeman Butts who, in his praise for the CIVITAS framework for civic education in the United States and in a similar way to Maynor, employs the language of virtues as character. The CIVITAS framework is one of the very few to explicitly use the concept of civic virtue in its conceptual focus. Suggesting that CIVITAS 'revives the term "civic virtue" and the 'civic character needed by American citizens', Freeman Butts (2006: 15) includes within civic character the following: 'dispositions and commitments [such] as civility, individual responsibility and self-discipline, civic-mindedness and open-mindedness, compromise and negotiation, respect for the rights of others, respect for the law, critical mindedness, patience and persistence, compassion, generosity, and loyalty'. Similar sorts of values and principles are also found in the definition of 'moral and civic virtue' offered in the Carnegie Corporation and CIRCLE (2003: 10) report *The Civic Mission of Schools*. Presented as one of four characteristics of 'competent and responsible citizens',[68] citizens who possess moral and civic virtues are said to be 'concerned for the rights and welfare of others, are socially responsible, willing to listen to alternative perspectives, confident in their capacity to make a difference, and ready to contribute personally to civic and political action'. Furthermore, they 'strike a reasonable balance between their own interests and the common good. They recognize the importance of and practice civic duties such voting and respecting the rule of law'.

The capacities referenced in documents on civic education such as the CIVITAS framework and *The Civic Mission of Schools* are clearly central to any republican (and I would suggest any meaningful) approach to civic education, but again it is difficult to see how many of these (perhaps with the exception of the last two) are virtues in the fullest sense of the term. The CIVITAS framework (Quigley and Buchanan, 1991: 12) presents civic virtue as a combination of 'civic dispositions' and 'civic commitments'. The former 'refer to those attitudes and habits of the mind of the citizen that are conducive to the healthy functioning and common good of the democratic system'. The latter 'refer to the freely-given, reasoned commitments of the citizen to the fundamental values and principles of American constitutional democracy'. Nowhere, though, do these dispositions and capacities necessarily move beyond cognitive processes (habits of the mind) to deeper affective processes (habits of the heart). An understanding of this difference within republican thinking on civic virtue, between, that is, an education in the virtues and an education for civic principles, is useful in exploring the moral component of civic education. Although '[T]he language of virtues' is often used in 'discussion of the qualities citizens need' in relation to civic education (Haydon, 2003: 83), official curriculum and guidance documents have provided little detail concerning the educational implications of this for civic education. Current practice in civic education in Western nations is most commonly rooted in liberal approaches to moral education which seek to develop rational moral autonomy within pupils. Based on the work of Piaget (1965) and Kohlberg (1981, 1984), consideration of moral questions or concepts within civic education requires pupils to engage in both moral reasoning and clarification of values rather than in internalizing ways of acting within their character. In effect, pupils are encouraged to come to their own conclusions regarding value or ethical judgements, with the proviso that this process involves critical reasoning with others. Understanding the moral dimension of civic education in this way involves an implicit assumption that such reasoning will 'lead to certain results rather than others' (Haydon, 1997: 152), and relates more to the idea of civic principles than to deeper virtues of civic character. In this sense, the civic principles which can be found within official and policy documents act only as a general guide. Schools, teachers and, most importantly, pupils are able to discuss and re-define the content of the principles through processes of consideration and dialogue which follow certain procedural rules.

Typically, then, recognition of any moral element of civic education in curricular terms is expressed in terms of certain values, or what I have termed above 'civic principles'. In this sense they can be seen as commensurable with the instrumental republican idea of civility, and as concerned with developing 'particular "norm[s] or principle[s]" that 'we expect people to do or to refrain from doing' (Haydon, 2003: 86). Such norms and principles inform the actions of pupils but remain external to them. Pupils are in effect taught to recognize the idea of the common good, to be tolerant, to recognize human rights, without the expectation that such commitments necessarily become part of their character. In this sense pupils are asked to accept certain rules on the basis of reciprocity – the mutually beneficial idea that if we act in a particular way, so too will others. There are real benefits in forming the moral element of civic education around civic principles. First and foremost, civic principles, such as respect and tolerance, are undeniably fundamental to the effective operation of reflexive political communities. Moreover, approaches to civic education which appeal to civic principles avoid the need for the specified content to be based on faith or metaphysics (Haydon, 2003: 85). Instead, moral instruction becomes focused on Kohlbergian critical rationalism and on the following of certain procedures, rather than action deriving from internalized dispositions.[69] As Davies et al. (2005: 352) reflect, pupil learning is normally informed by an 'agreement that a genuine exploration of dilemmas to be solved within a democratic society is preferred' to any form of character education. This focus is reinforced by curricular approaches in which the objective of pupil learning is to discuss positions, both their own and those of others, on particular controversial issues.[70] There is a certain danger in this practice, however: that pupils become guided purely by their conformity to certain rules rather than by their desire to abide by them. To repeat from Chapter 4, as MacIntyre (1999: 131) warns us, '[W]hat the morality of the virtues articulated in and defended by the moral rhetoric of our political culture provides is, it turns out, not an education in the virtues but, rather, an education in how to seem virtuous, without actually being so'. The commitment to broad civic principles, rather than deeper civic virtues, also raises the extent to which the principles have permanency and applicability within the lives of pupils, as well as the connections between the principles and the wider political community. Critical of moral development approaches, Battistoni (1985: 94) presents the problem like this:

> ...the thrust of the moral development literature denies that part of citizenship characterized by caring for the affairs of one's community and by the mutual sharing of concern among community members which makes people able to engage in common political *action*. The overriding thrust... is with fostering cognitive skills and competencies, not with the important affective foundations... for working

out public policy disputes. In fact, by attempting to attach people to abstract universal principles of justice and right, Kohlberg's method of instruction may even have the effect of *extricating* people from localized bonds of community and political commitment, as these are seen as being too 'parochial'.

Whilst current approaches to civic education may go beyond a simple set of prescribed rules, and may encourage pupils to critically engage in the development of moral reasoning about core civic values, they often stop short of deeper commitments to a form of moral education within which pupils can develop and express their civic character, and in so doing become bonded to their communities.

I have argued earlier that there is a second formulation of republican civic virtue which calls for a deeper and more sustained form of moral instruction within civic education. As Oldfield (1990: 172) makes clear, citizenship involves the internalization of character dispositions: '[N]o amount of political participation and economic democracy, no level of civic education or national service, will suffice for the practice of citizenship in a political community – unless and until the external covenant becomes an internal one'. When civic virtue is understood in these terms, and as involving dispositions internalized within one's character, the connections between civic and what has become known as character education become stronger. The extent to which citizenship is a practice through which young people can form and express their character is an important question for those interested in civic education. At present, the identification of links between civic education and character education in some nations are developed (most notably in the USA) whilst in others (such as England) they are at an early stage (Arthur, 2003; Davies et al., 2005). Framing the moral component of civic education around virtues and character education has notable advantages over approaches which centre on civic principles. In the latter, pupils are likely to be confronted with a range of issues that involve them in making value judgements without having the necessary underpinning framework for doing so. In discussing controversial issues, pupils are involved in identifying positions, discussing and justifying them, and reflecting on the value of such dialogue. Whilst critical thought and personal judgements enable pupils to consider specific issues, more thought is required as to how pupils construct their understandings of values and ethics across the range of issues with which civic education is concerned. In other words, what a pupil thinks about one ethical issue or value, or how they choose to act in a certain situation, cannot stand in isolation from how that same pupil thinks or acts in other contexts. A key role of the curriculum must be to make links between such values and issues, and to construct dialogue around any similarities or tensions which may result from this. Without a clear moral framework from which to do this, pupils' understanding may remain limited to applying general notions of under-articulated concepts, such as tolerance and respect, to their interactions with others. When civic virtues are understood in the intrinsic sense, the internalization of specific dispositions provides such a framework. Rather than requiring pupils to critically discuss questions of right and wrong, education for civic character requires them to develop a sense of inner morality which, in turn, would find expression in moral reflection and action. Moreover, education for civic character is fundamentally rooted as a common endeavour of both the classroom and the school as a whole. Whilst character formation and expression is likely to take place in civic education lessons (whether citizenship education or incorporated within social studies), it is supported and extended by wider school structures, processes and ethos.

In order for this to occur effectively, however, the distinction which civic republicans make between civic virtues and virtues *per se* must be countered. It was suggested in Chapter 4 that civic republicans are solely interested in the civic attributes of citizens, and as a result have very little to say about personal morality. This raises an important tension for the civic education raised by civic republican models of citizenship. The specific focus on the civic role of the citizen represents, of course, a central element of contemporary republican thought, but this is to the detriment of close interplay between the civic and the personal. Some may argue that this separation is right and proper for educational reasons, and may seek to distinguish between civic education and educational programmes which focus more on personal development.[71] However, the view that civic education should reflect and relate to the personal moral education of pupils has received some attention within the literature (Tomasi, 2001; Best, 2002; Haydon, 2005). As Clarke (1996: 89) has suggested in relation to citizenship education in England, a clear relationship between the personal and civic realms means that 'citizenship becomes linked more directly to human relations and to the way or ways in which these relations are shared' (cf. Faulks, 2006a). Whilst there are clear differences in scope between civic education and education for personal development, and few would support blurring the boundaries between them, any attempt to separate the political from the personal has ramifications for the nature of moral learning in the former. In many facets of life, citizens are involved in decisions which *at the same time* involve public and private concerns. Without a corresponding recognition of personal character, any decisions reached by pupils in public – even those that account for a common interest – will remain limited and partial. Indeed, a wider goal of education is precisely to support pupils in reasoning about the relationship between 'individual well-being' and 'the good society' (Haydon, 2005: 34). Any attempt to separate personal values from public values is likely to limit the opportunity for pupils to think through how the influence of familial, spiritual and religious beliefs relate to and impact upon their civic engagement. If the moral parameters of civic education are separated from the personal moral development and education of pupils, there is a danger that pupils, in their moral thinking, are in effect being asked to separate personal values from public values and dispositions. This is an inherently liberal position, which prioritizes acting in accordance with certain principles over individual character. As MacIntyre (1984: 216) points out, from this liberal understanding, the question of 'what should I do?' is primary to the question 'who am I?'. A properly constituted form of moral education would involve pupils in both questions, and would include both a personal and civic content.

It is perhaps worth paying brief attention to the potential criticisms which educating for character within civic education is likely to provoke. The first is that character education is likely to be narrow, dogmatic and restrictive. Indeed, the idea that character education need have these faults at all is an unfortunate, and misguided, caricature of the approach. This misses, however, the critical rationality which lies at the heart of effective character education. It is true that the development of character through schooling starts from a particular conception of what it means to be virtuous, but this is not necessarily static and fixed. A child's character is individual to that child, and is likely to change and adapt over time. What might be viewed as a courageous act by one child might not be by another. Similarly, an eleven-year-old's idea of honesty may differ from that of a sixteen-year-old. What is important is that each child reflects on the nature of such virtues, and seeks to employ them as a standard for their actions. Part of the process of character education is therefore the development of rational deliberation capacities within pupils regarding what they should do and why in any given situation. Critics may also question the extent to which virtue, as a moral concept, is important to young people. In short, they may question whether what may seem to be traditional, even anachronistic, dispositions and attributes are capable of connecting with young people's lives. One possible response to this is to suggest that every day young people, in both their personal and civic lives, encounter questions of character and virtue. When a pupil considers who he will or will not be friends with, when a pupil questions the decisions and actions of an important figure in history, when a pupil is exposed to the work of those who stand up against injustice, and even when pupils discuss in the school playground whether to condone the adventures (or misadventures) of those in the public spotlight, character and virtues are central their thoughts. This does not necessarily mean that pupils are always aware of the role of character and virtues in their reasoning, nor that they always have the moral vocabulary to discuss these concepts in an explicit way (cf. Arthur, 2010; Peterson, 2010). But it is to suggest that the idea of character and virtues is not alien to young people. The task for civic educators is to build a reflexive capacity within pupils to consider character and virtue not only with regard to the actions of others, but in relation to their own civic (and indeed personal) lives.

Deliberative democracy and civic education

Civic education in Western states, particularly when organized around the concept of citizenship, possesses an important relationship to democracy (Enslin et al., 2001). It should be remembered, however, that the substantive nature of any education for democratic depends upon what kind of democracy is envisaged (Ross, 2002). It was suggested in Chapter 5 that a focus on a deliberative form of democracy represents a central political commitment of contemporary republican theorists. Links between deliberation and civic education have been made in a number of countries (UK: Enslin et al., 2001; Parry, 2003; Annette, 2005; US: Gutmann and Thompson, 1996; Parker, 2002; Sweden: Roth, 2006; Englund, 2000, 2006), and Gutmann and Thompson (1996: 359) suggest that '[I]n any effort to make democracy more deliberative, the single most important institution outside government is the educational system'. Indeed, talk is a fundamental component of recent civic education initiatives, which commonly require pupils to learn the give-and-take of dialogical interaction (Gutmann, 1987; Kymlicka and Norman, 1995; Gutmann and Thompson, 1996; Hess, 2009). Typically this consists of pupils engaging in enquiry-based work in order to support their thinking about, analysing, and justifying their ideas in relation to, matters of public interest or what are commonly termed 'controversial issues'. As part of this endeavour, pupils are involved in articulating their interests, and coming to know the interests of others, through dialogical processes (Maynor, 2003: 183). This broadly deliberative approach to dialogue within civic education is encapsulated by the Swedish National Agency for Education (2000: 8) who contend that '[D]ialogue allows differing views and values to confront one another and develop. Dialogue allows individuals to make their own ethical judgements by listening, reflecting, finding arguments and appraising, while it also constitutes an important point of developing an understanding of one's own views and those of others' (cf. Roth, 2006: 575). In other words, a central aim of civic education across Western nations is the expectation that pupils be taught the skills of 'democratic communication' (Englund, 2006: 503). But what does deliberative democratic communication comprise and what is its in terms of consensus? I will consider these two questions in turn.

Democratic communication within civic education involves pupils in deliberating with both peers and those in positions of power (whether in the school or the wider political community) (Barton and Levstik, 2004: 29–31). The work of Walter Parker (2003, 2006) and Diana Hess (2009) reminds us that communication and deliberation can have two main purposes within civic education classrooms. Hess (2009: 85; emphasis in the original) suggests that civic educators may aim at 'teaching *for* and *with* discussion' and that communication 'is both a desired outcome and a method of teaching', whilst Parker (2006: 12), on whom Hess draws, remarks that the 'two kinds of discourse are complimentary in school practice, and neither is sufficient alone'. For Parker, discussion aims at both 'enriching the mind and cultivating a democratic political community'. Recourse to contemporary republican thinking, and in turn to wider deliberative theory, reminds us that it is through such democratic communication that citizens, and therefore pupils, can publicize their own interests and understand those of others (Maynor, 2003: 183). Civic republican models of deliberative engagement suggest that a variety of capacities are required for effective deliberation, and these provide a useful template for approaches to dialogical interaction within civic education.

The first and most rudimentary capacity required for effective deliberation can be understood in terms of the *civic commitment* required by pupils to participate in open and unforced democratic dialogue. Central to this commitment is an acceptance that democratic dialogue is a co-operative rather than a necessarily competitive enterprise. This does not mean that there will not be disagreement and tensions, but does suggest that there should be a sense and spirit of common pursuit. Without this sense of commitment to civic deliberation 'the rational individual whose cognitive abilities have been educated may not be predisposed to listen to others, or to resolve conflicting interests in the final formulation of public policy' (Battistoni, 1985: 160). Elizabeth McGrath (cited in Nash, 1997: 147) makes the observation that:

> Many people seem compelled to jump into a heated argument the moment they have sensed a different opinion... This tendency may be natural, but it need not be controlling. We can learn to acknowledge, without feeling threatened, the value of ideas that do not fit our system... [when I acknowledge the other] I am simply offering to that person the dignity, support, and encouragement that I myself need as I inch my way along the path. In short, we can choose to act as effective catalysts and staunch supports for one another or we can make [dialogue] even more difficult and painful by fuelling the fires of self-doubt in ourselves and others.

To develop this civic commitment within pupils is to seek to differentiate collective deliberation from other, at times more structured, forms of talk of the sort McGrath criticizes, in which pupils in civic education classrooms or in other school activities score points or seek to somehow outstrip or trump the arguments of their peers in order to gain a higher status or grade. In the more collaborative sense in which I am referring to, pupils are joint and equal participants in a social and civic endeavour.

A second vital capacity for republican deliberation that has resonance for civic education is *civic knowledge*. Civic knowledge is central to civic education, and properly constituted refers to the ability of students not only to know and understand certain civic facts, but to apply such learning to their actions and deliberations. Civic knowledge is synonymous with what in the English context has become known as political literacy, or the idea that the pupil must be able to 'use his or her knowledge, or at least see how it could be used and have a proclivity for using it' (Crick and Porter, 1978: 37). It is not a sufficient condition of democratic and deliberative civic education simply for pupils to have knowledge – they must be able to apply it appropriately in their discursive interactions. To this end, pupils require access to, and to have researched themselves, the necessary and important sources of information and data about a given topic or issue. In this sense, pupils require knowledge in order to engage in deliberation effectively, but also to develop their knowledge and understanding through their dialogical experiences.[72]

Civic commitment and civic knowledge are necessary conditions of *civic speaking*. Explicitly referencing civic speaking may appear somewhat tautological. To enter into public dialogue, or talk, by definition requires pupils to speak. However, in the sense I am using the term here, civic speaking has particular meanings, drawn from republican thinking, which render it a particular form of pupil talk. Civic speaking draws on the language of reason, but does not eschew the use of rhetoric and rhetorical devices in order, when appropriate, to stir the emotions of others. Whilst civic republicans typically prioritize reason within public discourse, the republican tradition reminds us that rhetoric plays an important role in civic dialogue. For this reason civic speaking is a particular brand of talk which aims to make clear one's own position and interests, but in a way that invites others to respond in the spirit of civic commitment as defined above. The skills, confidence and self-esteem necessary for civic speaking are not innate, and take time to cultivate. Closely intertwined with the notion of civic speaking is the notion of *civic listening*. I have written elsewhere that civic listening is central to republican forms of deliberation and, as such, forms an important component of the deliberative aim of civic education (Peterson, 2009). The clearest illustration of civic listening comes from Benjamin Barber (1998: 118), who asserts that '[T]he public not only has a voice, but an ear: the skills of listening are as important as the skills of talking', and that '...talk as communication... involves receiving as well as expressing, hearing as well as speaking, and emphasizing as well as uttering' (2003: 174). Related to the notion of civic listening is a second attribute necessary for understanding the interests of others – *civic empathy*. Again, the work of Benjamin Barber (2003: 175) is useful. He explains that the process involves a commitment that 'I will put myself in his place. I will try to understand. I will strain to hear what makes us alike, I will listen for a common rhetoric evocative of a common purpose or a common good'. In educational terms, empathy has been the subject of a great deal of discussion in relation to history education (see, for example, Wineburg, 2001), and has received some attention within social studies in the USA (Davis et al., 2001),[73] but is not always recognized explicitly within programmes for civic education. This is surprising, given the prerequisite for effective republican deliberative democracy that citizens enter dialogical forums in order that they come to understand the perspectives and interests which others hold dear. Republican models of citizenship suggest that pupils should learn to empathize not only with the interests of others, but also with the public interest, particularly when these may be in conflict with their own. As citizens interact, they are required to take on board and reflect upon how their actions and interests affect other citizens, as well as the manner in which other citizens are affected by actions of the state. In this sense, the empathy envisaged is civic and does not degenerate into sympathy or, worse still, pity[74] (cf. Davis, 2001: 3). This robust concept of civic empathy involves pupils in developing a knowledge and understanding of contexts and personal narratives (cf. Yeager and Foster, 2001), and is concerned with pupils understanding the interests of others from the perspective of others (Davis, 2001).

Whilst republican models of citizenship place a high premium on deliberation with others, they also account for the *internal reflection* that occurs within citizens when they engage in dialogue. Recognition of the internal-reflective element of deliberation holds significance educationally, particularly in terms of the need to *reflect* upon citizenship experiences in a meaningful way (Peterson, 2009). This aims at more than a simplistic evaluation of what went well and what did not. Rather it approaches the process which Dewey (1933: 9) describes as the 'active, persistent and careful consideration of any belief or supposed form of knowledge in the light of grounds that support it and further conclusions to which it tends'. This reminds us that when pupils engage in dialogue with each other, they are likely to be involved in reflecting upon and amending their views, based on the interests and evidence they are subjected to. This will inevitably involve a number of complex, and not always comfortable, stages, including the challenging of prejudices, the development of new prejudices and the changing of opinions as a result of new ideas and information. The processes involved are likely to be demanding on pupils, and will involve both cognitive and affective domains.

In addition to the composition of democratic communication, civic republican models of citizenship are useful in shedding light on what the aim of such dialogical interaction may be. In Chapter 5 it was suggested that republican approaches to deliberation have typically sought to combine dialogical interaction based on certain procedural criteria with a concern for the substantive outcomes achieved. This commitment to consensus through deliberation can also be identified in the work of the Swedish National Agency for Education (2000; cited in Englund, 2006: 504–5) which claimed that deliberative practice within education should include 'an endeavour to ensure that each individual takes a stand by listening, deliberating, seeking arguments and evaluating, while at the same time there is a collective effort to find values and norms that everyone can agree upon'. It was further argued that instrumental republican thought prioritizes the procedural element of deliberation and conceives of the general aim of deliberation in terms of political agreements. In contrast, intrinsic republican models place greater emphasis on the role deliberative practice can play in helping citizens to come to understand certain shared, substantive values that inform and bond civic communities.

The central distinction within republican thinking between agreed principles and shared values reminds us that involving pupils in deliberative practices can be structured around two distinct learning outcomes[75] (Peterson, 2009). In the first instance, participation in deliberative practices may aim at ensuring that pupils *learn the shared values of their political communities*. This understanding is based on the intrinsic republican model, and has parallels with communitarian conceptions of education. Pupils would be involved in coming to understand those shared values, based on a common political history and culture, which have already been formed by the political community. Understood in this way, civic education would involve the transmission to young people of core, shared political values, which they come to understand through dialogical interaction. Wringe (1988: 282–3) explains this in the following way: '[T]o speak of a group's values may be to imply that the holding of those values is definitive of membership of the group in question. Not to be committed or to conform to those values is simply not to belong to the group'. The difficulty in providing a basis for, and content of, certain specified values has informed a second learning outcome of pupil engagement in deliberation as part of civic education. Involvement in deliberative citizenship education may require pupils to learn *how deliberation concerning certain values and principles may benefit from unforced dialogue, within which unforced agreement may be reached*. This involves pupils in coming to shape and forge their own understandings of values, which become agreed within the context of the classroom or school community. It is this sense of deliberation which instrumental republicans would understand as central to civic education, with pupils expected not only to 'tolerate and respect others, but to engage with them' in order to understand their interests (Maynor, 2003: 183). For this reason, instrumental republicans understand dialogue and compromise as essential to civic education (Skinner, 1996; Pettit, 1997; Maynor, 2003). It is this second form of deliberative education that largely resonates with curricular approaches to civic education in Western democratic nations. Pupils are expected to be engaged in discussion concerning the meaning and importance of certain concepts deemed inimical to effective civic engagement. This is summarized by the Council of Europe (cited in Bottery, 2003: 116, emphasis in the original; cf. Halstead and Pike, 2006) which asserted that *'Education for Democratic Citizenship* is not mainly and essentially the inculcation of democratic norms, but more essentially the development of reflective and creative actors, the strengthening of the ability to participate actively and to question'. In effect, pupils are asked to account for the importance of these values within wider political communities, whilst also articulating their own understandings within their own political communities, including perhaps that of the school (Peterson, 2009).

Seeking democratic consensus through deliberation has much value in the classroom and in whole-school settings, but the nature of this value requires further analysis. The respective learning outcomes outlined above – the first based on shared values, the second on unforced political agreements – are likely to result in differentiated goals and pedagogies for civic education. They suggest that governments, schools, teachers, parents and communities need to be mindful as to the precise purpose of requiring and encouraging pupils to deliberate on public and community matters. This focus is one which may involve more sustained and rigorous thinking about the potential benefits that different republican accounts of consensus confer. It is also likely to involve the replacement of a simple skills-based approach to dialogue, particularly those approaches which value only those skills easily quantifiable in learning outcomes, in favour of generating for pupils more fluid, open and effective forms of deliberative experience. Teachers and schools should be mindful as well that, as research conducted in the United States suggests, 'public deliberation is more than "just talk". It is an important aspect of democratic citizenship, not only in its own right, but also in its ability to stimulate and facilitate further political and civic action' (Jacobs et al., 2009).

Conclusion

A feature common to a large number of civic education programmes and initiatives in Western democracies over the last twenty years has been the structuring of such education around the concept of citizenship. Most of these programmes of education for citizenship have used the language of civic republicanism and, and we have seen here, there has been much interest in teaching pupils about civic obligations, the common good, civic virtue and deliberative practices. The suggestion I have made here is that these terms, as they are used within civic republican theory, are not static and unitary. Although they often use the same language, intrinsic republicans have in mind different understandings of these core republican principles from those of instrumental republicans. That such terms can be understood differently raises questions and issues of interest to civic educators that relate to the aims and purposes of their endeavour. At times, civic education programmes use the language of republicanism with a lack of clarity about the actual meanings which are inferred and intended. We have seen how these key republican concepts, when considered in terms of civic education, can be suggestive of rather different foci in terms of depth and permanence. An important task for civic education programmes drawing on civic republican language is, therefore, to seek greater clarity in both the language used and the intentions behind it.

7
A Civic Republican Theory
of Civic Education?

As the arguments in the previous chapter have suggested, there is a strong sense in which civic education curricular programmes and initiatives in a number of Western democratic nations are influenced by a civic republican agenda. Is it possible, therefore, to delineate and clearly elucidate a singular and unified civic republican theory for civic education? Given the complexity of contemporary civic republican standpoints, which can at best be simplified into two differing strands, I doubt that such a task is possible, beyond a set of broad commitments. There is great value, however, in educationalists familiarizing themselves with these civic republican commitments and, in addition, with the key debates around them, to think more clearly about the nature, goals and content of civic education programmes. To do this will not necessarily present clear and finite answers, but instead will provide a range of questions, issues and ideas which will provoke further deliberation. The first task of this concluding chapter is to summarize the main tenets of civic republican models of citizenship, each of which raise significant issues for how we approach the aims, purposes and content of civic education. The second task of this chapter is to consider, in brief terms, additional areas of civic republican thought which have so far not received detailed attention and which seem to me to have the potential to provide an even fuller and more rounded republican agenda for civic education. In considering these, I focus on the three concerns of pluralism, globalization and patriotism, and point to the need for further investigation of the ways in which civic republicanism can conceive these concerns. At the end of the chapter, a conclusion provides a summary of the main arguments of the book.

Civic republican models of citizenship

Civic republican political thought is not an easily definable entity. The principles and ideas which comprise civic republican commitments find expression in a range of political writings. Whilst some proponents, such as Michael Sandel and Philip Pettit, offer sustained republican theories for the contemporary age, others include some elements of republican thought in their work whilst rejecting others. Nor is civic republicanism clearly related to, or easily differentiated from, other leading theoretical positions within political science, such as liberalism and communitarianism. Whilst some (Heater, 1999, for example) consider *a* civic republican model of citizenship as a simple concept not requiring further analysis, others (including myself, as I have argued here) point towards greater complexity and disagreement within the field. Nevertheless, there are commonalities that suggest that civic republicanism is more than a simply burgeoning (or re-surfacing) province of political thought. Civic republicans are united in their call for a re-awakening of the civic mind through dedication to the practice of citizenship, and recognize that liberal models of freedom as non-interference are limited. They remind us that there is an important and necessary public life beyond our private interests, and that engagement in this public life carries with it a number of benefits. This public life, according to the republican thesis, is one characterized by practice, deliberation and an interest in the common good of the political community. Civic republicanism therefore represents something of a call to action. A central suggestion advanced throughout this book is that this civic republican vision is dependent upon, and is therefore intimately linked to, educational processes. The type and depth of civic education which the civic republican project both necessitates and entails is complex. It occurs through a range of systems and processes which are at times formal and at others informal. In other words, republicans recognize that in their lives citizens are subject to a complex of experiences which shape (either to build or to limit) the extent and nature of their engagement in public life. I believe there to be five summarizing tenets of contemporary civic republican models of citizenship. Given the increasing prominence of a civic republican agenda within civic education in Western democratic nations, critical engagement with each of these will be of benefit for those with an interest in forms of education for citizenship.

The replacement or supplementing of the liberal notion of freedom as non-interference with notions of freedom as self-government or freedom as non-domination: Civic republicans challenge the orthodoxy of the liberal notion of freedom as non-interference. Rejecting the passivity and limited nature of the liberal tenet, they argue for alternative notions of freedom which place a greater expectation on citizens as active participants in public life. Republicans differ from each other, however, in stressing particular forms of freedom. For civic republicans who join communitarians in identifying an intrinsic benefit to civic life, freedom is best understood in the positive sense of self-government. For civic republicans, who join liberals in valuing the politically active life for instrumental reasons, freedom is best understood in the negative sense of the absence of domination. As I have argued here, it is these respective notions of freedom, both bound up with the principles of active citizenship, which underpin civic republican theories. In the context of civic education, freedom is an under-analyzed concept. Often cited, but largely undefined, freedom should be the concept which gives meaning to any form of civic education framed around the principle of citizenship. This, at least, is one of the central lessons that civic education can learn from a closer inspection of civic republican ideas.

The recognition of obligations which arise from the status and practice of citizenship: Civic republicans are keen to point out the obligations that result from the status of citizenship. It is the recognition and acceptance of these ties, duties and responsibilities that provides republican conceptions citizenship with their essential sense of practice. Such obligations result not just from a reciprocal relationship with rights. Rather, they exist independently of rights and in relation to citizens' sense of community. This strong sense of civic obligation to our political communities is understood by republicans as a necessary counter-balance to the individualizing and atomizing tendencies of liberal political thought and practice. In educational terms, the civic republican agenda has infused civic education programmes in the last twenty years with a common aim to develop an awareness and commitment to social and moral responsibility within young people. It was noted in the introduction that a common element of civic education programmes has been the bringing together of civic knowledge with service. As a result, most civic education programmes require some sense of service to the community in the social sense of charitable and philanthropic activity or in the political sense of affecting the decision-making process in the civic realm.

The importance and role of the common good within political communities: The concept of the common good is central to civic republican thought. Although proponents of the field do not understand the concept of the common good in unified terms, republicans typically posit an interdependent and mutually advantageous relationship between individual rights and the common good. Whilst there is some sense within republican theory that the common good has a moral basis in terms of political action as the, or one of the, highest forms of living, republicans largely conceive the concept in terms of what is in the public interest. The republican call in regard to the public interest is two-fold. First, that the public interest, rather than factional interests, should find expression in the discourse and shaping of public policy, and second, that individual citizens should have a mind to the public interest, rather than simply their narrow self-interest, in their civic deliberations and actions. It is this latter element of the republican concern for the common good which finds foremost expression in civic education programmes. It is a conception, however, which owing to its continual shaping and moulding through deliberation is inherently dynamic. In other words, the common good is not static and formed, but rather is shaped and revised through civic discourse. Such discourse occurs not only within public forums, but also within the classrooms of our schools. We must remember, however, that for pupils to debate the common good and to have a mind to the public interest, they must have some understanding of the basis of and for this. The public interest can be a somewhat abstract term, which civic educators will need to consider carefully in terms of how it can be meaningfully applied to educational programmes.

The requirement that citizens possess requisite civic virtue and the view that civic virtue needs to be inculcated within the citizenry: Virtue, or more precisely civic virtue, is a problematic term for contemporary civic republicans. It is clear that republicans are concerned with the attitudes, dispositions and behaviour of citizens, and that these are guided positively toward civic concerns. It is less clear, however, whether what civic republicans have in mind can be understood, in a true and ancient sense, as virtues. This difference is not without importance. To be concerned with virtues in the classical sense is to give prominence to 'habits of the heart' and is to have a particular picture of human character and life. To be concerned with less deeply ingrained attitudes and dispositions is to suggest, albeit forcefully, that public life places particular demands on the behaviour of citizens, but not that these become ingrained features of their character. This latter claim makes less rigorous demands on citizens than does the former. Moreover, republicans do not provide a clear set of civic virtues, nor do they provide a meaningful explanation as to why civic virtues should necessarily be distinct from more personal virtues or character traits. The problematic nature of virtues within civic republican thought is mirrored in the concern for civic virtue in civic education programmes. Typically in these programmes, the term 'civic virtue' suffers from much the same problem as it does in republican theory; namely, a sense of vagueness, a thinning out of the term 'virtue', and a lack of relation to more personal character traits. These problems are heightened when civic educators seek to reject any form of character development within civic education. This reminds those with an interest in civic education to pay much greater attention, particularly in terms of curricular expression, to the moral purposes and ends of the subject.

The role and centrality of deliberative forms of political engagement as a key source of democratic practice and as a central source of legitimacy: Republicans envisage a form of politics which permits and encourages citizens to deliberate with each other on matters of public importance. This is a necessary condition of an effective political system for a number of reasons. First, through dialogue in public forums, citizens and the state come to share their own, and to learn each other's, interests. Second, whilst it recognizes difference, this deliberative practice works toward consensus, including that which constitutes the common good. Third, it is through their engagement in public debates that citizens can check and affect the work of those who hold and wield power. In this sense, deliberation forms part of the requirement of vigilance placed upon citizens. Fourth, decisions that have been made in a way which takes citizen perspectives and deliberations into account possess legitimacy precisely by virtue of their shaping and scrutinizing by citizens. A further notable feature of republican deliberation is its openness to the inclusion of a range of viewpoints (whether comprehensive or otherwise) within public discourse. Republicans do not seek to deny those beliefs based on metaphysics or expressions of faith, but instead open them up to discursive practice. In addition, republicans are not closed to the role of rhetoric within deliberative practices. Deliberative practice is a central common feature of civic education programmes. Pupils are expected to enter dialogue in order to advance their particular viewpoints and to hear the viewpoints of others. Deliberative practices extend from the classroom throughout the school, and can meaningfully comprise a number of elements concerning what is now generally termed 'pupil voice'. Republican models of citizenship remind civic educators that a number of capacities need to be fostered in pupils in order to inform their discursive practice, including empathy and reflection. Crucially, republican models also point to the idea that entering into debate and dialogue should be considered as a collective and co-operative process rather than one characterized by competition between individuals.

Toward more rounded civic republican models of citizenship?

Recent civic republican political theory is capable of providing, and to a large extent has provided, detailed models of citizenship for civic education. As I have suggested throughout this book, there is a clear civic republican agenda behind recent programmes of civic education in a number of Western democratic nations. At the present time, however, there are elements of importance to civic education which are not fully detailed in civic republican political theory and which, if fully rounded civic republican models of citizenship are to be attained, require some further consideration. I view three specific concerns of civic education as particularly prescient – the existence of plural interests, the process of globalization and the nature of patriotism. Each of these finds expression in recent civic republican thinking, but without the cohesiveness of the main commitments set out above.

It was considered in Chapter 3 that a key challenge for civic republicans, particularly those who offer an intrinsic form of the theory and in doing so advocate a particular conception of the good life, is the *existence of plural interests*. From the liberal perspective, it is the 'fact' of pluralism' which renders coercive the promotion by the state of any particular concept of the good. To restate this in alternative terms, liberals (at least of the contractual variety considered in Chapter 1) seek to prioritize individual rights over the common good. Whilst many republicans reject this and seek to reverse the relationship in favour of recognition of the good, this does not mean that they are indifferent or hostile to the expression of plural interests. The challenge republicans face is encapsulated by Michael Walzer (1998: 180) in his reflection on Sandel's republicanism: '...the plurality of cultural commitments, if they are strong commitments, will pull people away from the republic, while if they are weak, they will weaken republicanism in turn. So: what *can* be done?' It is a particular feature of contemporary republican theories that although they respond to this question, the attention they give it is rather limited. As a result, we can only make some tentative points about the republican relationship with pluralism. It is clear that republicans accept that individuals have diverse and multiple interests to which they are committed, only one of which is being a citizen of particular political community, and they do not seek to deny such differences or to assimilate them into a cohesive singular entity. For example, in his brief consideration of the challenge of plural interests, Sandel presents what is described by Connolly (1998: 210) as a form of 'civic pluralism'. In effect, he suggests that plural interests are recognized once the gaps or differences between social groups are filled with civic forums and institutions. His argument is Tocquevillian, and he claims that 'republican politics...does not despise differentiation. Instead of collapsing the space between persons, it fills this space with public institutions that gather people together in various capacities, that both separate and relate them'. Sandel (1996: 321) continues, 'these agencies of civic education inculcate the habit of attending to public things. And yet given their multiplicity, they prevent public life from dissolving into an undifferentiated whole'. Pettit (1999: 144) presents similar arguments in making the case that his republican goal of freedom as non-domination 'has a reason and a capacity to cater for the claims of those in minority cultures'. His suggestion, however, is that members of minority communities and cultures may need to be provided with specific and additional 'attention and support' in order to ensure that they are willing and able to 'share in the common republican good of non-domination – the common good, if you like, of citizenship' (145).

The recognition of diverse and plural interests is a central theme of civic education; it is also one of its most contested concerns. How concepts of multiculturalism and diversity relate to citizenship is a thorny issue, but these initial civic republican ideas of civic pluralism may be able to form the basis of an approach to diverse and heterogeneous interests within political communities that go beyond 'a pedagogy of acceptance' and pupils learning about diversity, toward pupils 'operationalising this with respect to participative skills' (Kiwan, 2008: 54). This is what Kiwan (2008: 53) has in mind when she proposes the 'concept of 'institutional' multiculturalism, which she describes as:

> a process which attempts to address issues relating to the public/private sphere distinction. This would entail an active and constructive process of ensuring a diversity of identities represented with the public professional, political and legal spheres of society, thereby challenging the assumption that ethnic and religious identities operate only in the private sphere, and that the public sphere is culturally neutral.

Civic republicans do not state explicitly a progressive approach to the recognition of plural interests, but at least hint at one in a way that keeps the good of the community intact.

A second element of citizenship to which civic republicans pay limited attention, and which has educational importance, is the ***process of globalization***. Nation-states increasingly operate in a global world, in which inter-governmental and supranational forms of governance mean that they have become interconnected. This globalizing process is mirrored in terms of media, human capital, social action and social networking. For some, the process of globalization increasingly renders national forms of government, politics and citizenship as, at best, less important and, at worst, somewhat redundant. How do civic republicans respond to this challenge? The issue of size has always been of central importance for republicans. As the exploration of the civic republican tradition in Chapter 2 suggested, whilst some (Aristotle, Cicero and Rousseau, for example) considered republican politics as attainable only in small-scale states, others (Harrington and Madison, for example) considered them applicable to larger, modern nation-states. In some ways, the challenge of globalization is a contemporary restatement of this age-old republican concern, as it centres on the extent to which the obligations and practice of republican citizenship are stretched and compromised by the enlargement of the republican state. Contemporary republicans are rather silent on this important issue. It is only in the republicanism of Sandel that the challenge (or 'obstacle' as he terms it) of globalization is really addressed in detail. Sandel (1996: 339) expresses the challenge, and his response to it, as follows:

> If the global character of the economy suggests the need for transnational forms of governance, however, it remains to be seen whether such political units can inspire the identification and allegiance – the moral and civic culture – on which democratic authority ultimately depends. In fact there is reason to doubt that they can. Except in extraordinary moments, such as war, even nation-states find it difficult to inspire the sense of community and civic engagement self-government requires.

The difficulty lies in the absence of a common cultural tradition and a sense of shared histories, which, as we have seen, are prerequisites for the form of republican citizenship to which Sandel subscribes. Sandel suggests that, in order to overcome this obstacle, there may be some benefit to be gained from fortifying 'global governance' in order to 'cultivate a corresponding sense of global, or cosmopolitan citizenship'.[76] Further variations of, and extensions to, this suggestion regarding the possibility of transnational republican governance and citizenship can be found in the work of those who seek some sort of union between cosmopolitanism and republicanism (see, for example, Bohman, 2001, 2004; Hudson, 2006).

Educationally these issues are significant, and raise the question of how pupils come to understand national and transnational allegiances of citizenship. The global dimension of civic education has been much discussed, and there is likely to be some benefit in a more detailed consideration of the extent to which civic republican models of citizenship can inform this than is possible here. The challenge for those wishing to link republicanism to civic education is to counter the position of those who deny the importance of the nation-state as the primary source of community attachment and obligation. Martha Nussbaum (1994: 3), whom Sandel cites in his consideration of the global challenge, is a notable example of this stance. Nussbaum questions the educational place of national identity in civic education, which she describes as 'a morally irrelevant characteristic'. She argues instead for a cosmopolitan form of civic education in which pupils learn that their 'primary allegiance is to the community of human beings in the entire world'. Such arguments confront republican political theory, which remains steadfast in its square-on commitment to the nation-state. A republican-informed approach to the global dimensions of civic education is likely to take as its starting point Sandel's (1996: 343) counter argument to cosmopolitans such as Nussbaum that the 'cosmopolitan ethic is wrong, not for asserting that we have certain obligations to humanity as a whole but rather for insisting that the more universal communities we inhabit must always take precedence over more particular ones'.

A third concern which is under-defined in contemporary republican theory is the idea of **patriotism**. Patriotism is a prominent feature in the republican tradition, but does not feature significantly in most contemporary formulations of the theory. The one exception to this is Maurizio Viroli (1999: 79) who cements patriotism as a key element of his republicanism and who defines it in terms of 'a charitable love of the republic (*caritas reipublicae*) and of one's fellow citizens (*caritas civium*)'. Viroli presents patriotism as a form of glue which bonds the republic together in a similar way to religion. In fact, Viroli goes so far as to argue that a properly constituted form of patriotism within the citizenry may, in fact, render any civic benefits of religion redundant.

Whilst many would question this suggestion, there is much of interest in Viroli's republican patriotism. First, Viroli (1999: 86) is keen to draw a distinction between patriotism and nationalism, suggesting that '[C]lassical political writers were quite clear on this point: the political and cultural values of the fatherland differ from the non-political values of the nation'. It is clear, as is the case with any contemporary notion of patriotism, that Viroli is keen to avoid charges of supporting a negative, narrow and uncritical form of nationalism. Second, and for this reason, Viroli advocates a commitment to 'civic patriotism' which is not blind and uncritical, but rather is 'seasoned by a sense of proportion and a healthy dose of irony and doubt' (86). Third, and here there are clear links to educational processes, Viroli reinforces the recurring republican principle that the capacities required of citizens do not necessarily occur naturally by asserting that the 'most daunting problem that republican politics faces remains [the] issue of causing, encouraging, and diffusing the rebirth of a civic patriotism' (92). It is precisely this inculcation of a sense of patriotism that has gained recent attention in the field of civic education. Indeed, this burgeoning work has some similarities with Viroli's position in that there is a sense in which patriotism needs to be developed in citizens, and that critical and open forms of patriotism are preferred to, and are differentiated from, blind nationalism. This distinction is expressed clearly in relation to the teaching of patriotism in American schools by Michael Merry (2009: 1), which in his view is characterized by '[A] myopic understanding of one's national history as well as its contemporary role in a globalized society; [A]n unhealthy attitude of superiority relative to other cultures and polities; [and] [A] coerced (rather than freely given) sense of attachment to one's homeland'. In contrast, the former and more acceptable form of patriotism that might be taught embrace 'what is wonderful about one's homeland on the understanding that its ideals extend to all citizens irrespective of one's color, sexual orientation, creed or political affiliation' and accepts that where 'it is sensibly allowed, critical patriotism will foster the capacity to express dissent and moral outrage' (p. 2).[77] Commentators like Merry support the teaching of patriotism in schools in a way in which republicans are likely to support. Patriotism is inclusive and critical, but remains focused on a commitment to, and love of, the republic. The question remains as to the extent to which a clear republican meaning of patriotism is able (and perhaps is required) to support the other main republican commitments considered in this book.

Conclusion

The importance of educating citizens into their role is a longstanding feature of the civic republican tradition. It is a process which starts in childhood and continues throughout adult life. Contemporary republicans make use of this historical republican idea to inform their own ideas about the formative project which lies behind any successful application of republican principles of citizenship and governance. As has been pointed out on a number of occasions throughout this book, the development of citizens with the requisite knowledge, skills and capacities to play an active and purposeful role in public life is not the preserve of schooling and the formal education system alone, but rather results from a interconnected set of processes and practices which act upon citizens as they fulfil their civic role. We must be mindful from an educational point of view, however, that such interconnectedness is not lost. As Freeman Butts (2006: 15) starkly points out 'schools alone cannot instill these necessary values of personal obligation and responsibility when other major social institutions concentrate on promoting their private interests'. This reminds us that more needs to be done to understand how what goes on in our schools in the way of civic education draws upon, relates to, and combines with other formative processes that act on young people and adults as they proceed through life. To make such connections places a particular, although I would argue a necessary, burden on schools and teachers. Civic republican models of citizenship, when thought through and not treated uncritically, open up the possibility for models of citizenship that value these interconnections and that, as such, have much to offer civic educators. My aim here has been to introduce the work and ideas of contemporary civic republicans to civic educators in an accessible way, and to point to some of the issues within the field which may impact on curricular intentions, curricular policy and, to a lesser extent, on curricular implementation.

Whilst the focus here has been on the issues raised by civic republicanism for civic education in schools, we should not forget that there is an increasing concern in a number of nations to discover (or more correctly, in some instances, to rediscover) the role of further and higher education institutions in developing citizenship amongst students. Recognition that education for citizenship should be part of further, higher and lifelong learning reminds us that, when the existence of civic decline in the nation's youth is lamented, what we are really suggesting is that there is a need to engender the capacity for citizenship, not just in pupils in schools, but in the citizenry more widely. As Barber (1998:

217) asserts so potently, any observation about the societal 'illiteracy of the young turns out to be our own reflected back to us with embarrassing force'. In other words, attempts to engender civic capacities in young people are likely to suffer if they observe in adults a general trend toward incivility as well as a lack of civic engagement in society more generally. The civic republican tradition reminds us that it is to education (understood in general terms) that societies must look to address such concerns. As Thomas Jefferson (cited in Barber, 1998: 175fn1) suggested,'[T]here is no safe depository of the ultimate powers of the society but the people themselves... and if we think them not enlightened enough to exercise their control with a wholesome discretion, the remedy is not to take it from them, but to inform their discretion by education'. At a time of increasing complexity and political-economic challenge, there are compelling reasons to suggest that national governments will increasingly look to 'the people themselves' to play a more active role in their political communities. For this reason, there is a strong possibility that civic republican ideas will find increasing recognition within both political and public philosophy over the coming years.

This book began by pointing to a concern that through the use of a common language, civic republican ideas of citizenship are, at times explicitly and at times implicitly, informing and shaping civic education programmes in a number of Western democratic nations, sometimes without an accompanying analysis of what the precise nature of such ideas may be. We have seen that any attempt to operationalize civic republican ideas into civic education (or indeed education more generally) is not unproblematic, and requires a careful consideration of differences within the field. I have also suggested that in order to make the most of the potential which civic republican theories offer civic educators by way of models of citizenship, more thought is required as to their content, nature and form. Whilst no full and complete civic republican theory of civic education currently exists, I hope to have shown here that there is a great deal within civic republicanism that will be of interest to civic educators. In this respect, the analysis and suggestions offered here should be considered in a republican spirit – as intended to invite deliberation from others about the value and extent of appropriating civic republican ideas for the ends of civic education. That readers view them in this way is, at least, my hope.

Notes

1. This point is a notable feature of civic republican ideas, but it is not specific to republican politics. John Rawls (2001: 146) makes a similar point from his liberal position: '[T]hose who grow up in [a politically liberal] society will in good part form their conception of themselves as citizens from the public political culture and from the conceptions of the person and society implicit in it... The conceptions of the person and society are more fully articulated in the public charter of the constitution and more clearly connected with the basic rights and liberties it guarantees. Citizens acquire an understanding of the public political culture and its traditions of interpreting basic constitutional values. They do so by attending to how these values are interpreted by judges in important constitutional cases and reaffirmed by political parties'.
2. Arthur (2003: 3) terms this concern a 'litany of alarm'. Writing in the US, and citing the work of Barber (1992) and Coles (1993), Nash (1997: 35) challenges the view that young people have become increasingly apathetic. He argues that he could 'conceivably postulate that America is in the midst of a "character *incline*", given the rise of volunteerism and community service among young people'. Davies and colleagues (2005: 334) have made a similar point in relation to character education, contending that commentators 'make use of this "litany of alarm"...without any real basis for doing so' and that there is 'some evidence that there is no crisis'.
3. Professor David Hargreaves (1996: 15) expresses this link in the following terms: '[A]ctive citizens are as political as they are moral; moral sensibility derives in part from political understanding; political apathy spawns moral apathy'.
4. John Maynor (2003: 3) makes a similar point, stating that his own theory of republicanism is influenced by a concern for 'the operationalization of political philosophy and the degree to which important theoretical considerations may become ill considered as they become concrete policy remedies'. He continues: 'I am alarmed by the degree to which the ideals and values of classical republicanism are spread around by both philosophers and politicians without a clear and consistent sense of their historical pedigree and their relevance to the modern world'.
5. See, for example, Callan (1997); Arthur (2000); Keeney (2007).
6. Kymlicka (2002: 287) claim that '"new" debates about citizenship are often "old" debates over justice dressed up in new clothing' reminds us that whilst civic republican ideas hinge on the central principle of citizenship, they are not blind to wider conceptions of justice.
7. According to Viroli (1999: 4), civic republicanism is often mistakenly categorized as a 'theory of participatory democracy. It is, rather, a theory of political liberty'.
8. This does not mean that Constant understood the liberty of the ancients and the liberty of the moderns to be mutually exclusive. Rather, for Constant (1988: 327), a key task was 'to learn how to combine the two together' (cf. Maynor, 2003).

9. See, in particular, Maynor (2003) and Viroli (1999).

10. The type of claim Viroli is making should not be taken to mean that civic republicans are in some way against the nourishment and benefit which citizens can gain from their experiences and activities in the private scheme. Republicans would agree with Macedo's (1990: 39) view that 'the benefits of private citizenship are not to be sneezed at: they place certain basic goods (security, prosperity, and freedom) within the grasp of nearly all, and that is nothing less than a fantastic human achievement'. The claim of republicans is that citizens need to supplement this private enjoyment with action in the civic realm.

11. It is worth briefly noting that this perception of civic decline has found representation in the discourse of political leaders in a number of nations over the last two decades. Though few would label him as a civic republican, in his inaugural address as President of the United States, George W. Bush (2001) urged Americans to take an active role in civic life: '[W]hat you do is as important as anything government does. I ask you to seek a common good beyond your comfort, to defend needed reforms against easy attacks, to serve your nation, beginning with your neighbour. I ask you to become citizens. Citizens, not spectators. Citizens, not subjects. Responsible citizens, building communities of service and a nation of character... When this spirit of citizenship is missing, no government program can replace it. When this spirit is present, no wrong can stand against it'. For Bush, the educational need was clear: '[W]e are bound by ideals that move us beyond our background, lift us above our interests and teach us what it means to be citizens. Every child must be taught these principles... If we do not turn the hearts of children toward knowledge and character, we will lose their gifts and undermine their idealism'. Bush is not alone in using the rhetoric of greater citizen involvement in public affairs. Elected in 2010, the Prime Minister of the United Kingdom, David Cameron (2010), has made clear that 'citizenship isn't a transaction, in which you put your taxes in and get your services out. It's a relationship – you're part of something bigger than yourself and it matters what you think and you feel and you do'. Such sentiments are common to the discourse of a number of political leaders of Western democratic nations in recent times.

12. Although the focus in this book is on civic education in Western nations, there has also been a great deal of significant interest in the subject in a number of non-Western nations including Japan, Pakistan, Singapore, South Korea and Hong Kong. For two excellent collected editions which include coverage of developments in civic education across a number of nations see Arthur, Davies and Hahn (2008) and Reid, Gill and Sears (2010). Civic education practices across many nations have also been the subject of two extensive international comparative studies in recent years through the IEA CIVED study (1994–2002) and the IEA ICCS study (2009).

13. In France, civic education (*Éducation civique, juridique et sociale*) was introduced into the curriculum of *collèges* (11–15 year olds) in 1999 (Ruget, 2006).

14. In Germany, civic education comes under the jurisdiction of state governments and is further supported by the Federal Agency for Civic Education.

Most states have their own agency for civic education, with civic education often taught through classes in civics and/or social studies.

15. Civic education, based around the concept of citizenship, is not a subject *per se* in the National Curriculum in Northern Ireland, but rather is a composite part of some of the nine Areas of Learning to be followed by pupils at Key Stage Three (11–14 year olds) and Key Stage Four (14–16 year olds), most notably 'Learning for Life and Work' and 'Environment and Society'.

16. In Ireland, the subject 'Civic, Social and Political Education' became part of the mandatory curriculum within the Junior Certificate examination taken by pupils at the end of their junior cycle (12–15) in the late 1990s (Bryan, 2010).

17. In Scotland, education for citizenship represents one of the four 'capacities' to be developed in all children in the *Curriculum for Excellence*. Education for citizenship is not a stand-alone subject, but rather is a cross-curricular theme and goal as well as forming part of the subject 'Modern Studies' (for 5–14 year olds). This was proceeded by Learning and Teaching Scotland's (2002) paper *Education for Citizenship in Scotland: A Paper for Discussion and Development*, which Biesta (2008: 39) identifies as 'the most detailed account [in Scotland] of what citizenship is and how education can contribute to the development of the capacity for citizenship', and as 'clearly influence[ing] the positioning of citizenship within *Curriculum for Excellence*. The *Education for Citizenship* (LTS, 2002: 10) document emphasized the cross-curricular and whole-school nature of the subject in Scotland, asserting that 'each young person's entitlement to education for citizenship can be secured through combinations of learning experiences set in the daily life of the school, discrete areas of the curriculum, cross-curricular experiences and activities involving links with the local community'.

18. In Wales, education for citizenship forms part of the subject 'Personal and Social Education', which became a statutory requirement for students from 5–16 year olds in state schools (see Andrews and Mycock, 2007).

19. The *Statements of Learning* document makes clear that it is 'not a curriculum in itself' but rather is 'primarily intended for curriculum developers'.

20. The aim of producing responsible citizens also featured in two previous statements of Australian educational goals: the Declarations on National Goals for Schooling in the Twenty-First Century issued in 1988 (Hobart) and 1999 (Adelaide) (cf. Hughes, Print and Sears, 2009).

21. Honohan (2002) approaches her own historical interpretation by identifying four key periods in the development of the civic republican tradition. Each of these periods, Honohon argues, provides us with a central concept of civic republicanism. The first period, that of ancient Greece and Rome, saw the development of *virtue* in the writings of Aristotle and Cicero. The second period, from the fifteenth to the seventeenth centuries, saw the development of *freedom* in the writings of Machiavelli and Harrington. The third period, in the eighteenth century, saw the development of *participation* in the writings of Madison and Rousseau. The fourth, contemporary, period has seen the development of *recognition* in the writings of Arendt (1963) and Taylor

(1995). For alternative historical analyses, see Oldfield (1990), Rahe (1992), Skinner (1992), Held (1996, 1997), Honohan (2002) and Maynor (2003).

22. Not all commentators agree on the exact composition of the republican tradition. Whilst Held (1996, 1997) locates both Marx and Hegel within his depiction of the 'tradition', Honohan omits them from hers, but includes Mary Wollstonecraft.

23. In considering differing definitions of '[w]hom shall we call a citizen?' Aristotle (1992: 1275a2, 169) mentions the lack of a common definition. In setting out his own position, he rejects residence as the central criterion for citizenship, as 'resident foreigners' and slaves would thus be considered as citizens. In addition, and more importantly, Aristotle also rejects 'those who have access to legal processes, who may prosecute or be prosecuted' as this status may, at least partially, be open to what he terms a 'resident foreigner' through the terms of a 'commercial treaty'.

24. In the *Politics* he argues that '[N]o one would dispute the fact that it is a lawgiver's prime duty to arrange for the education of the young. In states where this is not done the quality of the constitution suffers' (1992: 1337a11: 452).

25. The full list of issues reads as follows: 'decisions as to war and peace, the making and dissolving of alliances, legislation, the penalties of death, exile and confiscation of goods, the choosing of officials, and the scrutiny of their conduct on expiry of tenure' (1992: IV, xiv. 1298a3. 277). In the *Art of Rhetoric* (1991: 1.4, 1359b. 84; emphasis in original) Aristotle identified the five 'most important subjects of deliberation' as *'revenue, war and peace, the defence of the realm, imports and exports* and *legislation'*.

26. Throughout the majority of Book Two of *The Republic*, Cicero outlines his ideal constitution with clear reference to the development of the governmental system of Rome (Book Two, 1–64: 35–56). Cicero argues that '[A]s for using my own state as a model, that had value, not for defining the best constitution (for that could have been done without a model), but for illustrating, from the actual experience of the greatest state, what was being described in my theoretical exposition' (*On the Republic*. 1998, Book Two, 66: 57). Cicero's preference for a mixed system of government is derived from the influence on his work of Polybius, a Roman historian of the second century BC (Honohan, 2002: 35).

27. Cicero contends that '[P]rovided the bonds hold firm, which in the first place fastened the people to each other in the fellowship of a community, any of these three may be, not indeed perfect, nor in my view the best, but at least tolerable, though one may be preferable to another. A just and wise king, or a select group of leading citizens, or the populace itself (though that is the least desirable type) can still, it seems, ensure a reasonably stable government, provided no forms of wickedness or greed find their way into it' (*On the Republic*. 1998, Book One, 42: 20). As part of the dialogue, Cicero actually devotes a substantial section of Book One to considering the defence of the three 'simple' forms of government (*On the Republic*. 1998, Book One, 46–64: 21–30). Of the three forms of government, despite recognizing its limitations, Cicero maintains his preference for a monarchy. This is based on the supposition that for man to be just, one element, namely reason, must be in control. Cicero also argues, through the dialogical exchanges

between Scipio (the main protagonist) and Laelius, that in practical areas of life citizens take individual control. This is correlated with the needs of one man, the just monarch, to control the decisions of the State (25–30).

28. Cicero's considerations of the limitations of democracies are insightful, and are clearly aimed at the Athenian model. Although the main interlocutor for Cicero's ideas in the *On the Republic* is Scipio, it is through Laelius that the criticism of unrestrained democracy is most forceful '[A]ctually there is no state to which I should be quicker to refuse the name of republic than the one which is totally in the power of the masses ... I don't see why there is any stronger case for applying the name of republic to a state enslaved by the mob ... That rabble is just as tyrannical as one man, and all the more repellent in that there is nothing more monstrous than a creature which masquerades as a public and usurps its name. (1998: 73).

29. The idea of a government of laws and not men has its roots in writers including Sallust and Livy as well as Cicero (Wirszubski, 1960; Skinner, 1998; Dagger, 2004).

30. Black (1997: 647–648) challenges the separation of civic republicanism and Christianity within commentaries on historical political thought, arguing that '...the Christian community started as a variant form of republic' and that early 'Christian theology referred unambiguously to a public life and a common good'.

31. Aquinas (1981: I–II q. 62. a. 1 – q. 63. a. 4. 87) described the four cardinal virtues as balancing certain faculties which guide human action. Prudence balanced the mind, justice balanced will, temperance the desire for pleasure and fortitude the desire to avoid pain or displeasure. Aquinas supplemented the learning of 'acquired virtues' through habituation with the theological principle of 'infused virtues', which are produced by good within humans.

32. In a speech to the British Humanist Association in 2006, the political theorist and architect of citizenship education in England, Bernard Crick, suggested that '[C]itizenship is secular, on historical and philosophical grounds' (cited in Arthur, Gearon and Sears, 2010: 2).

33. For an accessible analysis of the complexities of the political systems within Italian republics at this time, see Viroli (1999).

34. Although Pocock's analysis centres largely on Machiavelli, he also identifies elements of civic republican thought in the work of Girolamo Savonarola, Francesco Guicciardini, Donato Giannotti.

35. A number of writers have argued that Machiavelli's *The Prince* has been over emphasized at the expense of the *Discourses*, and that a reconsideration of the latter highlights a number of interesting arguments relating to civic republican ideas (Pocock, 1975; Skinner, 1981; Held, 1996).

36. Cicero's prioritizing of the liberty and freedom of the republic rather than the individual was also an important element of Machiavelli's main political manifesto *The Prince*. In *The Prince* Machiavelli (1974: 515; cf. Honohan, 2002: 54) observes that '[W]hen the safety of one's country wholly depends on the decision to be taken, no attention should be paid either to justice or injustice, to kindness or to cruelty, or to its being praiseworthy or ignominious. On the contrary, every other consideration being set aside, that alternative should be wholeheartedly adopted which will save the life and preserve the freedom of one's country'.

37. Although Machiavelli did not employ the term 'civil religion', in *The Discourses* he makes positive reference to the pagan religion of the ancient Roman republics (Bellah and Hammond, 1974: 447).

38. Although their main focus, Harrington is not the only English republican identified by those seeking to present republican historiographies. Central texts which have considered the field of 'English' republicanism, which Scott (2007: 1) considers as 'largely a creation of the past half-century', include Patrick Collinson, *De Republica Anglorum: Or, History with the Politics Put Back* (Cambridge, 1990); Mark Goldie, 'The Unacknowledged Republic: Officeholding in Early Modern England', in Tim Harris (ed.), *The Politics of the Excluded, c.1500–1850.* Pp. 153–194; Blair Worden, 'Classical Republicanism and the Puritan Revolution', in V. Pearl, H. Lloyd-Jones and B. Worden (eds.), *History and Imagination* (Oxford, 1981); Markku Peltonen, *Classical Humanism and Republicanism in English Political Thought 1570–1640* (Cambridge, 1995).

39. This characterization of Harrington's work as a reaction to Hobbes is challenged by Wettergreen (1988: 667, 682) who suggests that, particularly in relation to psychology, 'Harrington was Hobbesian in certain important respects', and that 'Harrington's... critique of Hobbes... is so polemical that its foundation in Hobbesian principles is obscured'. When the literature on Harrington is consulted, a range of influences can be identified, including: Plato (Blitzer, 1970), Aristotle (Pocock, 1975; Cotton, 1981), Machiavelli (Raab, 1964; Pocock, 1975), and Cicero (Skinner, 1998) (cf. Scott, 2007: 3).

40. In making this claim Harrington draws a distinction between the citizens of Lucca and those of Constantinople who, whilst subject to the rule of laws, he did not consider to be free in the fullest sense because the Sultan was above the law and, as such, was able to dominate citizen arbitrarily.

41. The precise virtues which Rousseau understood as central to this process are hard to identify. Rather than setting out a list of virtues Rousseau employed the term virtue to largely mean 'self-forced obedience to the law' (Melzer, 1990: 103; cf. Reizert, 2003: 12).

42. Madison (1992a: 47) asserts that a 'point of difference' between republic and democratic government is 'the greater number of citizens and extent of territory which may be brought within the compass of republican than of democratic government; and it is this circumstance principally which renders factious combinations less to be dreaded in the former than in the latter'.

43. Rahe (1992) viewed Madison's arguments for an extended republic as a fundamental rejection of Montesquieu's commitment to the limitation of the size of a republic. Montesquieu (1989: 124 [Book VIII, ch. 16; cited in Dagger, 2004: 170) argued that in large states '...the common good is sacrificed to a thousand considerations; it is subordinated to exceptions; it depends on accidents. In a small one, the public good is better felt, better known, lies nearer to each citizen; abuses are less extensive and consequently less protected'.

44. It was considered in Chapter One that writers broadly characterized as falling within the field of communitarianism have sought to reverse both the dominance of procedural liberal ideas within Western political theory and the problems associated with an increased focus on rights and a decreasing sense of civic duty, largely by stressing the obligations that citizens possess.

It was also suggested that, to a large extent because of this communitarian critique, a number of prominent liberal writers have looked to provide a more robust account of citizen obligation.

45. For Dagger (1999: 182), the relationship between Sandel's earlier and later work is so close that *Democracy's Discontent* should be considered as '*The Procedural Republic* writ large'.

46. The American political scientist Sheldon Wolin (1960: 43) explains that '[C]itizenship provides what other roles cannot, namely an integrative experience which brings together the multiple role activities of the contemporary person and demands that the separate roles be surveyed from a general point of view'.

47. The term 'weaker' derives from Sandel's (1982: 148) critique of liberal notions of community. The 'instrumental' form is weak because 'individuals regard social arrangements as a necessary burden and co-operate only for the sake of pursuing their private ends' (cf. Dagger, 1997).

48. Richard Dagger (1997: 79) uses this term in his theory of republican liberalism in relation to the need for liberal principles of political obligation to counter relationships between state and citizen based on provider-consumer. Dagger argues that a 'positive way to secure cooperation [within liberal states] is to cultivate the desire to do one's part in the cooperative endeavour'.

49. Raz (1995: 37) has argued that, understood as intrinsically important but not as the highest goal of human existence, political participation is best viewed as a '*framing* common good' (cf. Honohan, 2002: 156; for a discussion of republican approaches to the common good, see Honohan, 2002: 150–158).

50. A further and alternative argument regarding the abandonment of liberal neutrality is advanced by Dagger (1997: 187) in his liberal-republican theory, where he contends that '[A]nother possibility is that republicanism and liberalism *are* compatible...but only if one is willing to surrender the belief that liberalism is a neutral doctrine'. Dagger (1997: 192–3) argues for a liberal excellence which contains a 'distinctive' conception of the good which 'lies largely in the individual's ability to judge what is good'. This involves, however, a different ideal of excellence based on being good at something which is valued, rather than something which conforms to an external, objective foundation.

51. The methods advocated by Rousseau to produce commitment to the general will are multiple and complex. For a more detailed discussion of these in relation to civic republicanism, see Dagger, 1997: 83–97.

52. Connolly (1998: 206) makes this point in direct relation to Sandel's work suggesting that 'we hear...too little about specific virtues appropriate to the contemporary world'.

53. The concept of civility is not specific to republican political thought, and can be found in wider democratic theory. In *Civility: Manners, Morals and the Etiquette of Democracy*, Stephen Carter (1998: 229) defines civility as involving '...the discipline of our passions for the sake of living in a common life with others'.

54. In *Values and Teaching: Working with Values in the Classroom*, Raths et al. (1966) advocated a system of moral education in which values were not referenced to a universal moral standard, but rather focused on clarifying

the content of their own personal values. For Raths et al., the concern of moral education was perceived to be the development of *internally* consistent moral values. In this model, students were encouraged to discuss and debate the nature of their own moral views, whilst the values themselves remained 'situated', 'personal' and 'individual' (Yu, 2004: 50).

55. There are a number of detailed analyses of deliberation in the practice of particular nations. See, for example, John Uhr (1998) *Deliberative Democracy in Australia*; John Gatsil and Peter Levine (2005) (eds.) *The Deliberative Democracy Handbook: Strategies for Effective Civic Engagement in the Twenty-First Century*; Mark Warren and Hilary Pearse (2008: eds.) *Designing Deliberative Democracy: The British Columbia Citizens' Assembly*. In *Deliberation Day*, Bruce Ackerman and James Fishkin (2005) advance the idea of a new national holiday in each presidential election year in the United States, aimed at deliberation.

56. In 2001 the Organisation for Economic Co-operation and Development launched *Citizens as Partners*, a handbook on information, consultation and participation in policy-making. The use of deliberative processes and structures in practical political engagement forms the focus of the *Centre for Deliberative Democracy*, based at Stanford University, in the US (http://cdd.stanford.edu/).

57. The literature on civil society is extensive and wide-ranging. For important contributions to the field, see Cohen and Arato (1992); O'Connoll (1999) and Edwards (2004).

58. The idea of citizen juries found favour in the UK under the Labour government led by Gordon Brown (2007–2010). Speaking in 2007, Brown (BBC Today Programme 11 July) explained 'I'd like to have what are called citizens'juries, where we say to people "look, here is a problem that we are dealing with – today it's housing it could be drugs or youth services, it could be anti-social behaviour – here's a problem, this is what we are thinking about it, but tell us what you think and let's look at some of the facts, let's look at some of the challenges. Let's look at some of the options that have been tried in different countries around the world, and then let's together come to a decision about how to solve these problems". This is not sofa government, its listening to the people'.

59. This referencing of the importance for democratic engagement of participation within the structures and processes of civil society involves a wide definition of the scope of the 'political', and bears comparison with Macedo et al.'s (2005: 6–7) assertions that 'civic engagement includes any activity, individual or collective, devoted to influencing the collective life of the polity' and that 'a vibrant politics depends on a vibrant civil society'. From a republican perspective, Michelman (1988: 1531) draws similar connections in the context of the United States: 'much of the country's normatively consequential dialogue occurs outside the major, formal channels of electoral and legislative politics... [in] what we know as public life... in the encounters and conflicts, interactions and debates that are in and around town meetings, local government agencies, civic and voluntary associations, social and recreational clubs, [and] schools'.

60. The question and place of consensus has been much discussed in wider deliberative democratic theory (see, for example, Chambers, 1996; Smith

and Wales, 2000; Jacobs et al., 2009). The work of Gutmann and Thompson (2004: 7) who prioritize the 'economizing' or 'minimizing' of differences through deliberation, has been particularly influential.

61. It is worth noting here that there has been an increasing trend within wider political science to try and transcend the objective–relative dichotomy, a move on which civic republicans are largely silent. Barber (2003: 156) provides a useful example of this position in relation to his theory of Strong Democracy. He suggests that '[B]ecause it acknowledges that the condition of politics is the absence of an independent ground by which conflicts might otherwise be settled or common goods fashioned, Strong Democracy avoids reintroducing external criteria into the political process. Its central value is the autonomy of politics, and it therefore requires that participants put whatever moral codes, principles, interests, private ideas, visions, and conceptions of the good they may bring into the process as individuals as individuals or groups to the test of politics itself. This does not mean that values and ideas will not be drawn from religious and metaphysical systems of the kind offered by Christians or liberals. Rather, it means that such values will acquire their legitimacy from their political fecundity – from their acceptance into and transformation through, the democratic process'.

62. Here Pettit draws on the historical basis for viewing agreement as a regulative ideal suggested by Skinner (1996: 15–16). In particular, Pettit (1999: 189) cites Skinner's understanding that for instrumental republicans '[T]he appropriate model will always be that of dialogue, the appropriate stance a willingness to negotiate over rival intuitions concerning the applicability of evaluative terms. We strive to reach understanding and resolve disputes in a conversational way'.

63. One of the leading proponents of deliberative democracy, Joshua Cohen (1996: 106) makes a similar point: '[I]t is common ground, however, that citizens have substantial, sometimes compelling reasons for addressing public affairs. Because they do, the failure to acknowledge the weight of those reasons for the agent and to acknowledge claims to opportunities for effective influence that emerge from them reflects a failure to endorse the background idea of citizens as equal'.

64. Michael Walzer (1999: 58) describes the process as 'a particular way of thinking: quiet, reflective, open to a wide range of evidence, respectful of different views. It is a rational process of weighing the available data, conceiving alternative possibilities, arguing about relevance and worthiness, and then choosing the best policy or person'.

65. Whilst there has been much admirable comparative work in civic education, this has generally been focused on policy, the content of curricular provision, and student learning outcomes. It is the case that, at the present time, there is too little empirical research evidence to enlighten academics as to precisely what does take place within civic education classrooms and, perhaps even more importantly, how teachers themselves understand and approach the core aims and content of civic education. Despite Pajares' (1992) review of research which indicated that teachers' beliefs shape their classroom practices, current research reveals little about civic educators' perceptions of key elements of the subject discipline. This finding supports

data taken from the IEA civic education study, which suggests that teachers of civic education in England were likely to agree with the statement that 'there cannot be agreement on what should be taught in civic education' (Torney-Purta, 2005: 43). This reflection is pertinent given further evidence from the IEA Civic Education study that teachers' conceptions of citizenship may be 'inconsistent with models laid out by social studies researchers, national associations, education ministries, or community groups' (Torney-Purta et al., 2005: 37).

66. The Scottish *Curriculum for Excellence* (2004: 12; cf. Biesta, 2008: 38), for example, presents the responsible citizen as one who has 'respect for others' and who has a 'commitment to participate responsibly in political, economic, social and cultural life'. The Australian *Statement of Standards in Civics and Citizenship* includes as two of its aims 'an appreciation of the local, state, national, regional and global rights and responsibilities of citizenship and civic life' and 'the knowledge, skills and values that support active citizenship and the capacity to act as informed and responsible citizens' (MCEETYA, 2007: 2). The CIVITAS framework in America includes the need to develop 'competent and responsible participation' as central to the rationale for civic participation (Quigley and Buchanan, 1991: 5).

67. In England, the concept of the common good is referred to as a key value and disposition within the Advisory Group's Report. Citing the then Lord Chancellor, the last word of the report asserts that citizenship education should 'nurture a concern for the common good' (QCA, 1998: 61, 11.1).

68. The three others features of competent and responsible citizens are that they are 'informed and thoughtful', 'participate in their communities' and 'act politically'.

69. The Spirit of Democracy Programme (www.spiritofdemocracy.com), a co-operative project between democratic educationalists in Canada and Russia, provides an example of a curricular approach which requires pupils to actively consider democratic values as an explicit focus of learning. The values include loyalty, responsibility, freedom of speech and privacy.

70. The materials produced by the Deliberating in a Democracy (www.deliberating.org) project, based in the US but involving a number of European countries, are indicative of this approach.

71. This separation between the public concerns of civic education from the private concerns of personal development education is exemplified by the following example from England. Since the introduction of citizenship education in 2002, there has been a great deal of consternation at any attempt to blend the subject with what is known as Personal, Social and Health Education (commonly termed PSHE). The stance adopted by Chief Inspector David Bell of Her Majesty's Inspectorate (2005) is illustrative of this standpoint. Bell argued that 'PSHE is about the private, individual dimension, whereas citizenship concerns the public dimension. They do not sit easily together'.

72. In her excellent exposition of deliberation in classrooms in America, Diana Hess (2009: 17) remarks that learning takes place 'especially if the nature of talk is structured to make it more likely that people will share, hear, and interrogate a variety of different interpretations about such important

questions as what caused a problem and what the relative strengths and challenges associated with alternative solutions are'.

73. See Field (2001) for a useful summary of research into developing empathy within social studies programmes in the USA.

74. Barton and Levstik (2004: 206) draw a similar distinction in relation to history education.

75. I have drawn this distinction previously in relation to citizenship education in England, but, as I hope to demonstrate here, I believe that the two educational aims are pertinent to civic education initiatives outside England.

76. Cosmopolitanism has been defined by one of its leading proponents, David Held, as 'a way of specifying a democratic mutilayered, multilevel system of authority marked by mutilayered, multilevel citizenship enshrined by and defending the equal worth and dignity of each human being' (Thorup and Sorensen, 2004).

77. An alternative to this position is provided by Michael Hand and Joanne Pearce (2009: 77) who focus on the teaching of patriotism in British schools. In exploring the potential arguments both in favour of and against the teaching of patriotism in schools, they conclude that schools cannot ignore patriotism but 'are not in a position to promote or discourage it by rational means because compelling reasons for people to love or refrain from loving their countries are not available'. This leads them to suggest that the only justifiable course of action open to schools is to teach patriotism as a controversial issue. In other words, schools should ensure that students are presented with the arguments for and against patriotism in a fair and impartial way, allowing them to decide for themselves how they think and feel about it.

Bibliography

Ackerman, B. A. and Fishkin, J. S. (2005) *Deliberation Day*. New Haven, CT: Yale University Press.

Allen, A. and Regan, M. (1998) *Debating Democracy's Discontent: Essays on American Politics, Law, and Public Philosophy*. Oxford: Oxford University Press.

Andrews, R. and Mycock, A. (2007) 'Citizenship education in the UK: Divergence within a multi-national state', in *Citizenship Teaching and Learning*. 3(1). 73–88.

Annette, J. (1999) 'Education for citizenship, civic participation and experiential and service learning in the community', in *The School Field*. X (3/4). 85–102.

Annette, J. (2003) 'Community, politics and citizenship education', in Lockyer, A., Crick, B. and Annette, J. (eds.) *Education for Democratic Citizenship: Issues of Theory and Practice*. Aldershot: Ashgate.

Annette, J. (2005) 'Character, civic renewal and service learning for democratic citizenship in higher education', in *British Journal of Educational Studies*. 53 (3). 326–340.

Appleby, J. (1985) 'Republicanism and ideology', in *American Quarterly*. 37 (4). 461–473.

Aquinas, St. T. (1981 / [1265–1272]) *Summa Theologica: Volumes I & II*. Translated by Fathers of the English Dominican Province. Texas: Christian Classics.

Aquinas (2002) *De regimine principum*, in: R. W. Dyson (ed.) *Aquinas: political writings*. Cambridge: Cambridge University Press.

Arendt, H. (1958) *The Human Condition*. London: Cambridge University Press.

Aristotle (1991) *The Art of Rhetoric*. Lawson-Trancred, H. C. (trans.). London: Penguin.

Aristotle (1992)*The Politics*. Saunders, T. J. (ed.) London: Penguin.

Aristotle (1998) *The Nicomachean Ethics*. Ross, D. (ed.) Oxford: Oxford University Press.

Arthur, J. (1998) 'Communitarianism: What are the implications for education', in *Educational Studies*. 24 (3). 353–368.

Arthur, J. (2000) *Schools and Community: The Communitarian Agenda in Education*. London: Falmer Press.

Arthur, J. (2003) *Education with Character: The Moral Economy of Schooling*. London: Routledge.

Arthur, J. (2005) 'The re-emergence of character education in British education policy', in *British Journal of Educational Studies*. 53 (3). 239–254.

Arthur, J. (2010) *Of Good Character: Exploration of Virtues and Values in 3–25 Year Olds*. Exeter: Imprint Academic.

Arthur, J., Davies, I. and Hahn, C. (2008) *Sage Handbook of Education for Citizenship and Democracy*. London: Sage.

Arthur, J. Gearon, L. and Sears, A. (2010) *Education, Politics and Religion: Recognising the Civil and the Sacred in Education*. London: Routledge.

Association for Education in Citizenship (1936) *Education for Citizenship in Secondary Schools*. London: Oxford University Press.

Atkinson, R. (1994) *The Common Sense of Community*. London: Demos.

Bailyn, B. (1967) *The Ideological Origins of the American Revolution*. Cambridge, MA: Harvard University Press.

Barber, B. (1984) *Strong Democracy. Participatory Politics for a New Age*. Berkeley: University of California.

Barber, B. (1992) *An Aristocracy of Everyone: The Politics of Education and the Future of America*. New York: Ballantine.

Barber, B. (1996) 'Foundationalism and democracy', in Benhabib, S. (ed.) *Democracy and Difference: Contesting the Boundaries of the Political*. Princeton, NJ: Princeton University Press.

Barber, B. (1998) *A Passion for Democracy: American Essays*. Princeton, NJ: Princeton University Press.

Barber, B. (2003) *Strong Democracy. Participatory Politics for a New Age. 20th Anniversary Edition*. Berkeley: University of California.

Barber, B. and Battistoni, R. (1993) 'A season of service: introducing service learning into the liberal arts curriculum', in *Political Science*. 26(2). 235–240.

Barry, B. (1995) *Justice as Impartiality*. Oxford: Oxford University Press.

Barton, K. C. and Levstik, L. S. (2004) *Teaching History for the Common Good*. Mahwah, New Jersey: Lawrence Erlbaum Associates.

Battistoni, R. (1985) *Public Schooling and the Education of Democratic Citizens*. Jackson: University of Mississippi Press.

Bell, D. (1995) *What Does it Mean to be a Citizen?* Hansard Society / OfSTED Lecture. 17 January 2005.

Bellah, R. (2008) 'Yes he can: the case for Obama', in *Commonweal*. 14 March 2008.

Bellah, R. N. and Hammond, P. E. (1974) 'Le cinque religioni dell'Italia Moderna', in Luca, F. and Gaubard, S. R. (eds.) *Il Casa Italiano*. Milan: Garzanri editore.

Bellah, R. N., Madsen, R., Sullivan, W. M., Swidler, A. and Tipton, S. M. (eds.) (1985) *Habits of the Heart: Individualism and Commitment in American Life*. Berkely: University of California.

Benhabib, S. (1996) 'Toward a deliberative model of democratic legitimacy', in Benhabib, S. (ed.) *Democracy and Difference: Contesting the Boundaries of the Political*. Princeton, NJ: Princeton University Press.

Bennett, W. J. (1993) *The Book of Virtues: A Treasury of Great Moral Stories*. Simon & Schuster: New York.

Bennett, W. J. and Delattre, E. J. (1978) 'Moral education in schools', in *The Public Interest*. 50. 81–102.

Bentley, T. (2005) *Everyday Democracy*. London: Demos.

Berlin, I. (1998) *The Proper Study of Mankind: An Anthology of Essays*. Hardy, H. and Hausher, R. (eds.) London: Pimlico.

Bessette, J. (1980) 'Deliberative democracy: The majority principle in republican government' in Goldwin, R. (ed.) *How Democractic is the Constitution?*. Washington, D.C.: AEI Press.

Bessette, J. (1994) *The Mild Voice of Reason: Deliberative Democracy and the American National Government*. Chicago: University of Chicago Press.

Best, R (2002): Pastoral Care and Personal-Social Education - a Review of UK Research. Southwell (Notts): BERA.

Bickford. S. (1996) 'Beyond friendship: Aristotle and conflict, deliberation, and attention', in *The Journal of Politics*. 58 (2). 398–421.

Biesta, G. (2008) 'What kind of citizen? What kind of democracy? Citizenship education and the Scottish curriculum for excellence', in *Scottish Educational Review*. 40(2). 38–52.

Black, A. (1997) 'Christianity and republicanism: from St. Cyprian to Rousseau', in *American Political Science Review*. 91. 647–56.

Blattberg, C. (2000) *From Pluralist to Patriotic Politics: Putting Practice First*. Oxford: Oxford University Press.

Blitzer, C. (1970) *An Immortal Commonwealth: The Political Thought of James Harrington*. New Haven, Connecticut: Yale University Press.

Blunkett, D. (2003a) *Active Citizens, Strong Communities: Progressing Civil Renewal*. London: Home Office.

Blunkett, D. (2003b) *Civil Renewal: A New Agenda*. London: CSV/Home Office.

Bock, G., Skinner, Q. and Viroli, M. (eds.) (1990) *Machiavelli and Republicanism*. Cambridge: Cambridge University Press.

Bohman, J. (2001) 'Cosmopolitican republicanism', in the *Monist*, 84(1). 3–21.

Bohman, J. (2004) 'Republican cosmopolitanism', in *Journal of Political Philosophy*. 12(3). 336–352.

Bottery, M. (2003) "The end of citizenship' The nation state, threats to its legitimacy, and citizenship education in the twenty-first century', in *Cambridge Journal of Education*. 33 (1). 101–122.

Boyte, H. C. (2003) 'Civic education and the New American Patriotism Post-9/11', in *Cambridge Journal of Education*. 33(1). 85–100.

Boyte, H. (2004) *Everyday Politics: Reconnecting Citizens and Public Life*. Philadelphia, PA: University of Pennsylvania Press.

Braithwaite, J. and Pettit, P. (1990) *Not Just Deserts: A Republican Theory of Criminal Justice*. Oxford: Oxford University Press.

Brooks, B. D. and Kann, M. E. (1993) 'What makes character education programs work?', in *Educational Leadership*. November. 19–21.

Brown, G. (2007) BBC Today Programme. 11 July 2007.

Bryan, A. (2010) "Common sense citizenship', 'citizenship tourism' and citizenship education in the era of globalisation: the case of Ireland during the celtic tiger era', in Reid, A., Gill, J. and Sears, A. (eds.) *Globalization, the Nation-State and the Citizen*. London: Routledge.

Bull, B. L. (2006) 'Can civic and moral education be distinguished?', in D. Warren and J. J. Patrick (eds.) *Civic and Moral Learning in America*. Basingstoke: Palgrave.

Burtt, S. (1990) 'The good citizen's psyche: On the psychology of civic virtue', in *Polity*. 23. 23–38.

Bush, G. W. (2001) *First Inaugural Address*. 20 January 2001.

Callan, E. (1997) *Creating Citizens: Political Education and Liberal Democracy*. Oxford: Clarendon Press.

Cameron, D. (2010) *Together in the National Interest*. Speech to the Conservative Party Conference. 6 October 2010.

Carnegie Corporation of New York and The Centre for Information and Research on Civic Learning (2003) *The Civic Mission of School*. New York: Carnegie Corporation.

Carr, D. (1995) 'The primacy of virtues in ethical theory part I and II', in *Cogito*. 9 (3). 238–244 and 10 (1). 34–40.

Carr, D. (1996) 'After Kohlberg: some implications of an ethics of virtue for the theory of moral education and development', in *Studies in Philosophy of Education*. 14 (4). 353–370.

Carter, S. (1998) *Civility: Manners, Morals and the Etiquette of Democracy*. New York: Basic Books.

Chambers, S. (1996) *Reasonable Democracy: Jürgen Habermas and the Politics of Discourse*. Ithaca, NY: Cornell University Press.

Christman, J. (1998) 'Republicanism', in *Ethics*. 109 (1). 202–206.

Cicero (1998) *The Republic and the Laws*. Powell, J. and Rudd, N. (eds.) Oxford: Oxford University Press.

Clarke, D. (1996) *Schools and Learning Communities: Transforming Education*. London: Cassell.

Cohen, J. (1989) 'Deliberative democracy and democratic legitimacy', in Hamlin, A. and Pettit, P. (eds.) *The Good Polity*. Oxford: Blackwell.

Cohen, J. (1996) 'Procedure and substance in deliberative democracy', in Benhabib, S. (ed.) *Democracy and Difference: Contesting the Boundaries of the Political*. Princeton, NJ: Princeton University Press.

Cohen, J. (1997) 'Deliberative democracy and democratic legitimacy', in Goodin, R. and Pettit, P. (eds.) *Contemporary Political Philosophy: An Anthology*. Oxford: Blackwell.

Cohen, J. and Arato, A. (1992) *Civil Society and Political Theory*. Cambridge, Mass: Cambridge University Press.

Coles, R. (1993) *The Call of Service: A Witness to Idealism*. Boston: Houghton Mifflin.

Collinson, P. (1990) *De Republica Anglorum: Or, History with the Politics Put Back*. Cambridge: Cambridge University Press.

Connolly, W. E. (1998) 'Civic republicanism and civic pluralism: The silent struggle of Michael Sandel', in Allen, A. and Regan, M. (eds.) *Debating Democracy's Discontent: Essays on American Politics, Law, and Public Philosophy*. Oxford: Oxford University Press.

Constant, B. (1988) *Constant: Political Writings*. Fontana, B. (ed.) New York: Cambridge University Press.

Cotton, J. (1981) 'James Harrington and Thomas Hobbes', in *Journal of the History of Ideas*. 42 (3). 402–421.

Council of Europe (2002) *Recommendation 12 of the Committee of Ministers to Member States on Education for Democratic Citizenship*.

Crick, B. (2000) *Essays on Citizenship*. London: Continuum.

Crick, B. (2002) *Democracy: A Very Short Introduction*. Oxford: Oxford University Press.

Crick, B. (2003) 'The English Citizenship Order 1999: Context, context and presuppositions' in, Lockyer, A., Crick, B. and Annette, J. (eds.) *Education for Democratic Citizenship: Issues of Theory and Practice*. Aldershot: Ashgate.

Crick, B. and Porter, A. (1978) *Political Education and Political Literacy*. London: Longman.

Cromartie, A. (1998) 'Harringtonian virtue: Harrington, Machiavelli and the method of the *Moment*', in *The Historical Journal*. 41 (4). 987–1009.

Dagger, R. (1997) *Civic Virtues: Rights, Citizenship, and Republican Liberalism*. Oxford: Oxford University Press.

Dagger, R. (1999) 'The Sandelian republic and the unencumbered self', in *The Review of Politics*. 61 (2). 181–217.

Dagger, R. (2004) 'Communitarianism and republicanism', in *Handbook of Political Theory*. Gaus, G. and Kukathas, C. (eds.) London: Sage. 167–179.

Dagger, R. (2006) 'Neo-republicanism and the civic economy', in *Politics, Philosophy and Economics*. 5(2). 151–173.

Dahl, R. (1995) 'Participation and the problem of civic understanding', in A. Etzioni (ed.) *Rights and the Common Good: A Communitarian Perspective*. New York: St. Martin's Press.

Davies, I., Gorard, S. and McGuinn, N. (2005) 'Citizenship education and character education: similarities and contrasts', in *British Journal of Educational Studies*. 53 (3). 341–358.

Davis, O. L. (2001) 'In pursuit of historical empathy', in Davis Jr, O. L., Yeager, E. A, Foster, S. J. (eds.) *Historical Empathy and Perspective Taking in the Social Studies*. Oxford: Rowman & Littlefield Publishers.

Dejaeghere, J. and Tudball, L. (2007) 'Looking back, looking forward: critical citizenship as a way ahead for civics and citizenship education in Australia, in *Citizenship Teaching and Learning*. 3(2). 40–57.

Dewey, J. (1933) *How We Think*. London: D. C. Heath.

Dryzek, J. (2000) *Deliberative Democracy and Beyond: Liberals, Critics, Contestations*. Oxford: Oxford University Press.

Duncan, C. (1995) 'Civic virtue and self-interest', in *The American Political Science Review*. 89 (1). 147–151.

Dwight, T. (1887) 'Harrington', in *Political Science Quarterly*. 2 (1). 1–44.

Dworkin, R. (1978a) *Taking Rights Seriously*. Cambridge, MA: Harvard University Press.

Dworkin, R. (1978b) 'Liberalism', in Hampshire, S. (ed.) *Public and Private Morality*. Cambridge University Press: Cambridge.

Dworkin, R. (1986) *Law's Empire*. Cambridge, Mass.: Harvard University Press.

Edwards, M. (2004) *Civil Society*. Cambridge: Polity Press.

Englund, T. (2000) 'Rethinking democracy and education: towards an education of deliberative citizens', in *Journal of Curriculum Studies*. 32 (2). 305–313.

Englund, T. (2006) 'Deliberative communication: a pragmatist proposal', in *Journal of Curriculum Studies*. 38 (5). 503–520.

Enslin, P., Pendlebury, S. and Tjiattas, M. (2001) 'Deliberative democracy, diversity and the challenges of citizenship education', in *Journal of the Philosophy of Education*. 35 (1). 115–130.

Etizioni, A. (1995) *The Spirit of Community: Rights, Responsibilities and the Communitarian Agenda*. London: Harper Collins.

Etzioni, A. (1998) 'Moral dialogues: a communitarian core element', in Allen, A. and Regan, M. (eds.) *Debating Democracy's Discontent: Essays on American Politics, Law, and Public Philosophy*. Oxford: Oxford University Press.

Faulks, K. (2006a) 'Rethinking citizenship education in England: some lessons from contemporary social and political theory', in *Education, Citizenship and Social Justice*. 1 (2). 123–140.

Field, S. L. (2001) 'Perspectives and elementary social studies: practice and promise', in Davis Jr, O. L., Yeager, E. A, Foster, S. J. (eds.) *Historical Empathy and Perspective Taking in the Social Studies*. Oxford: Rowman & Littlefield Publishers.

Fishkin, J. (1991) *Democracy and Deliberation: New Directions for Democratic Reform.* London: Yale University Press.

Frazer, E. (1999) *The Problems of Communitarian Politics: Unity and Conflict.* Oxford: Oxford University Press.

Freeman Butts, R. (2006) 'The politics of civic and moral education', in D. Warren and J. J. Patrick (eds.) *Civic and Moral Learning in America.* Basingstoke: Palgrave.

Galston, W. (1995) 'Liberal virtues and the foundation of character', in Glendon, M. A. (ed.) *Seedbeds of Virtue: Sources of Competence, Character and Citizenship in American Society.* Lanham, Maryland: Madison Books.

Gatsil, J. and Levine. P. (2005) (eds.) *The Deliberative Democracy Handbook: Strategies for Effective Civic Engagement in the Twenty-First Century.* San Francisco, CA: Jossey-Bass.

Gey, S. (1993) 'The unfortunate revival of civic republicanism', in *University of Pennsylvania Law Review.* 141 (3). 801–898.

Ginsborg, P. (2005) *The Politics of Everyday Life.* Yale: Yale University Press.

Goldie, M. (2001) 'The Unacknowledged Republic: Officeholding in Early Modern England', in Tim Harris (ed.) *The Politics of the Excluded, c.1500–1850.*

Goodin, R. (2003a) 'Democractic deliberation within', in Fishkin, J. S. and Laslett, P. (eds.) *Debating Deliberative Democracy.* Oxford: Blackwell. 54–79.

Goodin, R. (2003b) *Reflective Democracy.* Oxford: Oxford University Press.

Gutmann, A. (1987) *Democratic Education.* Princeton: Princeton University Press.

Gutmann, A. and Thompson, D. (1996) *Democracy and Disagreement.* Cambridge, MA: Harvard University Press.

Gutmann, A. and Thompson, D. (2003) 'Deliberative democracy beyond process', in Fishkin, J. S. and Laslett, P. (ed.) *Debating Deliberative Democracy.* Oxford: Blackwell. 31–54.

Gutmann, A. and Thompson, D. (2004) *Why Deliberative Democracy?* Oxford: Princeton University Press.

Habermas, J. (1994) 'Three normative models of democracy', in *Constellations.* 1. 1–10.

Habermas, J. (1995) *Between Facts and Norms: Contributions to a Discourse Theory of Law and Democracy.* Cambridge, MA: MIT Press.

Halstead, J. M. and Pike, M. A. (2006) *Citizenship and Moral Education: Values in Action.* London: Routledge.

Hand, M. and Pearce, J. (2009) 'Patriotism in British schools: principles, practices and press hysteria', in B. Haynes (ed.) *Patriotism and Citizenship Education.* Chichester: Wiley and Sons.

Hargreaves, D. (1996) *The Mosaic of Learning.* London: Demos.

Harrington, J. (1992 / [1656]) *The Commonwealth of Oceanea.* Pocock. J. G. A. (ed.) Cambridge: Cambridge University Press.

Haydon, G. (1997) *Teaching About Values: A New Approach.* London: Cassell.

Haydon, G. (2003) 'Aims in citizenship education: responsibility, identity, inclusion' in Lockyer, A., Crick. B. and Annette, J. (eds.) *Education for Democratic Citizenship: Issues of Theory and Practice.* Aldershot: Ashgate.

Haydon, G. (2005) *The Importance of PSHE: A Philosophical and Policy Perspective on Personal, Social and Health Education.* Impact No. 10. London: Philosophy of Education Society of Great Britain.

Heater, D. (1999) *What is Citizenship?* Cambridge: Polity Press.

Hébert, Y. (2009) 'Responsibility and citizenship education: shifting meanings, policy and curricula', in *Citizenship Teaching and Learning.* 5(2). 4–15.

Held, D. (1996) *Models of Democracy.* 2nd Edition. Cambridge: Polity Press.

Held, D. (1997) 'Democracy: From city-states to a cosmopolitan order', in Goodin, R. and Pettit, P. (eds.) *Contemporary Political Philosophy: An Anthology.* Oxford: Blackwell.

Hess, A. (2000) *American Social and Political Thought: A Concise Introduction.* Edinburgh: Edinburgh University Press.

Hess, D. E. (2009) *Controversy in the Classroom: The Democratic Power Discussion.* Abingdon: Routledge.

Hirst, P. (1993) *Associative Democracy.* Cambridge: Polity.

Honohan, I. (2002) *Civic Republicanism.* London: Routledge.

Hudson, C. W. (2006) 'Globalization and cosmopolitan republicanism', in *Tamkang Journal of International Affairs.* 9(3). 1–32.

Hughes, A., Print, M. And Sears, A. (2010) 'Curriculum capacity and citizenship education: a comparative analysis of four democracies', in *Compare.* 40(3). 293–309.

Hulliung, M. L. (1984) *Citizen Machiavelli.* Princeton: Princeton University Press.

Ireland, E., Kerr, D., Lopes, J. and Nelson, J., with Cleaver, E. (2006) *Active Citizenship and Young People: Opportunities, Experiences and Challenges in and Beyond School.* Citizenship Longitudinal Study, Fourth Annual Report. London: DfES.

Jacobs, L. R., Cook, F. L. and Delli Carpini, M. X. (2009) *Talking Together: Public Deliberation and Political Participation in America.* Chicago, Il: University of Chicago Press.

Jochum, V., Pratten, B. and Wilding, K. (2005). *Civil Renewal and Active Citizenship: a Guide to the Debate* online]http://www.ncvovol.org.uk/asp/uploads/uploadedfiles/1/637/civilrenewalactivecitizenship.pdf(accessed   on 23 July 2010).

Keeney, P. (2007) *Liberalism, Communitarianism and Education: Reclaiming Liberal Education.* Aldershot: Ashgate.

Kilpatrick, W. (1992) *Why Johnny Can't Tell Right From Wrong: Moral Literacy and the Case for Character Education.* New York: Simon and Schuster.

Kiwan, D. (2008). 'Citizenship education at the cross-roads: four models of citizenship and their implications for ethnic and religious diversity', in *Oxford Review of Education.* 34 (1). 39–58.

Kohlberg, L. (1981) *Essays on Moral Development: The Philosophy of Moral Development.* Vol. I. San Francisco: Harper & Row.

Kohlberg, L. (1984) *Essays on Moral Development: The Philosophy of Moral Development.* Vol. II. San Francisco: Harper & Row.

Kohn, A. (1997a) 'The trouble with character education', in Molnar, A. (ed.) *The Construction of Children's Character.* Chicago: University of Chicago Press. 154–162.

Kohn, A. (1997b) 'How not to teach values: a critical look at character education', in *Phi Delta Kappan.* 78 (6). 428–439.

Kymlicka, W. (1988) 'Rawls on teleology and deontology?', in *Philosophy and Public Affairs'.* 17 (3). 173–190.

Kymlicka, W. (1998) 'Liberal egalitarianism and civic republicanism: friends or enemies?', in Allen, A. and Regan, M. (eds.) *Debating Democracy's Discontent: Essays on American Politics, Law, and Public Philosophy.* Oxford: Oxford University Press.

Kymlicka, W. (2002) *Contemporary Political Philosophy.* Oxford: Oxford University Press.

Kymlicka, W. and Norman, W. (1994) 'Return of the citizen: a survey of recent work on citizenship theory', in *Ethics.* 104. 352–381.

Lane, F. (1966) 'At the roots of republicanism', in *The American Historical Review.* 71 (2). 403–420.

Larmore, C. (1996) *The Morals of Modernity.* Cambridge: Cambridge University Press.

Learning and Teaching Scotland (2002) *Education for Citizenship in Scotland: A Paper for Discussion and Development.* Dundee: Learning and Teaching Scotland.

Leming, J. (1997) 'Whither goes character education? Objectives, pedagogy and research in education programs', in *Journal of Education.* 179 (2). 11–34.

Levinson, M. (1999) 'Liberalism, pluralism and political education: paradox or paradigm?' in *Oxford Review of Education.* 25(1/2). 39–58.

Lickona, T. (1991) *Educating for Character: How Our Schools Can Teach Respect and Responsibility.* New York: Bantam.

Lickona, T. (1999) 'Religion and character education', in *Phi Kappa Delta.* 81 (1). 21–27.

Lickona, T. and Davidson, M. (2005) *Smart and Good High Schools: Integrating Excellence and Ethos for Success in School, Work and Beyond.* A Report for the Templeton Foundation.

Little, A. (2002) *The Politics of Community.* Edinburgh: Edinburgh University Press.

Lockyer, A. (2003) 'Introduction and Review', in Lockyer, A., Crick, B. and Annette, J. (eds.) *Education for Democratic Citizenship: Issues of Theory and Practice.* Aldershot: Ashgate.

Lovett, F. and Pettit, P. (2009) 'Neo-republicanism: A normative and institutional research program', in *Annual Review of Political Science.* 12. 11–29.

Macedo, S. (1990) *Liberal Virtues, Citizenship, Virtue and Community in Liberal Constitutionalism.* Oxford: Clarendon.

Macedo, S. (1999) (ed.) *Deliberative Politics: Essays on Democracy and Disagreement.* Oxford: Oxford University Press.

Macedo, S. (2005) *Democracy at Risk: How Political Choices Undermine Citizen Participation, and What We Can Do About It.* Washington, DC: Brookings Institution Press.

Machiavelli, N. (1970) *Discourses.* Crick, B. (ed.) Harmondsworth: Penguin.

Machiavelli, N. (1974) *The Prince.* Bull, G. (ed.) Harmondsworth: Penguin.

MacIntyre, A. (1981) *After Virtue: A Study in Moral Theory.* London: Duckworth & Co.

MacIntyre, A. (1988) *Whose Justice? Whose Rationality?* Duckworth: London.

MacMahon, C. (2005) 'The indeterminacy of republican policy', in *Philosophy and Public Affairs.* 33 (1). 67–93.

Madison, J. (1992a) 'The union as a safeguard' Federalist Paper 10, in Madison, J., Hamilton, A. and Jay, J. (eds.) *The Federalist.* London: Phoenix Press.

Madison, J. (1992b) 'The conformity of the plan to republican principles' Federalist Paper 39, in Madison, J., Hamilton, A. and Jay (eds.) *The Federalist.* London: Phoenix Press.

Madison, J. (1992c) 'The senate *continued'* Federalist Paper 63, in Madison, J., Hamilton, A. and Jay, J. (eds.) *The Federalist.* London: Phoenix Press.

Manin, B. (1987) 'On legitimacy and political deliberation', in *Political Theory.* 15 (3). 338–368.

Marquand, D. (2004) *The Decline of the Public.* Cambridge: Polity Press.

Martí, J. L. and Pettit, P. (2010) *A Political Philosophy in Public Life: Civic Republicanism in Zapatero's Spain.* Princeton, NJ: Princeton University Press.

Mason, A. (2000) *Community, Solidarity and Belonging.* Cambridge: Cambridge University Press.

Maynor, J. W. (2003) *Republicanism in the Modern World.* Cambridge: Polity Press.

MCEETYA (2007) *National Statements of Learning in Civics and Citizenship.* Carlton: Curriculum Corporation.

MCEETYA (2008) *Melbourne Declaration on Educational Goals for Young Americans.* MCEETYA.

McLaughlin, T. and Halstead, J. (1999) 'Education in character and virtue', in Halstead and McLaughlin (eds.) *Education and Morality.* London: Routledge. 132–163.

Melzer, A. M. (1990) *The Natural Goodness of Men: On the System of Rousseau's Thought.* Chicago: University of Chicago Press.

Merry, M. (2009) 'Patriotism, history and the legitimate aims of American education', in B. Haynes (ed.) *Patriotism and Citizenship Education.* Chichester: Wiley and Sons.

Michelman, F. (1986) 'Foreward: traces of self-government', in *Harvard Law Review.* 100. 4–77.

Michelman, F. (1988) 'Law's Republic', in *The Yale Law Journal.* 97 (8). 1493–1537.

Miller, D. (1995) *On Nationality.* Oxford: Oxford University Press.

Montesquieu (1989 / [1748]) *The Spirit of the Laws.* Cohler, A. M., Miller, B. C. and Stone, H. S. (eds.) Cambridge: Cambridge University Press.

Moon, D. (1993) *Constructing Community: Moral Pluralism and Tragic Conflicts.* Princeton: Princeton University Press.

Mouffe, C. (1999) (ed.) *The Challenge of Carl Schmitt.* London: Verso.

Mouffe, C. (2000) *The Democratic Paradox.* London: Verso.

Mulgan, G. (1991) 'Citizens and responsibilities', in Andrews, G. (ed.) *Citizenship.* Lawrence and Wishart: London.

Nash, R. J. (1997) *Answering the Virtuecrats: A Moral Conversation on Character Education.* New York: Teachers College Press.

Nelson, J., and Kerr, D. (2005) *International review of curriculum and assessment frameworks. Active citizenship: Definitions, goals and practices. Background paper.* (http://www.inca.org.uk/pdf/Active_citizenship_background_paper.pdf; accessed 20 November 2009).

Nelson, J., and Kerr, D. (2006). Active citizenship in international review of curriculum and assessment frameworks countries: Definitions, policies, practices and outcomes. Final report. (http://www.inca.org.uk/pdf/Active_Citizenship_Report.pdf; accessed 20 November 2009).

Noddings, N. (1995) *Philosophy of Education*. Boulder, CO: Westview Press.

Norman, R. (1983) *The Moral Philosophers*. Oxford: Oxford University Press.

Nozick, R. (1977) *Anarchy, State and Utopia*. New York: Basic Books.

Nussbaum, M. (1994) 'Patriotism and cosmopolitanism', in *Boston Review*. October/November. 3.

O'Connell, B. (1999) *Civil Society: The Underpinnings of American Democracy*. Medford, MA: Tufts University Press.

Oldfield, A. (1990) *Citizenship and Community, Civil Republicanism and the Modern State*. London: Routledge.

Pajares, F. (1992) 'Teachers' beliefs and educational research: cleaning up a messy construct', in *Review of Educational Research*, 62. 307–332.

Pangle, T. (1988) *The Spirit of Modern Republicanism: The Moral Vision of the American Founders and the Philosophy of Locke*. Chicago: University of Chicago Press.

Pangle, T. (1998) 'The retrieval of civic virtue: a critical appreciation of Sandel's *Democracy's Discontent*', in Allen, A. and Regan, M. (eds.) *Debating Democracy's Discontent: Essays on American Politics, Law, and Public Philosophy*. Oxford: Oxford University Press.

Parry, G. (1999) 'Constructive and reconstructive political education', in *Oxford Review of Education*. 25 (1/2). 23–38.

Parker, W. C. (2002) 'The deliberative approach to education for democracy: problems and possibilities', in *The School Field*. XIII (3/4). 25–42.

Parker, W. C. (2003) *Teaching Democracy: Unity and Diversity in Public Life*. New York: Teacher's College Press.

Parker, W. C. (2006) 'Public discourses in schools: purposes, problems and possibilities', in *Educational Researcher*. 35. 8–18.

Parker, W. C. (2010) 'Oppositions and possibilities', in Reid, A., Gill, J. and Sears, A. (eds.) *Globalization, the Nation-State and the Citizen*. London: Routledge.

Patten, A. (1996) 'The republican critique of liberalism', in *British Journal of Political Science*. 26. 25–44.

Peltonen, M. (1995) *Classical Humanism and Republicanism in English Political Thought 1570–1640*. Cambridge: Cambridge University Press.

Peterson, A. (2009) 'Civic republicanism and contestatory deliberation: Framing pupil discourse within citizenship education'. *British Journal of Educational Studies*. 57(1). 55–69.

Peterson, A. (2010) 'The formation and expression of character: schools, families and citizenship', in J. Arthur (ed.) *Citizens of Character: New Directions in Character and Values Education*. Exeter: Imprint Academic.

Pettit, P. (1993) *The Common Mind: An Essay on Psychology, Society and Politics*: Oxford: Oxford University Press.

Pettit, P. (1999) *Republicanism: A Theory of Freedom and Government*. Oxford: Oxford University Press.

Pettit, P. (2001) 'Deliberative democracy and the discursive dilemma', in *Philosophical Issues*. 11. 268–299.

Pettit, P. (2002) 'Keeping republican freedom simple: On a difference with Quentin Skinner', in *Political Theory*. 30. 339–356.

Pettit, P. (2006) 'The determinacy of republican policy: A reply to McMahon', in *Philosophy and Public Affairs*. 34. 275–283.

Piaget, J. (1965) *The Moral Judgement of the Child*. New York: The Free Press.

Pitkin, H. (1981) 'Justice: on relating private and public', in *Political Theory*. 9 (3). 327–352.

Pocock, J. G. A. (1975) *The Machiavellian Moment: Florentine Political Thought and the Atlantic Republican Tradition*. Princeton, NJ: Princeton University Press.

Pocock, J. G. A. (1992) 'Introduction' in James Harrington, *The Commonwealth of Oceana and A System of Politics*, (Pocock, ed). Cambridge: Cambridge University Press.

Print, M. and Coleman, D. (2003) 'Towards an understanding of social capital and citizenship education', in *Cambridge Journal of Education*. 33 (1). 123–149.

Putnam, R. D. (2000) *Bowling Alone: The Collapse and Revival of American Community*. New York: Simon and Schuster.

Qualifications and Curriculum Authority (1998) *Education for Citizenship and the Teaching of Democracy in Schools* (Crick Report). London: QCA.

Qualifications and Curriculum Authority (1999) *National Curriculum for England* (Key Stages 3 and 4). London: HMSO.

Qualifications and Curriculum Authority (2007) *The National Curriculum for Citizenship* (Key Stages 3 and 4). http://curriculum.qca.org.uk/subjects/citizenship/index.aspx (accessed on 10 August 2010).

Quigley, C. N. and Buchanan. J. H. (1991) *CIVITAS: A Framework for Civic Education*. Calabasas, CA: Centre for Civic Education.

Raab, F. (1964) *The English Face of Machiavelli: A Changing Intrepretation 1500–1700*. London: Routledge.

Radford, R. (2002) *Cicero: A Study in The Origins of Republican Philosophy*. New York: Rodopi B. V.

Rahe, P. (1992) *Republics Ancient and Modern: Classical Republicanism and the American Revolution*. Chapel Hill, NC: University of North Carolina Press.

Raths, L., Harmin, M. and Simon, S. (1966) *Values and Teaching – Working with Children in the Classroom*. Columbus, OH: Merrill.

Rawls, J. (1971) *A Theory of Justice*. London: Oxford University Press.

Rawls, J. (1980) 'Kantian constructivism in moral theory', in *Journal of Philosophy*. 77 (9). 515–572.

Rawls, J. (1985) 'Justice as fairness: political not metaphysical', in *Philosophy and Public Affairs*. 14 (3). 223–251.

Rawls, J. (1988) 'The priority of the right and ideas of the good', in *Philosophy and Public Affairs*. 17 (4). 251–276.

Rawls, J. (1996) *Political Liberalism*. New York: Columbia University Press.

Rawls, J. (2001) 'Justice and fairness: A restatement', E. Kelly (ed.) Cambridge, MA: Harvard University Press.

Raz, J. (1995) 'Rights and politics', in *Indiana Law Journal*. 71 (1). 27–44.

Reid, A. and Gill, J. (2010) 'In whose interest? Australian schooling and the changing context of citizenship', in Reid, A., Gill, J. and Sears, A. (eds.) *Globalization, the Nation-State and the Citizen*. London: Routledge.

Reid, A., Gill, J. and Sears, A. (2010) 'The forming of citizens in a globalising world', in Reid, A., Gill, J. and Sears, A. (eds.) *Globalization, the Nation-State and the Citizen*. London: Routledge.

Reizert, J. R. (2003) *Jean-Jacques Rousseau: A Friend of Virtue*. Ithaca, New York: Cornell University Press.

Rodgers, D. T. (1992) 'Republicanism: The career of a concept', in *The Journal of American History*. 79(1). 11–38.

Ross, A. (2002) 'Citizenship education and curriculum theory', in Scott, D. and Lawson, H. (eds.) *Citizenship Education and the Curriculum* (International Perspectives on Curriculum Series: Vol 3). Westport, CA: Greenwood Publishing.

Roth, K. (2006) 'Deliberation in national and post-national education', in *Journal of Curriculum Studies*. 38 (5). 569–589.

Rousseau, J. J. (1968 / [1762]) *The Social Contract*. Cranston, M. (ed.) Harmondsworth: Penguin.

Rousseau, J. J. (1993) *The Social Contract and the Discourses*. London: Dent.

Ruget. V. (2006) 'The renewal of civic education in France and in America: comparative perspectives', in *The Social Science Journal*. 43. 19–34.

Russell, I.M. (2005). A national framework for youth action and engagement. Report of the Russell Commission. London: The Stationery Office.

Ryan, K. (1989) 'In defence of character education', in Nucci, L. (ed.) *Moral Development and Character Education: A Dialogue*. Berkley, CA: McCutchan. 3–17.

Sacks, J. (1997) *The Politics of Hope*. London: Jonathan Cape.

Sandel, M. (1982) *Liberalism and the Limits of Justice*. Cambridge: Cambridge University Press.

Sandel, M. (1984) *Liberalism and its Critics*. Oxford: Basil Blackwell.

Sandel, M. (1996) *Democracy's Discontent: America in Search of a Public Philosophy*. London: Belknap Harvard.

Sandel, M. (1998) 'A reply to my critics', in Allen, A. and Regan, M. (eds.) *Debating Democracy's Discontent: Essays on American Politics, Law, and Public Philosophy*. Oxford: Oxford University Press.

Sandel. M. (1999) *Justice: What's the Right Thing to do?* London: Penguin.

Schaap, A. (2006) 'Agonism in divided societies', in *Philosophy and Social Criticism*. 32 (2). 255–77.

Selbourne, D. (1997) *The Principles of Duty*. London: Little Brown.

Selznick, P. (1992) *The Moral Commonwealth: Social Theory and the Promise of Community*. Berkeley, California: University of California Press.

Scott, J. (2000) *England's Troubles: Seventeenth-Century Political Instability in European Context*. Cambridge: Cambridge University Press.

Scott, T. and Cogan, J. (2010) 'A paradigm shift in the political culture and in educating for citizenship? The case of the United States of America', in Reid, A., Gill, J. and Sears, A. (eds.) *Globalization, the Nation-State and the Citizen*. London: Routledge.

Sears, A. (2010) 'Possibilities and problems: Citizenship education in a multinational state: The case of Canada', in Reid, A., Gill, J. and Sears, A. (eds.) *Globalization, the Nation-State and the Citizen*. London: Routledge.

Shapiro, I. (1990) *Political Criticism*. California: University of California Press.

Sherry, S. (1995) 'Responsible republicanism: Educating for citizenship', in *The University of Chicago Law Review*. 62(1). 131–208.

Shklar, J. (1990) 'Montesquieu and the new republicanism', in Bock, G., Skinner, Q. and Viroli, M. (eds.) (1990) *Machiavelli and Republicanism*. Cambridge: Cambridge University Press.

Shklar, J. (1998) *Redeeming American Political Thought.* Chicago: Chicago University Press.

Skillen, T. (1997) 'Can virtue be taught – especially these days?', in *Journal of Philosophy of Education.* 31 (3). 375–393.

Skinner, Q. (1990a) 'The republican ideal of political liberty', in Bock, G., Skinner, Q. and Viroli, M. (eds.) (1990) *Machiavelli and Republicanism.* Cambridge: Cambridge University Press. 291–309.

Skinner, Q. (1990b) 'Pre-humanist origins of republican ideas', in Bock, G., Skinner, Q. and Viroli, M. (eds.) (1990) *Machiavelli and Republicanism.* Cambridge: Cambridge University Press.

Skinner, Q. (1992) 'The Italian city-republics', in *Democracy: The Unfinished Journey, 508BC to AD1993.* Dunn, J. (ed.) Oxford: Oxford University Press.

Skinner, Q. (1997) 'The State', in *Contemporary Political Philosophy: An Anthology.* Goodin, R. and Pettit, P. (eds.) Oxford: Blackwell.

Skinner, Q. (1998) *Liberty Before Liberalism.* London: Cambridge University Press.

Skinner, Q. (2002) 'A third concept of liberty', in *London Review of Books.* 4 April. 16–18.

Smith, G. and Wales, C. (2000) 'Citizen juries and deliberative democracy', in *Political Studies.* 48. 51–65.

Steutal, J. (1997) 'The virtue approach to moral education: some conceptual clarifications', in *Journal of Philosophy of Education.* 31 (3). 395–407.

Stoker, G. (2006) *Why Politics Matters: Making Democracy Work.* Basingstoke: Palgrave.

Stoner, J. (2007) 'Was Thomas Aquinas a republican?' *Paper presented at the annual meeting of the Southern Political Science Association, Hotel InterContinental, New Orleans.*

Sunstein, C. (1988) 'Beyond the republican revival', in *Yale Law Journal.* 97 (8). 1539–1589.

Sunstein, C. (1993a) *The Partial Constitution.* Cambridge, Mass: Harvard University Press

Sunstein, C. (1993b) *Democracy and the Problem of Free Speech.* New York: Free Press.

Sunstein, C. (1993c) 'The enduring legacy of republicanism', in S. E. Elkin and K. E. Soltan (eds.) *A New Constitutionalism: Designing Political Institutions for a Good Society.* (Chicago: University of Chicago Press).

Sunstein, C. (1999) 'Agreement without theory', in Macedo, S. (ed.) *Deliberative Politics: Essays on Democracy and Difference.* Oxford: Oxford University Press. 123–150.

Swedish National Agency for Education (2000) *Democracy in Swedish Education.* Stockholm: National Agency for Education.

Taylor, C. (1979) *Hegel and Modern Society.* Cambridge University Press: Cambridge.

Taylor, C. (1985) *Philosophy and the Human Sciences: Philosophical Papers.* (Vol II). Cambridge University Press: Cambridge.

Taylor, C. (1995) *Philosophical Arguments.* Cambridge: Harvard University Press.

Theobold, P. and Snauwaert, D. T. (1995) 'Education and the liberal communitarian debate', in *Peabody Journal of Education.* 70(4). 119–138.

Tomasi, J. (2001) *Liberalism Beyond Justice.* Princeton, New Jersey: Princeton University Press.

Torney-Purta, J., Richardson, W. K. and Barber, C. H. (2005) 'Teachers' educational experience and confidence in relation to students' civic knowledge across countries', in *International Journal of Citizenship and Teacher Education,* 1 (1). 32–55.

Tyler, T. R. and Mitchell, G. (1994) 'Legitimacy and the empowerment of discretionary legal authority: The United States Supreme Court and abortion rights', in *Duke Law Journal.*43. 703–815.

Uhr, J. (1998) *Deliberative Democracy in Australia: The Changing Face of Parliament.* Cambridge: Cambridge University Press.

Victoria Costa, M. (2004) 'Rawlsian civic education: political not minimal', in *Journal of Applied Philosophy.* 21(1). 1–14.

Viroli, M. (1999) *Republicanism.* New York: Hill and Wang.

Walzer, M. (1983) *Spheres of Justice.* New York: Basic Books.

Walzer, M. (1998) 'Michael Sandel's America', in in Allen, A. and Regan, M. (eds.) *Debating Democracy's Discontent: Essays on American Politics, Law, and Public Philosophy.* Oxford: Oxford University Press.

Warren, M. and Pearse, H. (2008) (eds.) *Designing Deliberative Democracy: The British Columbia Citizens' Assembly.* Cambridge: Cambridge University Press.

Wettergreen, J. A. (1988) 'James Harrington's liberal republicanism', in *Polity.* 20 (4). 665–687.

Wirszubski, C. (1960) *Libertas as a Political Idea at Rome During the Late Republic and Early Principate.* Cambridge: Cambridge University Press.

Wolin, S. (1960) *Politics and Vision: Continuity and Innovation on Western Political Thought.* Princeton, NJ: Princeton University Press.

Wood, G. (1969) *The Creation of the American Republic, 1776–1787.* Chapel Hill, NC: University of North Carolina Press.

Worden, B. (1981) 'Classical republicanism and the puritan revolution', in V. Pearl, H. Lloyd-Jones and B. Worden (eds.) *History and Imagination.* Oxford: Oxford University Press.

Wringe, C. (1998a) 'Reasons, values and community in moral education', in *British Journal of Educational Studies.* 46 (3). 278–288.

Wringe, C. (1998b) 'Reason, rules and virtues in moral education', in *Journal of Philosophy of Education.* 32 (2). 225–237.

Wringe, C. (2000) 'The diversity of moral education', in *Journal of Philosophy of Education.* 34 (4). 659–672.

Wynne, E. (1982) *Character Policy: An Emerging Issue.* Lantham, MD: University Press of California.

Wynne, E. (1985) 'The great traditions in education: transmitting moral values', in *Educational Leadership.* 45 (5). 4–9.

Wynne, E. (1986) 'Character development: renewing an old commitment', in *Principal.* 65 (3). 28–31.

Wynne, E. (1988) 'Balancing character development and academics in the elementary school', in *Phi Delta Kappa.* 69 (6). 424–426.

Wynne, E. (1997) 'For character education', in Molnar, A. (ed.) *The Construction of Children's Character.* Chicago: National Society for the Study of Education.

Yeager, E. A. and Foster, S. J. (2001) 'The role of empathy in the development of historical understanding', in Davis Jr, O. L., Yeager, E. A, Foster, S. J. (eds.) *Historical Empathy and Perspective Taking in the Social Studies*. Oxford: Rowman & Littlefield Publishers.

Yu, T. (2004) *In the Name of Morality: Character Education and Political Control*. New York: Lang.

Index

Ackerman, B. 102, 164n
Advisory Group on Education for
    Citizenship and the Teaching of
    Democracy 25, 122, 125, 166n
Altruism 69, 74, 130
Annette, J. 22, 25, 26, 122, 127, 137
apathy 2, 157n
Aquinas, St. T. 40, 41–3, 73, 81, 161n
Arendt, H. 8, 53, 159n
Aristotle 8, 32, 33, 34–43, 51, 52, 56,
    73, 81, 84, 97, 108, 152, 159n,
    160n, 162n
Arthur, J. 13, 25, 41, 42, 63, 85, 91, 116,
    128, 134, 137, 157n, 158n, 161n
Atomism 78
Augustine, St. 40–2
Australia, civic education in 27, 127,
    166n; goals of education in 29,
    159n

Barber, B. 1, 8, 11, 24, 59, 65, 69, 73,
    74, 89, 100, 102, 117, 126, 140,
    155, 156, 157n, 165n
Battistoni, R. 74, 121, 133, 139
Bellah, R. 20, 23, 162n
belonging 23, 107, 123
Benhabib, S. 100, 107, 117
Berlin, I. 11, 15, 17, 18, 137
Blair, T. 22
Blunkett, D. 22–3
Boyte, H. 2, 13, 127
Brown, G. 164n
Burtt, S. 78, 114
Bush, G. 158n

Callan, E. 83, 96, 157n
Cameron, D. 158n
Canada, civic education in 27, 28,
    121, 124, 166n
character 13, 40, 43, 46, 51, 66, 75,
    78–82, 84–8, 100, 148–9, 157n,
    158n; character education 78,
    90–8, 125, 130–7

checks and balances 53, 103; see also
    mixed government, separation of
    powers
children 122, 158n, 159n
Cicero 8, 32, 33, 38–40, 44, 45, 46,
    51, 52, 56, 152, 159n, 160n, 161n,
    162n
citizens' juries 102, 164n
civic religion 47, 51, 162n; see also
    religion
civic virtue see virtue
civil society 48, 53, 58, 72, 90,
    101–2, 104, 107, 164n; and civic
    education 124–7; see also
    society
civility 82–4, 89, 95–6, 105, 130–2,
    163n
CIVITAS 27–8, 131–2, 166n
coercion 71–4
Cohen, J. 99, 100, 112, 164n, 165n
common good 3, 4, 6, 7, 13, 23, 28,
    30, 38–46, 49, 55, 56, 62–76,
    108, 146, 148–51, 158n, 161n,
    162n, 163n, 165n; in civic
    education 29, 120, 127–33, 143,
    166n; as a civic virtue 80, 86, 118;
    deliberation about the 17, 109;
    relation to rights 12
commonwealth 38, 48
communitarianism 5, 7, 9, 11–14, 20,
    58, 61, 63, 67, 75, 80, 85, 107, 116,
    142, 146–7, 162n, 163n; see also
    liberal-communitarian debate
community/communities 1, 3,
    12, 13, 58, 62, 115–56, 147–8,
    158n, 163n; Aristotle's view
    of 34–6; Cicero's view of 39,
    160n; and civic education,
    123–30, 133–4, 138, 142,
    159n, 166n; and deliberation
    within 100–2, 107–10; the
    general welfare of 69–70;
    Harrington's view of 48–9; lack

183